nt Settlement

Public Policy and Immigrant Settlement

Edited by

Deborah A. Cobb-Clark and
Siew-Ean Khoo

Research School of Social Sciences
Australian National University, Australia

Edward Elgar
Cheltenham, UK • Northampton, MA, USA

Published by
Edward Elgar Publishing Limited
Glensanda House
Montpellier Parade
Cheltenham
Glos GL50 1UA
UK

Edward Elgar Publishing, Inc.
136 West Street
Suite 202
Northampton
Massachusetts 01060
USA

A catalogue record for this book
is available from the British Library

Library of Congress Cataloguing in Publication Data
Public policy and immigrant settlement / edited by Deborah A. Cobb-Clark and Siew-Ean Khoo.
p. cm.
Includes bibliographical references and index.
1. Australia--Emigration and immigration--Economic aspects. 2. Australia--Emigration and immigration--Social aspects. 3. Immigrants--Australia--Social conditions. I. Cobb-Clark, Deborah A. II. Khoo, Siew-Ean, 1949-
JV9120.P83 2006
325.94--dc22 2006005890

ISBN-13: 978 1 84542 245 5
ISBN-10: 1 84542 245 7

Printed and bound in Great Britain by MPG Books Ltd, Bodmin, Cornwall

Contents

List of Figures

List of Tables

Contributors

Barry R. Chiswick is Distinguished Professor and Head of the Department of Economics at the University of Illinois at Chicago and Program Director for Migration Studies, IZA-Institute for the Study of Labor (Bonn). He has published twelve books and monographs and over 140 journal articles and book chapters in economics, statistics and demography. His research on various aspects of the economics of immigration and the economics of minorities has been seminal. This research includes studies on the major immigrant receiving countries, including numerous studies for Australia. He has lectured at all of the major research universities in Australia. Professor Chiswick's research has earned him numerous honours and awards.

Deborah A. Cobb-Clark is the former Director of the Social Policy Evaluation, Analysis and Research Centre in the Research School of Social Sciences at the Australian National University. She is currently co-editor of the *Journal of Population Economics*. Dr. Cobb-Clark's research centres on the use of economics and applied, econometric methods to evaluate the impact of social policy – particularly immigration policy – on the labour market outcomes of individuals. This emphasis on rigorous evaluation of policy outcomes has led to a number of projects linked to various government agencies, both in Australia and abroad. She has published extensively on the subject of immigration in top international journals, including *American Economic Review, Journal of Labor Economics, Journal of Human Resources* and *Journal of Population Economics.*

Tue Gørgens is a Research Fellow of the Social Policy Evaluation, Analysis, and Research Centre, Research School of Social Sciences, the Australian National University. His research fields are applied labour economics and econometrics. He is especially interested in labour market issues related to individual behaviour and outcomes, such as the impact of business cycles and the influence of social policy. In addition to social implications, he is also interested in developing econometric methods that can be used to analyse behaviour and outcomes. Recently, he has become involved in a number of projects on the behaviour and outcomes of young Australians including, for example, projects on the choice of job search methods and unemployment duration, on persistence in labour market histories, on the educational choices of young people, and on intergenerational welfare dependence.

Steven Kennedy is the General Manager of the Domestic Economy Division at the Australian Treasury. He leads a division responsible for preparing the Government's macroeconomic forecasts, providing policy advice on economic developments, and liaising with the Australian business community about current economic conditions. He obtained his PhD in economics from the Australian National University, and has a Bachelor degree in Economics (Honours) from the University of Sydney. Steven's research interests include labour and health economics, applied macroeconomics, income inequality and poverty measurement, and productivity analysis.

Siew-Ean Khoo is Senior Fellow in the Demography and Sociology Program in the Research School of Social Sciences at the Australian National University. A graduate of Harvard University, she has worked with the East-West Population Institute at the East-West Center, the Bureau of Immigration, Multicultural and Population Research and the Australian Government's Department of Immigration and Multicultural Affairs. She has published widely on international migration and immigrant settlement issues and is joint editor and contributing author of the recent book, *The Transformation of Australia's Population, 1970–2030* (Sydney: University of New South Wales Press, 2003).

Anh T. Le is Senior Lecturer in the School of Economics and Commerce at the University of Western Australia. She has a Bachelor of Business from Curtin University of Technology and a PhD in Economics from the University of Western Australia. She has undertaken research in a number of areas related to labour economics including employment outcomes of female migrants, educational attainment, unemployment, gender wage differential and self-employment. Her papers have appeared in a range of journals, including *Economics of Education Review, Education Economics, Economic Record, Australian Economic Papers, Australian Economic Review and International Migration Review.*

James Ted McDonald is an Associate Professor of Economics at the University of New Brunswick in Fredericton, Canada. He has an MCom and PhD from the University of Melbourne and was previously a senior lecturer at the University of Tasmania. He has published on a wide range of topics in journals such as *Social Science and Medicine* and the *Journal of Human Resources*. His current research interests are focused on the health behaviours, health services use and health outcomes of immigrants in Canada, the United States and Australia.

Paul W. Miller is a Professor in the School of Economics and Commerce at the University of Western Australia. His primary research interest is labour market performance, particularly as it relates to educational attainment, gender and ethnic and racial origin. In 1997 he was elected as a Fellow of the Academy of the Social Sciences in Australia. In 1994, and again in 2004, he was awarded the Economic Society of Australia's Best Paper Prize, and in 2001 he received (together with Barry Chiswick) the US based Milken Institute Award for Distinguished Economic Research for the paper 'Do Enclaves Matter in Immigrant Adjustment?'

Prem Jung Thapa is a Fellow in the Economics Program at the Research School of Social Sciences at the Australian National University. He has a PhD in Economics from ANU and an MA in Economics from the University of California at Berkeley. Dr Thapa's main research interests are in labour economics and development and regional economics. He was previously a research economist at the Institute for Integrated Development Studies in Kathmandu, Nepal, working mainly in the areas of population and development and poverty analyses. He was also a Research Fellow at the Centre for Regional Economic Analysis at the University of Tasmania, where his primary research focus was on the construction and application of general equilibrium simulation modelling of the regional economies of Australia.

Preface

Australia has had a formal immigration program for more than fifty years. During this time immigration has contributed to nearly half of the country's total population growth. Today, nearly one-quarter of the population are foreign-born; most of them are either naturalised citizens or have rights to permanent residence. The immigration program has always emphasised permanent settlement for migrants. Therefore, besides the setting of numerical targets, immigration policy in Australia also includes the setting of immigrant selection criteria and programs to assist migrants in their settlement after migration. These immigrant selection and settlement policies have evolved over the years in response to demographic, social, economic and political considerations.

As an initiative to provide more information to better evaluate its immigrant selection and settlement policies, the Australian Government's Department of Immigration and Multicultural Affairs in 1993 commissioned a longitudinal survey of recently arrived immigrants. The Longitudinal Survey of Immigrants to Australia tracked a sample of these immigrants, interviewing them about their settlement experiences three times over the first three and half years of their residence in Australia. A second group of immigrants who arrived some six years later were also interviewed twice during the first one and half years after their arrival in Australia.

In the interim period between the arrival of the two cohorts of immigrants, there were some changes to immigrant selection policy and criteria as well as changes in migrants' access to welfare benefits. Furthermore, economic and labour market conditions in Australia improved considerably. These changes in public policy and the economic environment provide an interesting case for comparing the two cohorts of immigrants in the longitudinal survey in order to provide important information on whether, and how, immigrants' early settlement experiences were affected. This is essentially the issue addressed by the chapters in this book.

The book is an outcome of a research project – Public Policy and Immigrant Settlement in Australia – funded by a Discovery Project grant from the Australian Research Council. The aims of the project were to explore the role of labour market conditions, income support policy and immigrant selection criteria in promoting immigrant settlement in Australia through an examination of the two immigrant cohorts in the Longitudinal Survey of Immigrants to Australia. Immigrant settlement outcomes to be examined included labour market participation, job search behaviour, language skills, health and housing arrangements.

Drafts of the chapters were initially presented at a workshop at the Australian National University in 2004. We thank the workshop participants for their thoughtful comments, which have helped all the authors in revising their chapters for publication. Comments from participants at the Economics Program seminar at the University of Western Australia and from our other colleagues are also gratefully acknowledged.

ARC funding has been crucial in providing research assistance for data management and analysis. We are most grateful to Sue Fong Kong for her work in organising the very complex longitudinal datasets into a format that has made the data analysis phase of the research so much easier. Financial assistance from the School of Economics and Commerce, University of Western Australia, and administrative support from the Social Policy and Economic Analysis and Research Centre and the Demography and Sociology Program of the Research School of Social Sciences, Australian National University, are also acknowledged.

We also thank Elisa Birch, Grace Chan, Susan Lindsay and Derby Voon for their research assistance and Alice Summers and David Osborne for provision of background information on Australia's immigration policy and the Longitudinal Survey of Immigrants to Australia. Our special thanks go to our Managing Editor, Cristene Carey, for her invaluable assistance in the final editing of the chapters and in preparing the book manuscript, and Margaret-Ann Williams for editorial assistance and to Lynne Payne for formatting the text, tables and charts.

The Longitudinal Survey of Immigrants to Australia was the first longitudinal survey of recently arrived immigrants to be undertaken in any country. Since the completion of this survey other countries, including the United States of America, Canada and New Zealand, have embarked on similar surveys. It is to be hoped that these initiatives will lead to similar studies of immigrant settlement as in this book. With many countries today being immigrant destination countries, knowledge about the factors contributing to the successful settlement of immigrants that emerge from such studies will be important for policy development in these countries.

Siew-Ean Khoo and Deborah Cobb-Clark
The Australian National University

Glossary

ABS	Australian Bureau of Statistics
BS	Business Skills visa category
CES	Commonwealth Employment Service
DIMA/DIMIA	Department of Immigration and Multicultural Affairs, later Department of Immigration and Multicultural and Indigenous Affairs
ENS	Employer Nomination Scheme visa category
ES(B)	English-speaking (background)
HUM	Humanitarian visa category
IND	Independent visa category
LSIA	Longitudinal Survey of Immigrants to Australia
NES(B)	Non-English-speaking (background)
PA	Principal Applicant
SAL	Skilled – Australian Linked visa category (later SAS)
SAS	Skilled – Australian Sponsored visa categor

PART ONE

INTRODUCTION

1. Immigration to Australia During the 1990s: Institutional and Labour Market Influences

Barry R. Chiswick and Paul W. Miller

INTRODUCTION

Australia is often described as a land of immigrants, and government policy has addressed both selection of immigrants and the immigrant settlement process. To provide an informed basis for this, in the 1990s the Department of Immigration and Multicultural Affairs initiated the Longitudinal Survey of Immigrants to Australia (LSIA). This is a set of two longitudinal surveys of immigrants who received their visas for permanent residence in Australia. The two surveys are referred to as Cohort 1 and Cohort 2 in this book. The population represented in the first survey (Cohort 1) is all Principal Applicants for immigration visas aged 15 years and over who arrived in Australia in the two-year period between September 1993 and August 1995.[1] The population represented in the second survey (Cohort 2) is all Principal Applicants aged 15 years and over who arrived in Australia between September 1999 and August 2000. The LSIA data are described in detail in the Technical Appendix.

Immigrants in Cohort 1 were interviewed three times. The first interview took place between three and six months after arrival, the second interview one year later (1995–1996) and the third interview a further two years later (1997–1998), or 3.5 years after immigration. However, immigrants in Cohort 2 were interviewed only twice, with the first interview being held after three to six months of residence in Australia, and the second one year later.

This chapter presents an overview of both immigration policy and some changes in the points test used in the selection of skilled immigrants to Australia during the 1990s. It also details the changing labour market circumstances of the 1990s that may have impacted on immigrants who arrived during that period. Finally, aspects of the institutional support offered to immigrants are reviewed. Particular attention is given to the entry periods of immigrants in the two cohorts, 1993 to 1995 for the first cohort, and 1999 to 2000 for the second cohort. Figure 1.1 displays a chronology of the significant dates and events highlighted in this chapter.

IMMIGRATION POLICY AND POINTS TESTING OF SKILLED IMMIGRANTS

The inflow of persons (other than New Zealand citizens[2]) seeking permanent residence in Australia is currently regulated through the Humanitarian and Migration (non-Humanitarian) programs.[3] The Humanitarian program is for people from refugee or refugee-like situations in urgent need of resettlement. Within the migration program there are three broad categories: a Family stream, a Skilled stream, and a relatively minor Special Eligibility stream (covering former residents and those with close ties to Australia). The general characteristics of the Family and Skilled streams are as follows.

The Family stream allows for the migration of immediate family members of Australian citizens, permanent residents or eligible New Zealand citizens. Until 1996–1997 this category was demand driven, that is, the number of visas issued annually was determined by the number of successful applicants in each category, without government imposed numerical limits.[4] Since then, however, the category has been subject to planning levels, with this policy shift being driven by a desire to achieve a more balanced migration program.[5] Applicants must be sponsored by a close family relative. There are four main sub-categories: spouses (legally married or in a de facto relationship of more than one year duration), child, parent and other family (for example, aged dependent relatives). Many of these categories are subject to the provision of an Assurance of Support statement. This is either mandatory, as in the case of parents, or discretionary where, based mainly on the applicant's characteristics and employment history, the applicant is assessed as being at risk of becoming a charge on Australia's welfare system. The Assurance of Support statement is a legal commitment by a person to repay to the Australian Government any welfare payments made during the period covered by the statement. Generally the period is two years, although it can be as long as ten years in some instances. There is no other test for the applicant's likely benefit to Australia in the Family stream.

Migrants entering Australia under the Skilled stream must satisfy a points test regarding their skills; have specific work skills; be nominated by particular employers; or otherwise have the potential to bring benefits to Australia. There are a number of categories in this stream. The Business Skills category caters to people with a successful business background who can be expected to go into business within a short time after arrival.[6] The Employer Nomination Scheme enables employers to nominate skilled

Figure 1.1 Time line for policy changes and the business cycle, Australia 1991–2001

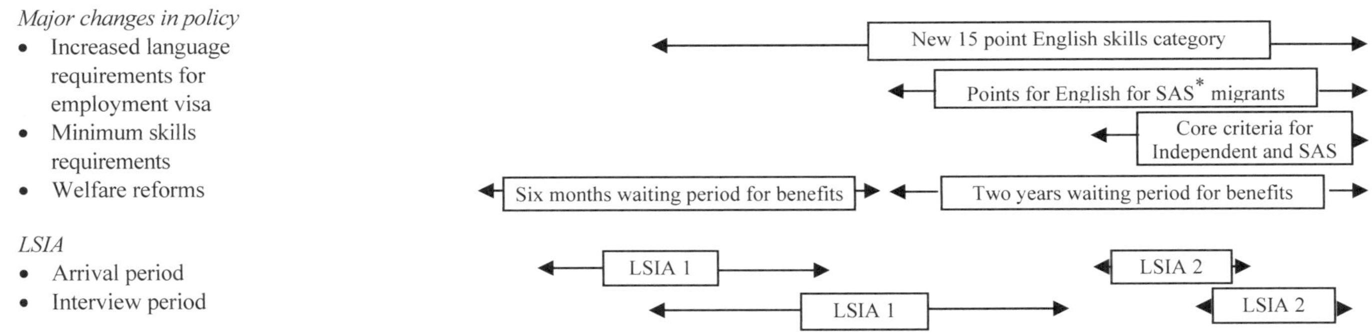

Year	1991	1992	1993	1994	1995	1996	1997	1998	1999	2000	2001
Business Cycle											
Unemployment rate of males born:											
• In Australia	9.2	10.6	10.7	8.7	7.7	8.4	8.3	8.0	6.7	6.3	6.9
• Abroad in English-speaking country	10.1	11.0	10.4	9.3	7.5	7.9	8.1	7.2	6.3	5.3	5.9
• Abroad in Non-English-speaking country	14.6	14.6	15.9	13.1	13.0	11.5	10.6	9.2	8.8	7.0	7.6

Note:
*SAS–Skilled – Australian Sponsored.

personnel for permanent residence into Australia to fill positions they have been unable to fill from the Australian labour market. The Independent and Skilled – Australian Sponsored categories of skilled migrants are selected mainly on the basis of their skills (that is, education/occupation and work experience), age, and English language proficiency. Skilled – Australian Sponsored immigrants must be sponsored by a relative already living in Australia who also needs to provide an Assurance of Support.[7] Independent migrants are not sponsored by an employer or relative in Australia. Both Skilled – Australian Sponsored and Independent categories are subject to a points test.[8]

Points test overview

The planning levels set by the Australian Government for the Migration and Humanitarian Programs described above, the quality of immigrants attracted into them, and the likely success of these immigrants after arrival in Australia, depend on three main factors. First, the government's immigration policy seeks to balance social, economic, humanitarian and environmental objectives. Accordingly, labour market conditions play a role in the determination of planning levels. Labour market conditions may also influence the success of immigrants when they enter the Australian labour market. Chiswick and Miller (2002), for example, show that in the United States there is a temporary adverse effect on the earnings of immigrants entering the labour market during a period of high unemployment. Immigrants entering during a recession compete with natives for jobs and are less likely to be able to support themselves. Second, the points test used in immigrant selection in the Skilled stream is expected to play a role in determining immigrant labour market outcomes. Miller (1999, p.196), for example, concludes:

> The points systems used in a number of the components of the immigration program in Australia offer a means of selecting immigrants who will adjust rapidly to the circumstances of the Australian labor market and bring benefit to Australia. The analyses reported in this paper show that the tests relating to employability are useful screens.

Finally, the institutional support offered to immigrants by way of welfare or settlement policies will also influence both the attractiveness of Australia as a destination country and post-arrival immigrant labour market outcomes. While Reitz (1998), in a paper based on comparisons of the United States, Canada and Australia, argued that differences in the welfare systems were unlikely to exert a major influence on differences in labour market outcomes across countries, the period of his analysis did not cover some of the important exclusions from eligibility for welfare assistance that had been introduced in Australia. These are reviewed below, and comparative studies of immigrants in Cohort 1 and Cohort 2 discussed in this book attempt to quantify their impact.

Points testing in the skilled migration categories in Australia was introduced in 1989.[9] The major aim of this type of selection mechanism is to identify characteristics in a potential migrant that will benefit Australia or assist with the settlement process. The criteria used to select immigrants in this points test are largely those which have been identified in applied labour market research as being associated with more rapid adjustment among immigrants (for example, educational attainment, labour market experience, English language proficiency, and age). The main changes to the points test over the first few years of operation were to the occupations included in the Priority Occupation List (a list of occupations where there may be job opportunities in Australia, and for that reason were awarded additional points)[10] and the list of occupations requiring English. A Principal Applicant whose occupation was on the list of occupations requiring English was required to speak and write English fluently as well as pass the points test.[11] The components of the points tests at August 1993, which were relevant for many migrants in Cohort 1, are presented in Table 1.1.[12]

In 1993 Independent applicants in the Skilled stream needed to achieve 110 points to pass the test. The Skilled – Australian Sponsored category (which has points for family links) had a pass mark of 100. A second threshold that is important is the 'pool' mark.[13] In 1993 this was 10 points lower than the pass mark for both the Independent category and the Skilled – Australian Sponsored category. Applications that did not achieve the 'pool' mark were refused outright, while those that fell short of the pass mark but which achieved the 'pool' mark were held in reserve in case a lower pass mark was set.[14] Applications that passed the points test for the Independent and Skilled – Australian Sponsored categories, but which would have resulted in the yearly immigration planning limit being exceeded, were processed up to visa stage. Visas were not issued, however, until a place became available in subsequent years. This is termed 'cap and queue' and is the mechanism for visa processing in place at the current time.

Points testing and English language ability

Since August 1993 there have been various changes to the points tests. These were of a relatively minor nature until 1 July 1999, when the recommendations of a major review of the points test were implemented.[15] The minor changes to the points test from 1993 to 1999 included a number that related to English skills. First, the points available for various levels of English ability were altered on 23 May 1994, when a 15 point category was inserted between the existing 10 points and 20 points categories.[16] Second, points were introduced for English language ability for immigrants in the Skilled – Australian Sponsored category on 1 July 1997. Third, there was expansion in the number of occupations included on the Occupations Requiring English list, so that by 1998 it covered almost all skilled occupations. Fully 85 per cent of points-tested applicants had to meet this requirement.[17] Fourth, in 1996 there was a change in the language requirements for these occupations to 'vocational English', defined as the ability to communicate effectively in

Table 1.1 Migrant characteristics awarded points and points available: Skilled migration to Australia, August 1993

	Characteristics	Points as at August 1993[a]
Age	18–29 years:	30
	30–34 years:	20
	35–39 years:	10
	40–49 years:	5
	50+ years:	0
English language[b]	Able to handle basic communication in English on familiar everyday topics or bilingual in languages other than English.	5
	Reasonably proficient in English but some training required.	10
	Proficient in English (able to speak and write English well).	20
Relationship factor[c]	Applicant was the parent, brother, sister, non-dependent child, nephew or niece of sponsor.	15
Citizenship factor[c]	Sponsor had been an Australian citizen for fewer than 5 years.	5
	Sponsor had been an Australian citizen for 5 years or more.	10
Settlement factor[c]	Sponsor has been resident in Australia for 2 years and in continuous employment in Australia for the last 2 years.	10
Location factor[c]	Sponsor has lived in one of a number of special designated areas for the last two years.	5

Notes:

a General requirements related to age (the applicant needed to be less than 65 years if male and less than 60 years if female) and language (proficient in English if the applicant's occupation was listed in the Occupations Requiring English list).

b Applies to Independent immigrants only.

c Applies to Skilled – Australian Sponsored immigrants only.

Source: Department of Immigration and Ethnic Affairs, Form 958i, August 1993.

Table 1.2 Migrant characteristics awarded points and points available: Skilled migration in Australia, 1 July 1999

	Characteristics	Points from 1 July 1999[a]
Skills: Occupation	Occupations that require diploma or advanced diploma level qualifications.	40
	'Generalist' occupations which require degree level training.	50
	Occupations that require degree (or higher) qualifications and where training specific to the occupation is necessary.	60
Skills: Experience	Applicants who have been employed in a skilled occupation for 3 of the 4 years before applying.	5
	Applicants who have worked in a high-skilled occupation for three of the four years before applying.	10
Age	18–29 years	30
	30–34 years	25
	35–39 years	20
	40–44 years	15
	45+ years: ineligible for a visa.	-
English language	Vocational English.	15
	Competent English.	20
Occupational targeting	Skills in short supply in Australia.	5
	Further points for a job offer in a high-demand occupation.	5
Spouse skills	Where the spouse meets the core requirements.	5
Australian qualifications	Diploma, trade qualification or degree from an Australian institution.	5
	Higher degree from an Australian institution.	10
Bonus points	5 points for one of: • 6 months Australian work experience in a skilled occupation in the past 4 years; • commitment to bringing a large amount of capital to Australia; • a high level of fluency on one of Australia's major non-English community languages.	5
Sponsorship[b]		15
Settlement/location	Relaxation of pass mark.	

Notes:

a General requirements, known as core criteria, were a requirement to meet Australian standards for employment in one of a range of occupations, have recent work experience (of between 12 and 24 months, depending on the occupation nominated), be younger than 45 years at the time of lodging their application, and be proficient in English at the vocational level.

b Skilled – Australian Sponsored only.

Source: Department of Immigration and Multicultural and Indigenous Affairs, Fact Sheet 25, July 1999.

English in at least three of the four skills: reading, speaking, understanding and writing. In other words, applicants needed to attain at least 15 points of English skills to meet this threshold. Fifth, from 1997, where skilled Principal Applicants (or their family members aged 18 years or over) lacked functional English, they were required to pay for appropriate English language training. In total, these changes increased the English language requirements for entry into Australia in the Skilled Migration stream.

The recommendations of the major review of the points test in the late 1990s were implemented from 1 July 1999 (see DIMA 1999). From this date the points were as outlined in Table 1.2.

In 1999, to pass the test Independent applicants had to achieve 110 points. The Skilled – Australian Sponsored category also had a pass mark of 110. The 'pool' marks for these categories in 1999 were 70 and 110 respectively.

In addition to the points test, applicants in the Independent and Skilled – Australian Sponsored categories are now required to meet Australian standards for employment in one of a range of occupations, have recent work experience (of between 12 and 24 months, depending on the occupation nominated[18]), be younger than 45 years at the time of lodging their application, and be proficient in English at the vocational level. These minimum thresholds are termed core criteria, and represent a tightening of the former equivalent requirements which related to English proficiency in the Occupations Requiring English.

About 35 per cent of immigrants in the Independent visa category and 20 per cent of the immigrants in the Skilled – Australian Sponsored category in Cohort 2 entered on visas assessed under the post-1 July 1999 points test.[19] The remainder, and those in Cohort 1, entered on visas assessed under different points tests.

A comparison of the points tests that were in operation in 1999 and 1993 highlights four major differences.

First, minimum standards were not explicitly specified in relation to the skills, age and English language ability of either Independent or Skilled – Australian Sponsored immigrants prior to 1 July 1999. Consequently, skilled immigrants in Cohort 2 assessed under the post-1 July 1999 points test were expected to have at least vocational English. This was prescribed in terms of a minimum score of at least five in all four components (writing, reading, listening and speaking) on the International English Language Testing System.[20,21] There was, however, no such minimum threshold in place for all the immigrants in Cohort 1 or for those in the second cohort assessed under the pre-1 July 1999 points test.[22] The impact of this policy change is likely to have been moderated, however, by the fact that immigrants assessed under the pre-1 July 1999 points tests were required to possess vocational English if their usual occupation was on the Occupations Requiring English list. As noted above, this list had been expanded over time so that by 1998 around 85 per cent of all points-tested applicants had to meet this requirement.

Second, until 1 July 1997 points were not given for English language ability to immigrants in the Skilled – Australian Sponsored category (DIMA, 1999, p.50). Immigrants in this category in Cohort 2 are therefore expected to have initial English language skills superior to those of their counterparts in Cohort 1. Given that points were given for Independent immigrants in Cohort 1, the move to a common requirement for English language ability for skilled immigrants should be associated with a more pronounced improvement in initial English language skills for Skilled – Australian Sponsored immigrants than for Independent category immigrants.

Third, the other (seemingly more minor) changes to the role of English language ability in immigrant selection in Australia will impact positively on those immigrants in Cohort 2. This will reinforce the effects of the more pronounced policy changes noted above. These include, for example, the 23 May 1994 changes to the points available for various levels of English ability, which inserted a 15 points category between the existing 10 and 20 points categories.

Fourth, prior to 1 July 1999 the modest number of points – five – currently allocated when the applicant's spouse also meets the core criteria for skills were not available. This may have had a small positive impact on the language skills of the spouses of Principal Applicants and a negative impact on the Principal Applicant's proficiency at the time of application.

These changes to the points system used in the selection of immigrants in the Independent and Skilled – Australian Sponsored categories focused on immigrant characteristics that have been shown in research in Australia and overseas, and in the chapters in this volume, to be associated with labour market success. Accordingly, it would be expected that the skill level of immigrants in Cohort 2 for the points-tested visa categories will be greater than for the skills-tested immigrants in Cohort 1. No such improvement is expected for immigrants in the Family stream and the Humanitarian category. Comparisons of the English language proficiency and labour market outcomes of the two groups of immigrants from both the LSIA cohorts offer the opportunity to assess the impact on post-arrival outcomes that the points system can have.

THE AUSTRALIAN LABOUR MARKET DURING THE 1990s

The Australian labour market of the early 1990s has been described as 'poor by international standards' (Watts 2000, p.27). Double digit unemployment rates were experienced by most groups. Among men, the unemployment rate for the Australian-born and for immigrants from English-speaking countries was as high as 11 per cent in 1993, when immigrants from Cohort 1 started to arrive.[23] In the same year the unemployment rate for male immigrants from non-English-speaking countries was 16 per cent. As shown in Figure 1.2, since 1993 the labour market has been characterised by almost continual improvement. In 2000, when many immigrants in Cohort 2 arrived, the unemployment rate was around 7 per cent for male immigrants from non-English-speaking countries, 6.3 per cent for Australian-born males and 5.3 per cent for male immigrants from English-speaking countries. Figure 1.2 shows that changes in unemployment rates were similar for these three birthplace groups.

The 1990s also brought a continuation of the trends in labour force participation rates which have been such a strong characteristic of the Australian labour market since the early 1970s (see Norris and Wooden 1996). In particular, male labour force participation rates declined over much of the 1990s, whereas female participation rates increased. As illustrated in Figure 1.3, the changes in labour supply have not been neutral with respect to birthplace. Thus, whereas the decline in the participation rates for Australian-born men over the period represented in Figure 1.3 was only around 2 percentage points, and that for immigrants from English-speaking countries was just 3 percentage points, the decline for immigrants from non-English-speaking countries was close to 10 percentage points. Among women there was growth in the labour force participation rates of the Australian-born and of immigrants from English-speaking countries, but little change in the labour force participation rates of immigrants from non-English-speaking countries.

Labour market outcomes and duration of residence

Australian studies (for example, Miller and Neo 2003) have drawn attention to the changes in immigrant labour market outcomes with duration of residence in Australia. Miller and Neo (2003) argue that many recently arrived immigrants in Australia attempt to enter jobs covered by award conditions. To the extent that these conditions are determined largely with the native-born and longer-term immigrants in mind, and for that reason have above-market-clearing wage levels for recent arrivals, it is expected that recent immigrants will experience relatively high probabilities of being unemployed. As duration of residence in Australia increases, and the immigrants acquire Australia-specific skills, productivity tends to converge to the institutionally determined (above-market-clearing) rates and so the probability of unemployment diminishes. Thus, in Australia, because of wage rigidity, much of the adjustment of immigrants is observed in their employment status rather than in their relative wages (Miller and Neo 2003). This is unlike the United States and Canada which both have greater wage flexibility in their labour market.

Figure 1.2 Unemployment rates by gender and region of origin, 1991–2004

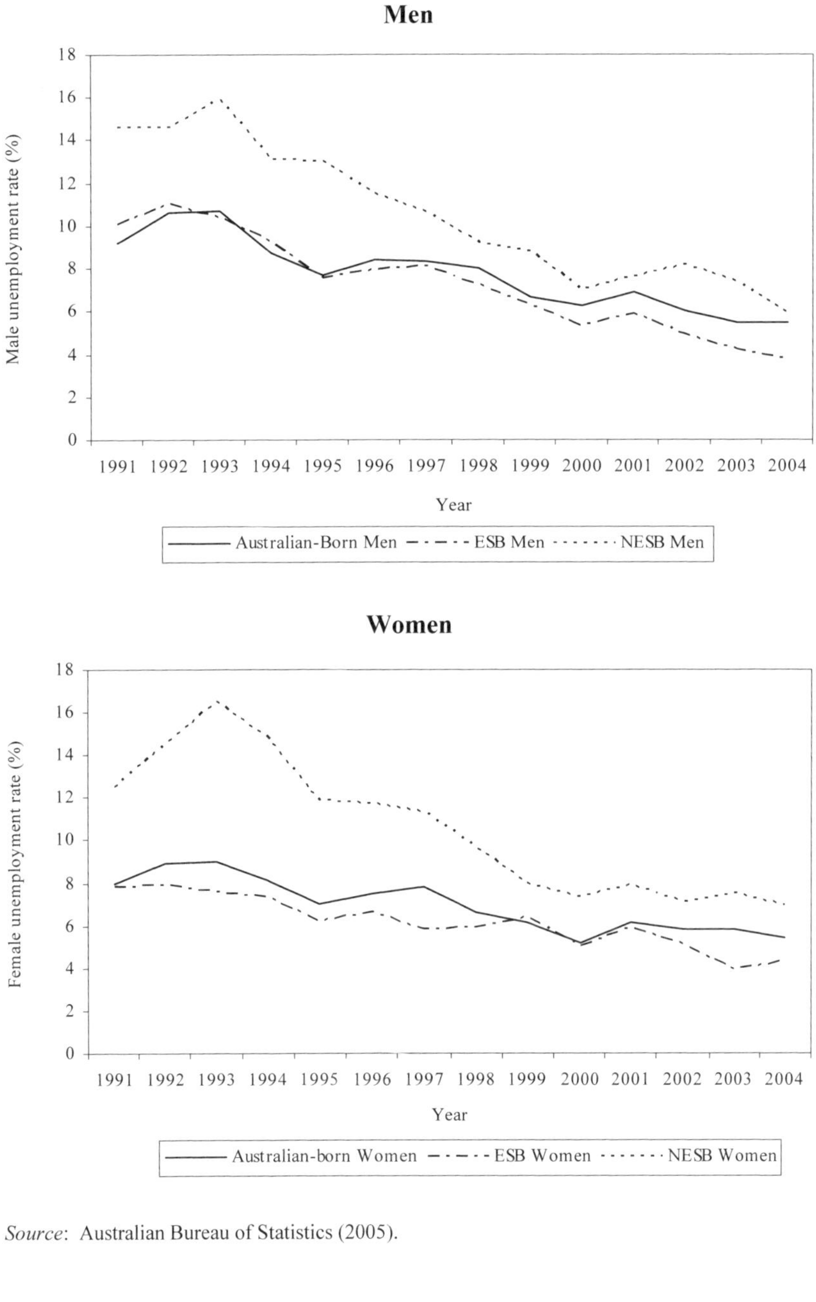

Source: Australian Bureau of Statistics (2005).

Figure 1.3 Labour force participation rates by gender and region of origin, 1991–2004

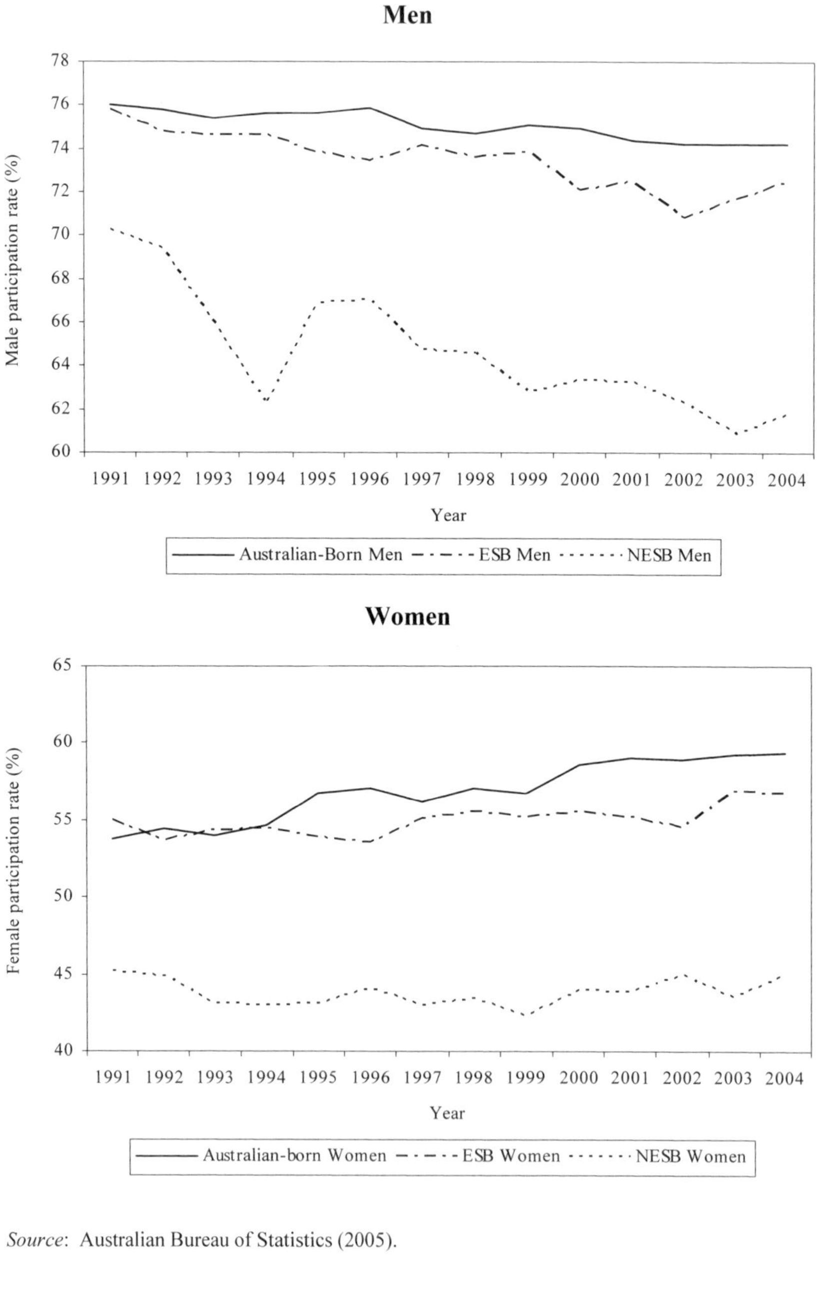

Source: Australian Bureau of Statistics (2005).

Figure 1.4 Unemployment rates by gender and duration of residence, 1995 and 2000

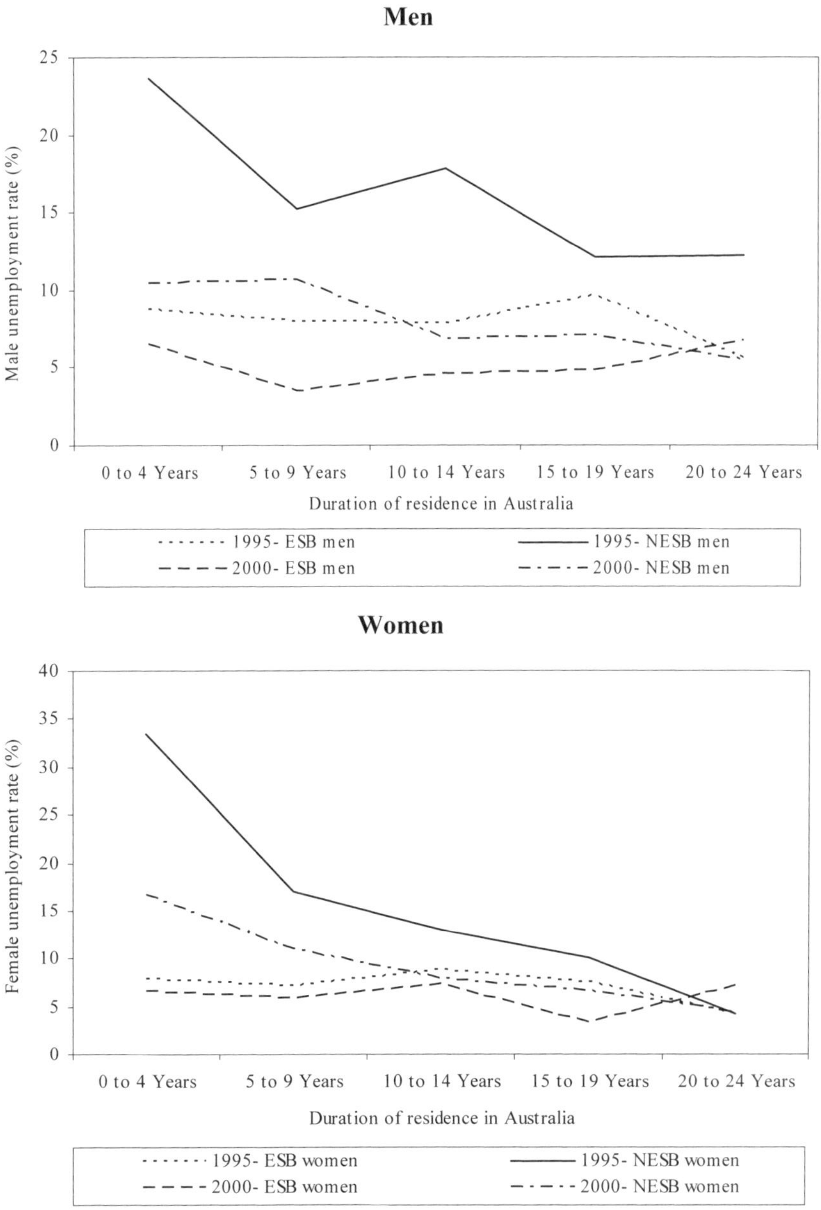

Source: Australian Bureau of Statistics (2005).

Figure 1.4 displays the unemployment rate/duration of residence profiles for immigrants in two years: 1995 and 2000. For each year separate profiles are presented for immigrants from English-speaking countries and for immigrants from non-English-speaking countries. These years represent different stages of the business cycle. The unemployment rate for Australian-born males was 7.7 per cent in 1995 and 6.3 per cent in 2000.

These data show that the inverse relationship between unemployment rates and duration of residence in Australia is particularly evident among immigrants from non-English-speaking countries, and is more pronounced during periods of relatively high unemployment than it is during periods of low unemployment. The aggregate unemployment rate for immigrants from non-English-speaking countries in 1995 was 13 per cent, whereas it was only 7.6 per cent for this group in 2001. The patterns in the data on unemployment rates by duration of residence for females are similar to those displayed for males. It is clear that the second cohort of the LSIA entered the Australian labour market under much more favourable conditions than the first cohort. The aggregate-level evidence in Figure 1.4 suggests that the 'equalising' effects that the tighter labour market appears to have across subgroups of the immigrant population will have more of an impact on the labour market outcomes of immigrants from non-English-speaking countries than it will on the labour market outcomes of immigrants from English-speaking countries.

Business cycle and participation rates

Labour force participation rates also appear to vary with the business cycle. The patterns evident in Figure 1.5 for males, however, suggest that influences other than the business cycle are operative. Among recent immigrants from English-speaking countries, the labour force participation rate was higher in the year of tighter labour markets (2000) but among other immigrants it was higher during the year of greater unemployment (1995) than in the year of tighter labour markets. This lower labour force participation rate in 2000 for immigrants from non-English-speaking countries was presumably associated with the factors that led to a lower unemployment rate in 2000 than in 1995. Changes in these immigrants' access to welfare support (which may have led to benefit-induced unemployment in 1995 but not in 2000) are prime candidates. These will be discussed later in the chapter.

Another feature of Figure 1.5 is the rapid improvement in labour force participation rates as duration of residence increases for male immigrants from non-English-speaking countries. This is also a feature of labour force participation rates among female immigrants.

Figure 1.5 Labour force participation rates by gender and duration of residence, 1995 and 2000

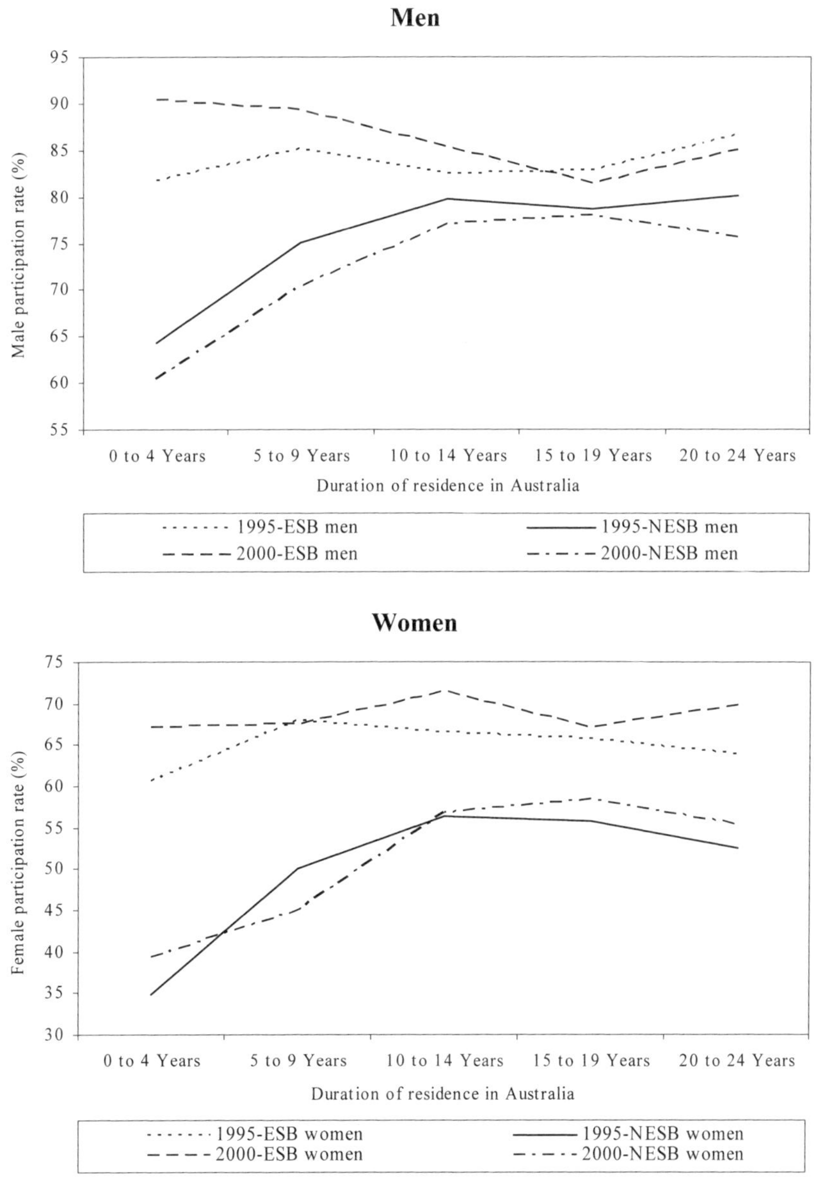

Source: Australian Bureau of Statistics (2005).

Unemployment and birthplace

Finally, Figure 1.6 presents information on male unemployment rates for a number of the major birthplace groups. There are three features of this graph.

First, each of the major birthplace groups experienced improvements in labour market outcomes in the 1990s. Second, the high unemployment groups in the early 1990s were typically also high unemployment groups in the late 1990s. Similarly, the foreign-born groups that had unemployment rates around that of the Australian-born in the early 1990s also had unemployment rates around that of the Australian-born in the late 1990s. Hence, with the exception of movements over the business cycle, there appears to be a degree of stability in the relative unemployment outcomes by birthplace group in the Australian labour market.

Summary

In summary, the Australian labour market improved rapidly during the 1990s. This improvement appears to have had a major impact on the labour market success of immigrants as measured by their unemployment rates, particularly immigrants from non-English-speaking countries. However, a review of the labour force participation rates of immigrants across the 1990s suggests that their participation may have been influenced by non-labour market factors. Two potential influences are the points test used in immigrant selection (reviewed earlier) and the arrangements for welfare payments, reviewed below.

IMMIGRANTS AND THE WELFARE STATE

Immigrants' access to social welfare benefits can be expected to affect both the decision to migrate to Australia and post-migration behaviour. According to Richardson et al. (2001, p.82), whenever immigrants' access to social welfare benefits is tightened, 'People who feel less confident of being able to support themselves, through employment, self-employment or income from assets, or do not have family on whom they could rely if necessary, will face a higher risk of serious hardship on migrating. Some will be deterred by this greater risk'. Those who do migrate, however, would be expected to feel greater urgency about securing employment when they are affected by any tightening in the eligibility criteria for welfare benefits. As well, there will be a greater return migration rate, especially in a recession, if migrants in economic distress have reduced access to the income transfer system (welfare).

Figure 1.6 Unemployment rates by country or region of birth, 1991–2003

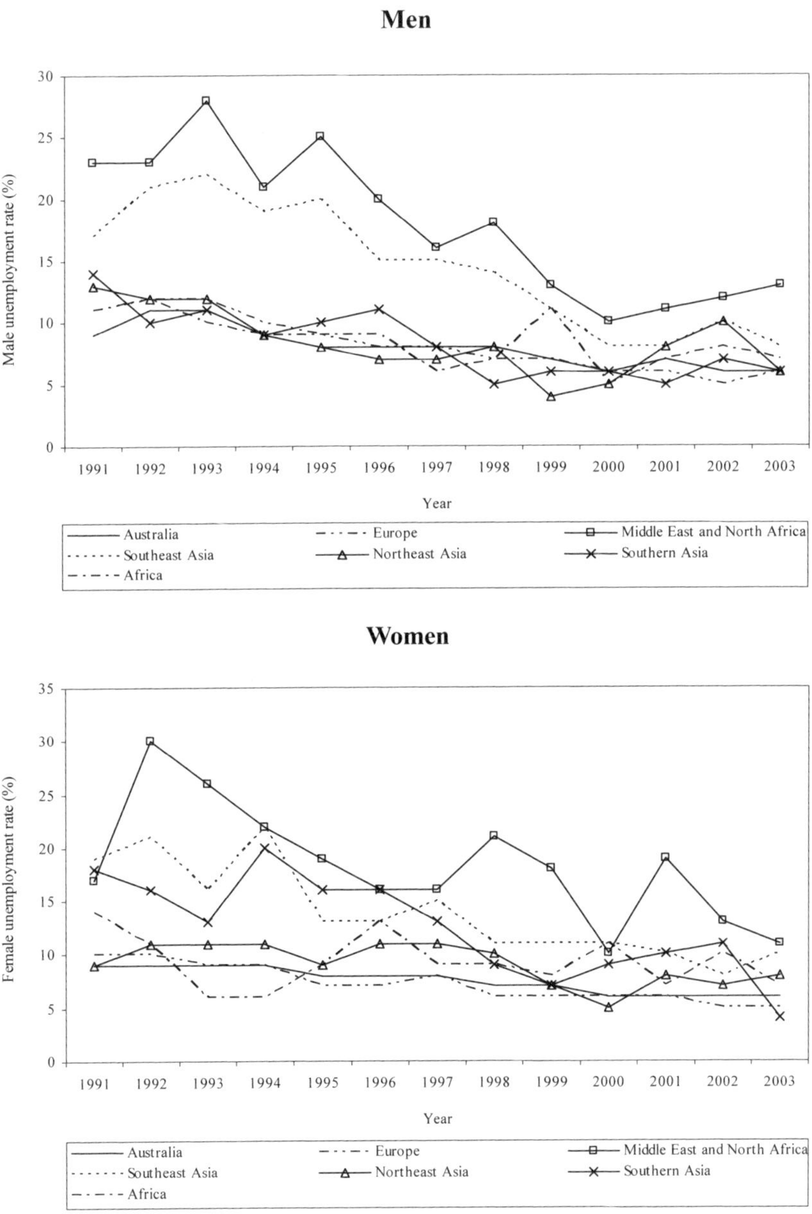

Source: Australian Bureau of Statistics (2005).

Birrell and Evans (1996), Murphy and Williams (1996) and Richardson et al. (2001) provide accounts of the effects of recent changes in immigrant access to social welfare benefits in Australia. It is apparent that the provision of welfare to recent arrivals is a controversial issue. Birrell and Evans (1996, p.1) argue 'What obligation does society owe to such immigrants, given that they have not yet contributed to the wealth which makes the payments possible? If the answer is that obligations to new arrivals are not the same as those owed to longstanding residents, will this create undesirable divisions within the national community?'

Policy changes and their impact

There are two dates of special significance in relation to recent immigrants' entitlements to social welfare in Australia: 1 January 1993 and 4 March 1997.[24]

Prior to 1 January 1993, immigrants, including recent arrivals, had access to social welfare benefits and were subject to the same waiting periods as the Australian-born.[25] Immigrants who arrived in Australia after 1 January 1993, however, were not eligible for Job Search Allowance, Newstart Allowance or Sickness Allowance until six months after their arrival or their receipt of their permanent residence visa, whichever was the later (Daniels 2004). This waiting period was also applied to the Youth Training Allowance and Parenting Allowance, introduced in 1995 (Parliamentary Library 1996). Murphy and Williams (1996, p.16) explain that 'The rationale for the waiting period, announced as part of the 1992–1993 budget, was that newly arrived migrants can be expected to make provision for their own needs for a reasonable period in Australia, before calling on taxpayer support'. Not all immigrants were subject to this waiting period, however. The first group of exceptions comprised immigrants entering Australia under the Humanitarian program. The second group was comprised of the partners of Australian residents with more than 26 weeks of permanent residence in Australia. In addition, immigrants who could demonstrate financial hardship were eligible for Special Benefit. As noted in Birrell and Evans (1996), all new arrivals gained immediate access to Medicare benefits, family payments and Austudy.

Murphy and Williams's (1996) study of welfare benefits received by immigrants in Cohort 1 shows there was considerable usage of these benefits by recent arrivals, and this extended to most major visa groups. The differences across visa groups appeared to reflect well the 1993 waiting period rules and exemptions.

Despite the introduction of the 26-week waiting period, Birrell and Evans (1996, p.1) described the welfare arrangements in Australia at the time (1996) as being relatively generous, with the gap between the entitlements in

Australia and in the immigrant-sending countries helping to create 'an enormous incentive to seek out migration opportunities'.

The second significant date in immigrants' eligibility for welfare was 4 March 1997. This was when a waiting period of 104 weeks was introduced for the Newstart Allowance, Sickness Allowance and a range of other allowances for immigrants arriving after that date (for example, Mature Age Allowance, Partner Allowance, Carer Payment, Youth Allowance, Austudy Payments, Mobility Allowance, Special Benefit, Commonwealth Seniors Health Card and the Health Care Card). Moreover, the exemption previously granted to spouses joining partners who had served the waiting period was no longer available. In other words, spouses had to serve their own two-year waiting period. The reason for these measures was, according to the Parliamentary Library (1996), 'The Government expects that new entrants to Australia should provide for their own support during their first two years (104 weeks) in Australia'.

A number of exemptions were, however, put in place. In particular, immigrants entering under the Humanitarian program were not affected by these changes. In addition, a Special Benefit was payable where the immigrant suffered severe hardship during the 104 weeks waiting period due to circumstances beyond their control. This payment was to be made at the discretion of the Secretary of the (then) Department of Social Security, and the circumstances under which it could be paid represented a significant tightening of eligibility compared to the 'demonstrate financial hardship' criterion that applied before the change. In particular, the inability to find employment was not viewed as a circumstance warranting the payment of Special Benefits. Access to both the Family Allowance and Medicare was retained, however.

Richardson et al. (2001, p.44) show that this tightening of the eligibility criteria for welfare benefits resulted in a marked reduction in the number of immigrants receiving benefits. However, while these changes appear to be quite major, their overall impact needs to be kept in perspective. The exemptions in place for immigrants entering under the Humanitarian program, the provision, albeit restricted, of Special Benefits, and the presence of Assurances of Support for immigrants such as those in the Family stream, minimised the overall impact. Consistent with this, assessments by Richardson et al. (2001, p.28) suggest that 'There is no support ... for the proposition that migrants in Cohort 2 have been forced to accept poor jobs by virtue of the unavailability of social welfare benefits'.

There were a number of other changes to welfare eligibility that may impact upon utilisation rates among immigrants in Cohort 1 and Cohort 2. Two that appear to be particularly important are described below.

First, in September 1994, the additional amount of Job Search Allowance/ Newstart Allowance/Sickness Allowance paid to recipients who had a dependent spouse was replaced by an allowance paid directly to the dependent spouse. This change was expected to increase the number of recent arrivals in the Family stream receiving Job Search Allowances, particularly in Cohort 1 (Murphy and Williams 1996).

Second, in 1997 the number of visas for aged parents was capped, and for 1997–1998 the cap was 1,000 visas, a considerable reduction on the number of visas issued in previous years. This was partially relaxed in 1998, although the 'parent' category was then subject to the payment of bonds to underwrite the required Assurance of Support and to higher non-refundable health care charges that needed to be paid before the parent entered Australia. The 1997 policy change was expected to alter the age-mix of immigrants in the Family migration category (Richardson et al. 2001).

The progressive tightening of recent arrivals' eligibility for social welfare benefits in Australia would be expected to affect their post-arrival activities. Benefit-induced unemployment should have declined, and job search in the immediate post-arrival period intensified. The changes will be more apparent for immigrants in Cohort 2 than they will be for the immigrants in Cohort 1. Comparisons across the two cohorts therefore provide an opportunity to assess the importance of the welfare state to immigrants' post-arrival activities.

CONCLUSION

The 1990s brought a number of significant changes to the methods used to select immigrants for entry into Australia, to conditions in the Australian labour market, and to the eligibility criteria for social welfare benefits in Australia. These changes are expected to have had a marked impact on the mix of immigrants coming to Australia, and to the experiences of immigrants in the Australian labour market, especially in the immediate post-arrival period.

The Australian labour market improved more or less continuously throughout the 1990s. This means that immigrants arriving later in the 1990s, and represented in Cohort 2, could be expected to have had an easier transition into the labour market than those in Cohort 1 who arrived earlier in the decade. The improvement in the labour market experiences of immigrants during the 1990s due to the cyclical upturn would have been reinforced by the changes to the points test used in immigrant selection in the Skilled stream. When formally introduced in 1989, the points test selected immigrants on the basis of characteristics linked to labour market success. The changes to the points test during the 1990s, and particularly the major changes introduced from 1 July 1999, strengthened the role of skills linked to better labour market outcomes in immigrant selection.

Finally, immigrants' access to social welfare benefits was restricted during the 1990s. This will have both altered the mix of immigrants seeking to migrate to Australia (those more prone to unemployment may have been deterred from migrating) and impacted on post-arrival labour market activity. The changes would have reduced benefit-induced unemployment and induced greater urgency in obtaining employment among those affected by the various waiting periods introduced. For immigrants who could not find a job or who had lost a job it would also have increased the incentive to consider returning to their origin country, or to consider migrating to another country.

These changes – in conditions in the Australian labour market, to the points test used in immigrant selection, and in eligibility for social welfare benefits – affected immigrants in the two cohorts of the LSIA to varying degrees. Accordingly, comparison of the personal characteristics (for example, English language skills) and labour market outcomes of immigrants in the two LSIA cohorts provides a basis for assessing the roles of these two factors in the post-arrival experience of immigrants in Australia. The chapters that follow provide these comparisons.

NOTES

1. Excluded from the scope of the survey were New Zealand citizens for whom there is unrestricted entry into Australia and those granted an immigrant visa while resident in Australia on other types of visas.
2. New Zealand residents are subject to the 1973 Trans-Tasman Travel Arrangement, which provides for unrestricted mobility between Australia and New Zealand.
3. This separation of the Humanitarian and Migration programs dates back to January 1993.
4. In the words of the National Population Council (1988, p.7), 'numbers were self-determining'.
5. Within the Family stream, some subclasses (for example, spouses, dependent children) remain exempt from capping.
6. Currently, most Business Skills immigrants enter Australia on a provisional or temporary visa for four years. After satisfactory evidence of business or investment activity, they may apply for permanent residence. Sub-visa categories set out minimum requirements in terms of net assets, business turnover, age, language proficiency and general requirements.
7. Until 1 July 1997 this category was included in the Family stream as the Concessional Family category.
8. The names of the visa groups have changed over time. For example, the Skilled – Australian Sponsored group was formerly termed the Skilled – Australian Linked category, and before that the Concessional Family category. The names used in this book are those in place in the late 1990s.
9. See Appendix 1 of Kan (1991) for information on changes in Australia's immigration policy leading up to 1989. As noted by Kan (1991), numerical scoring was used as an administrative arrangement as early as 1979. The importance of the change in 1989 was that the points system was recognised in law.
10. From October 1992 there were no occupations on the Priority Occupation List. The principle of targeting particular occupations was, however, re-introduced in the more recent post-1 July 1999 points test.
11. At this time, occupation was defined as usual occupation, namely the job in which applicants had worked continuously for at least six months in the two years prior to lodging their migration visa application.

12 When a visa is issued to a Principal Applicant, visas in the same category are also generally issued to the applicant's spouse and all minor or dependent children.

13 In 1993 there was also a 'Priority Mark'. As this had been set equal to the Pass Mark from 1990, and was abandoned in 1994, it is not included in this discussion.

14 Initially the applications in the pool were held until they were assessed against three different pass marks. Since 1994 pooled applications have been held for one year only.

15 See Department of Immigration and Multicultural Affairs (DIMA) (1999).

16 The points awarded were as follows: 'Able to communicate effectively in English in a range of situations' (20 points); 'At the level described for 20 points for three of the four skills of reading, speaking, understanding and writing, but at a lower level for the remaining skill' (15 points); 'Able to communicate effectively in English on familiar, everyday topics' (10 points); 'Able to handle basic communication in English on familiar everyday topics or fluent in at least two languages other than English' (5 points).

17 Department of Immigration and Multicultural Affairs (1999, p.50).

18 Under the new points test applicants are required to nominate the occupation against which they wish to be assessed, and for which they meet Australian standards. This does not have to be their 'usual' occupation, as defined above.

19 Immigrants in the newer visa classes were over-sampled. The respective population estimates are 17 per cent of Independent immigrants and 4 per cent of Skilled – Australian Sponsored immigrants respectively.

20 The International English Language Testing system is jointly managed by University of Cambridge ESOL Examinations, the British Council and IDP Education Australia: IELTS Australia. Further details are available from http://www.ielts.org/what.htm.

21 According to the IELTS website, a score of 5 indicates that the individual has partial command of the language, coping with overall meaning in most situations, though s/he is likely to make many mistakes. The individual should be able to handle basic communication in her/his own field. As a benchmark, an overall score of 6.0 on this test will satisfy immigration requirements (though not necessary those of individual institutions) for a student visa for enrolment in a higher education degree in Australia.

22 The importance of this has been noted by the Department of Immigration and Multicultural Affairs (1999, p.36), 'Under the current pass mark...(Skilled – Australian Sponsored applicants) may gain sufficient points...if their occupation is not on the Occupations Requiring English list, where they speak no English'.

23 The English-speaking countries, as defined by the Australian Bureau of Statistics in their publications, include New Zealand, the United Kingdom, the Republic of Ireland, the United States of America, Canada and South Africa.

24 For an excellent overview of changes to welfare payments (between 1942 and 2004), see Daniels (2004).

25 The names of specific forms of welfare benefits have changed over time. For instance, the Unemployment Benefit program was introduced in July 1945, and replaced by the Job Search Allowance and Newstart Allowance in July 1991 (see Daniels 2004). These two forms of assistance were subsequently amalgamated under the title Newstart Allowance in September 1996. Other name changes are outlined in Daniels (2004).

PART TWO

LABOUR MARKET ENTRY

2. Selection Policy and the Labour Market Outcomes of New Immigrants

Deborah A. Cobb-Clark

INTRODUCTION

The increasing complexity of large-scale movements of people across international borders has policymakers grappling with difficult issues surrounding the design and implementation of policies meant to ensure that the potential benefits of immigration are realised for the host country.[1] Selection policies – in which some potential immigrants are chosen over others – have historically been used, in conjunction with quotas on the level of immigration, as the primary means of achieving national objectives regarding immigration. Like Australia, other countries over the 1990s moved to place a greater emphasis on productive skills (including entrepreneurial skills) in the selection process.[2] These changes stem primarily from the belief that skill-based immigrants do better in some sense and provide greater economic benefits than immigrants admitted on the basis of their family relationships.

This chapter updates previous research exploring the potential for selection criteria, income-support policy and labour market conditions to facilitate entry into the Australian labour market (see Cobb-Clark, 2003). That research assessed initial outcomes (six months after migration) and concluded that the substantially improved outcomes for new arrivals over the 1990s resulted largely from changes in selection policy that led to enhanced skills amongst new immigrants. Still, changes in labour market conditions and income-support policy – which most likely altered the returns to human capital – appear to have been instrumental in reinforcing the effects of tighter selection criteria. This chapter re-examines these issues at a later stage – 18 months after migration – of the settlement process. The question is: are immigrant outcomes over the longer run related to selection policy?

Understanding the relationship between immigrant outcomes and selection criteria is important because the success of the migration decision rests for many immigrants on making a successful transition into the new labour market. This is especially true in the early stages of settlement, and continues to be the case even in later stages of family reunion and community formation (Wooden et al. 1994). It is, therefore, important to understand the capacity of immigrant selection policy to facilitate this transition. Selection policy also has implications beyond influencing outcomes for individual immigrants. By altering the skills of the immigrant flow – and consequently the extent to which immigrants and natives act as substitutes for one another – selection policy can affect macro-employment and wage outcomes. Selection policy may also have fiscal effects if it is used to influence the extent to which new immigrants are likely to be reliant on the income-support system. Finally, selection policy is inherently bound up in the formation of attitudes towards immigrants, in attempts to achieve a range of other social and demographic goals, as well as in the political economy of decision making regarding immigration policy generally.[3]

The results indicate that the increased emphasis on productive skills in the selection process led individuals entering Australia in the late 1990s to have more education, better language skills and more recent labour market experience than those individuals entering five years earlier. This expansion in skills explains completely the increased propensity for the second LSIA cohort to be labour market participants 18 months after migration. In contrast, the decline in unemployment – especially for women – is more closely related to differences in the returns to productive characteristics that stem from changes in both income-support policy and aggregate labour market conditions. On the whole, however, up to two-thirds of the gap in the proportion of new arrivals who have found employment 18 months after migration stems from inter-cohort differences in productive skills. These patterns provide strong evidence that immigrant selection policy does influence immigrant outcomes, not just immediately after migration, but also over the medium run.

SELECTION POLICY AND IMMIGRANT OUTCOMES

Is selection policy a useful tool for capturing the potential economic gains, to both the host nations and individual immigrants themselves, which could be derived from immigration? Many researchers in a number of different countries have addressed this question. The overarching conclusion is that selection criteria can be important in shaping immigration outcomes. However, while selection criteria – and settlement policy more broadly – can lead to improved economic outcomes, they may also have unintended effects.

Researchers have used the similarities in the Canadian, United States and (occasionally) Australian labour markets and the dissimilarities in their immigration policies to shed light on the ways in which selection criteria might matter (see Chiswick 1987, Duleep and Regets 1992, Borjas 1993, Antecol et al. 2003a, 2003b). These cross-national comparisons highlight the important role of the national origin mix in determining the skill level of the overall immigrant stream. Immigrants from newer source countries generally do less well than those from traditional sources (see Chiswick 1987, for example). However, the extent to which any differences in national origin mix stem from variation in immigrant selection policy is a matter of debate. Borjas (1993) concludes that the Canadian points system 'attracted' more educated immigrants because it altered the national origin mix. At the same time, Antecol et al. (2003a, 2003b) note that while much of the cross-national difference in immigrant skills does stem from the distribution across national origins, this distribution is similar for both men, who are often selected on the basis of skills, and women, who are not. The authors conclude therefore that factors other than selection policy per se – that is, geographic, historical and/or social forces – contribute to producing the national origin mix of immigrants.

Selection policy has also been linked to both the initial occupational distribution and the earnings of new arrivals. The introduction of the Canadian points system in 1967, for example, shifted the inflow of immigrants to Canada away from less-skilled occupations (such as labourers) and towards professions. However, subsequent changes in the entry-class and national-origin composition of immigrant admissions have reduced the tendency for immigrants to Canada to be assessed under the points system.[4] At the same time, entry class matters. Skill-based immigrants are more likely to enter skilled occupations both in Canada (Green 1995, 1999) and in the United States (Sorensen et al. 1992, Jasso and Rosenzweig 1995). Entry class is also related to immigrant earnings. Employment-based immigrants to the United States have higher initial earnings (Sorensen et al. 1992, Duleep and Regets 1996), while the fraction of individuals entering Canada as independent migrants is positively related to average entry wages (Wright and Maxim 1993).

Although research indicates that selection criteria are almost certainly related to immigration outcomes, it is useful to bear in mind three observations regarding this relationship. First, selection criteria are most closely related to outcomes at the time of arrival and over time distinctions become less sharp. Jasso and Rosenzweig (1995) note, for example, that with time the occupational distribution of family- and skill-based immigrants becomes more similar, while Sorensen et al. (1992) suggest that these two immigrant groups are actually quite similar in many respects, including in their labour market attachment, their rate of naturalization and their geographic distribution. Second, although more detailed individual-level survey data point to rather large differences in the outcomes of individuals in different visa categories, these differentials largely appear to reflect the underlying characteristics of immigrants themselves rather than immigration categories per se (Miller 1999, Cobb-Clark 2000, 2003). This is especially true for established – as opposed to recent – immigrants. While the observable characteristics of individuals within visa categories do seem to be correlated, there is little unobserved heterogeneity associated with visa category. To the extent that migration programs operate by selecting individuals on the basis of readily observable characteristics, this is perhaps not surprising. Finally, policies beyond selection criteria also matter. Edin et al. (2004) conclude, for example, that recent changes in immigrant settlement and integration policy in Sweden combined to produce substantial long run earnings losses for immigrants. Earnings losses are primarily the result of the changed integration policy that reduced the focus on labour market assimilation and expanded access to the income-support system. New settlement policies mitigated these losses somewhat, however, by dispersing immigrants across more geographic areas.

DATA SAMPLE AND VARIABLES OF INTEREST

Attention can be focused on the effects of policy by drawing comparisons between the two LSIA entry cohorts at a similar point in the settlement process. Consequently, this chapter will focus solely on outcomes measured at Wave 2, that is, approximately 18 months after migration.[5] A number of outcomes will be considered. Specifically, LSIA respondents were asked about their 'current main activity'. Individuals were coded as employed if they responded that their current main activity was working as a wage or salary earner or conducting a business. Labour market participants were employed individuals or individuals responding that they were unemployed and looking for either part-time or full-time work.[6] Further, all LSIA respondents – irrespective of current labour market status – were asked whether (and if so for how long) they had ever been unemployed and looking for work since arriving in Australia. 'Ever unemployed' is a dummy variable which equals one for individuals experiencing a period of unemployment since arrival, and zero otherwise. 'Months unemployed' captures, irrespective of current labour market status, the total duration of post-migration unemployment.

LABOUR MARKET OUTCOMES AND HUMAN CAPITAL ENDOWMENTS

Participation rates, employment-to-population ratios, and unemployment indicators for both cohorts are reported separately by gender and visa category in Table 2.1. Cohort differences 18 months after migration largely mirror differences earlier in the settlement process (see Cobb-Clark 2003) and show the dramatic improvement in immigrants' early labour market outcomes over the later half of the 1990s. There are large increases in the overall participation rate 18 months after migration from 57.2 per cent (Cohort 1) to 64.4 per cent (Cohort 2). This is driven largely by the behaviour of immigrant women. At the same time unemployment fell dramatically, leading to a substantial improvement in the employment-to-population ratio. The unemployment rate of Cohort 2 immigrants (9.9 per cent) is less than half that of Cohort 1 immigrants (22.3 per cent) at the same stage of the settlement process.

The end result is that somewhat less than half (44.4 per cent) of immigrants entering Australia between 1993 and 1995 had found employment 18 months after migration, while the employment-to-population ratio at the same point in the settlement process is 58.1 per cent for the cohort entering five years later. Finally, Cohort 2 immigrants are more likely to report experiencing some unemployment since arrival (59.9 per cent versus 56.8 per cent) – most likely the result of their greater tendency to enter the labour market – although, on average, immigrants arriving in Australia in the later part of the 1990s spent fewer months unemployed than did their counterparts who entered earlier.[7]

Table 2.1 also documents the variation across visa categories in the participation rates and unemployment experiences of men and women in the two cohorts. In order to illustrate these differences, participation rates, unemployment rates and employment-to-population ratios are shown in Figures 2.1–2.3. Irrespective of the type of visa they held, Cohort 2 immigrants are much less likely to have been unemployed 18 months after arriving in Australia. The fall in unemployment is particularly impressive (from 12.6 to 4.7 per cent for men and from 14.9 to 9.7 per cent for women) for skilled Independent migrants, who were subject to the new points test (see Chapter 1). It is also evident for Family stream and Humanitarian immigrants who were not subject to the test. These falls in unemployment are even more impressive in light of the increased labour market participation rate that led proportionately more Cohort 2 immigrants to seek employment in the first place. The sole exception to the trend in improving labour market outcomes is the substantial fall in the participation rate (see Figure 2.1) of men and women holding Humanitarian visas. Though the probability of being unemployed – conditional on labour market entry – is also substantially lower, the fall in participation dominates, leading the employment-to-population ratio for Humanitarian immigrants to be lower in Cohort 2 than in Cohort 1.[8]

Table 2.2 compares the productivity-related characteristics of the two LSIA cohorts. The distribution of LSIA immigrants across visa categories highlights the expansion of the skilled immigration program and the relative scaling back of the Family and Humanitarian streams. Amongst the immigrants interviewed at Wave 2, the proportion who entered on a skills-based visa increased from one in three (35.2 per cent) in the first cohort to one in two

Table 2.1 Labour market outcomes 18 months after migration: LSIA Cohort 1 and Cohort 2 by gender and visa category

	Participation rate %	Unemployment rate %	Employment to population ratio	Months unemployed	Percentage ever unemployed %
Total					
Cohort 1	57.2	22.3	0.444	2.80	56.8
Cohort 2	64.4	9.9	0.581	2.29	59.9
Men					
Cohort 1	78.6	22.4	0.610	3.30	62.0
Cohort 2	81.9	10.0	0.737	2.61	63.6
Women					
Cohort 1	39.6	22.2	0.308	2.40	52.5
Cohort 2	49.5	9.6	0.448	2.03	56.7
Men Cohort 1					
Family	72.6	19.7	0.583	2.82	55.2
SAS	88.1	18.5	0.717	3.38	75.4
BS/ENS	93.4	3.7	0.899	0.38	24.0
Independent	90.1	12.6	0.788	2.86	72.5
Humanitarian	65.6	56.8	0.283	5.64	64.4
Men Cohort 2					
Family	79.1	14.7	0.674	3.34	62.7
SAS	92.7	6.3	0.868	2.70	84.5
BS/ENS	91.5	0.3	0.913	0.77	23.0
Independent	89.4	4.7	0.852	1.61	66.4
Humanitarian	40.3	48.9	0.206	4.74	58.9
Women Cohort 1					
Family	35.6	23.0	0.274	2.17	42.5
SAS	57.1	22.1	0.445	2.93	75.2
BS/ENS	40.8	6.0	0.384	1.01	27.7
Independent	54.8	14.9	0.149	2.34	73.8
Humanitarian	26.5	42.2	0.153	3.42	59.2
Women Cohort 2					
Family	45.2	11.3	0.401	2.18	49.1
SAS	70.0	5.3	0.662	3.18	83.0
BS/ENS	45.6	0.5	0.454	0.63	22.4
Independent	62.5	9.7	0.565	1.75	70.8
Humanitarian	11.5	32.4	0.077	1.60	50.4

Note:
See Technical Appendix for variable definitions.

Source: Longitudinal Survey of Immigrants to Australia.

Figure 2.1 Labour force participation rate 18 months after migration, by gender and visa category

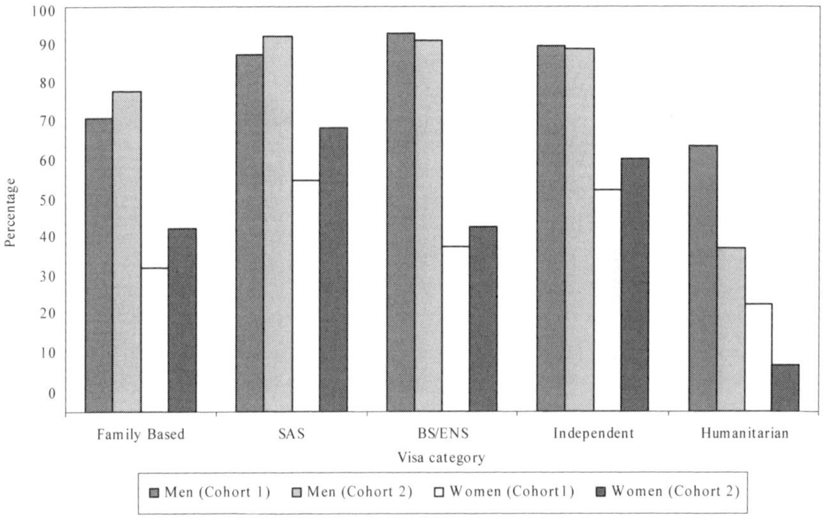

Figure 2.2 Unemployment rate 18 months after migration, by gender and visa category

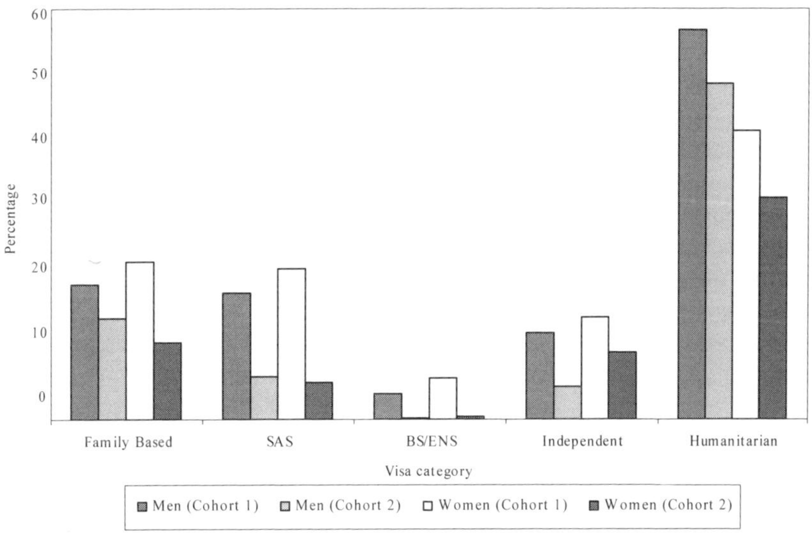

Note:
SAS – Skilled – Australia Sponsored
BS/ENS – Business Skills/Employer Nomination Scheme

Source: Longitudinal Survey of Immigrants to Australia.

Figure 2.3 Employment-to-population ratio 18 months after migration, by gender and visa category

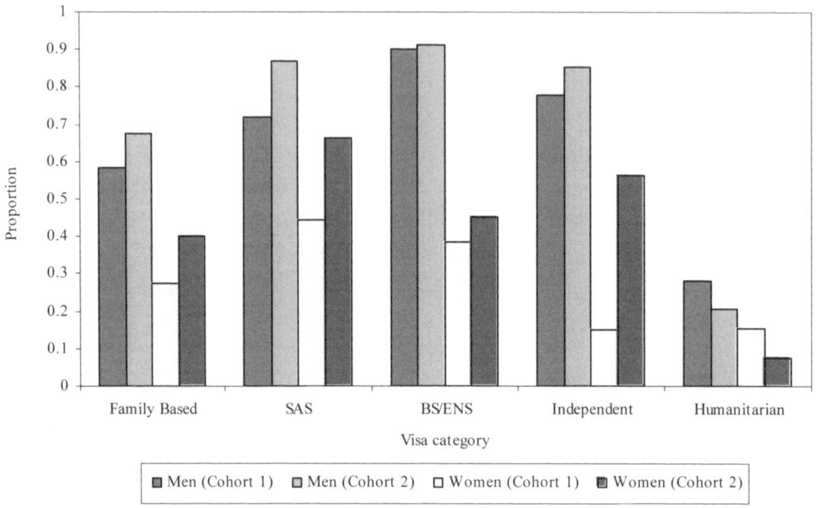

Note:
SAS – Skilled – Australia Sponsored
BS/ENS – Business Skills/Employer Nomination Scheme

Source: Longitudinal Survey of Immigrants to Australia.

(49.2 per cent) in the second. Individuals in the Family stream accounted for 48.2 per cent of Cohort 1, but only 42.0 per cent of Cohort 2, while the proportion of Humanitarian immigrants fell by almost half over the five years separating the two entry cohorts.

Although the demographic composition – average age, gender ratio and marital status – of the two cohorts is much the same (see Table 2.2), there are striking differences in human capital endowments. Consistent with changes in selection criteria, the cohort of individuals entering Australia in 1999–2000 is more educated and has better English language skills[9] than the previous cohort. In particular, native English speakers accounted for 42.3 per cent of Cohort 2 immigrants, but only 32.1 per cent of individuals entering in Cohort 1. Immigrants in Cohort 2 are more likely to have been working in a professional occupation and more likely to have been employed in their former home country in the year before migrating to Australia.[10] Overall, almost half (46.0 per cent) of immigrants entering in 1999–2000 had recent labour market experience in a professional occupation at the time of migration. This was true of just over one third (35.1 per cent) of individuals in the first cohort. Finally, there are differences in the source countries of the two cohorts. Cohort 2 immigrants are more likely (55.6 per cent versus 48.9 per cent) to come from a country where English is widely spoken and with cultural traditions and institutions that closely resemble Australia's.[11] These changes in human capital characteristics almost certainly facilitate employment and make the settlement process easier.

DETERMINANTS OF LABOUR MARKET PARTICIPATION, EMPLOYMENT AND UNEMPLOYMENT

Our goal is to shed light on both the desire for employment and the success in finding it for immigrants in the two LSIA cohorts. To what extent were the changes in selection policy helpful in facilitating entry into the Australian labour market? In addressing this question, it is necessary to first concentrate on three primary outcomes of interest to policy makers setting selection criteria: labour market participation rate; the unemployment rate; and the employment-to-population ratio. In this section, multivariate models of the determinants of each of these labour market outcomes are estimated. These results will highlight the relationship between immigrants' skills and their early labour market outcomes. They will also form the basis of the decomposition analysis that follows later in this chapter.

Empirical framework

The first step is to model the process through which immigrants enter the Australian labour market and begin seeking work. In particular, immigrants are assumed to participate in the Australian labour market whenever the return to market work exceeds the value of their time in alternative activities. Modeling participation effectively allows us to draw distinctions between individuals who are economically active and those who are not. Of course, not every new immigrant who wants a job will necessarily be successful in finding one. Some immigrants arrive in Australia with skills that do not completely translate into the Australian labour market. Making an investment in Australia-specific skills – for example, learning English – may increase the transferability of those skills acquired before migration (see Chiswick and Miller 1994, Khan 1997, Duleep and Regets 1999, Friedberg 2000). Moreover, job search efficiency may depend both on the transferability of skills and on knowledge (which may be gained differentially over time) about the local institutions and work environment (see Chapter 3 on the duration of job search and its determinants). Immigrants may need time to accumulate the skills that are relevant to finding Australian employment, including labour market information. Given this, the next step is to estimate the determinants of unemployment in order to understand how, conditional on having chosen

Table 2.2 Immigrants' visa status, demographic, and human capital characteristics 18 months after migration: LSIA immigrants by gender and cohort[a]

	Cohort 1			Cohort 2		
	Total	Men	Women	Total	Men	Women
Visa status						
Family – Principal Applicants	45.0	37.6	51.0	40.5	33.9	46.2
Family – Spouse	3.2	0.8	5.1	1.5	0.7	2.2
SAS – Principal Applicants	6.3	9.9	3.3	7.7	9.8	5.9
SAS – Spouse	3.9	1.9	5.5	4.7	4.7	4.8
BS/ENS-Principal Applicants	2.7	5.1	0.7	4.0	7.3	1.2
BS/ENS – Spouse	1.9	0.4	3.1	3.2	0.5	5.4
IND – Principal Applicants	13.6	22.8	6.1	18.3	26.3	11.5
IND – Spouse	7.0	2.2	10.9	11.3	7.4	14.6
HUM – Principal Applicants	11.2	16.1	7.1	5.6	7.5	4.0
HUM – Spouse	5.4	3.1	7.3	3.2	1.9	4.3
Weeks since migration	72.0	72.4	71.8	75.0	75.3	74.9
Demographic characteristics						
Female	54.9	–	–	54.1	–	–
Married	78.7	76.9	80.1	82.9	80.2	85.1
Age (years)	36.4	36.8	36.0	35.9	37.4	34.7
Education						
University	31.7	36.3	27.9	42.3	45.7	39.4
High school	28.1	34.1	23.2	27.3	31.6	23.6
Less than 10 years	26.9	20.7	32.0	22.0	16.7	26.6
Trade degree	12.6	8.6	15.9	8.0	5.6	10.0
English ability						
Native speakers	32.1	35.4	29.5	42.2	47.6	37.6
Speaks it well	37.0	39.5	35.0	34.2	34.0	34.4
Speaks it badly	30.8	25.2	35.5	22.6	17.2	27.2
Labour market experience in home country						
Professional	35.1	42.0	29.4	46.0	53.8	39.5
Other skilled	28.0	31.0	25.6	24.8	27.3	22.6
Unskilled	6.6	8.2	5.3	3.7	4.8	2.7
Not employed	30.3	18.8	39.7	25.1	13.7	34.9
English language proficiency group[b]						
Group 1	21.8	24.5	19.6	24.1	28.9	20.1
Group 2	27.1	25.8	28.1	31.5	29.6	33.1
Group 3	35.9	37.7	34.4	27.8	28.1	27.6
Group 4	15.2	12.0	17.9	16.6	13.2	19.3

Notes:

a Percentages except for time since migration (weeks) and age (years).

b Group 1 consists of those countries rating 98% or higher on the English proficiency index. Group 2 is made up of those countries with a rating of 80% or higher, while Group 3 contains countries with a rating between 5% and 80%. Countries with a rating of less than 50% comprise Group 4 (DIMA, 1999). See this section for other variable definitions.

Source: Longitudinal Survey of Immigrants to Australia.

to enter the Australian labour market, the characteristics of those who have been successful in finding employment 18 months after migration differ from those who have not. Finally, the factors behind the propensity to be employed generally must be considered. Examining the employment-to-population ratio allows the joint consideration of the factors related to both desiring, and successfully finding, employment.[12]

Models of labour force participation and employment status 18 months after migration (Wave 2) are estimated for male and female immigrants aged 22–60 using a standard probit model.[13] Using the working-aged sample of labour market participants, the propensity to be unemployed is also estimated using a probit model.[14] In each case, Model 1 restricts the coefficients to be the same for each cohort allowing for only a simple intercept shift, while Model 2 estimates separate slope coefficients for each cohort.

Each model includes a vector of human capital (education, English ability, English language background), demographic (age, marital status, children) and geographic (state of residence) variables thought to be related to the value of time in non-market activities and to labour market productivity. Although the data do not provide a direct measure of labour market experience, pre-migration occupation and employment status are included to take account of the effects of labour market experience immediately prior to migration. The model also includes controls for visa category, Principal Applicant status and the number of weeks since migration.

The results (probit marginal effects and standard errors) from each regression are reported in Tables 2.3–2.5.[15] In addition, Tables 2.3–2.5 report the results of Chi-square tests of significant differences in Cohort 2 and Cohort 1 coefficients.[16] Given the focus in this book on the potential role of public policy in facilitating labour market outcomes, the first step must be to consider the relative outcomes across Principal Applicant and visa status. Then explicit consideration can be given to the returns associated with those human capital characteristics (formal education, English language ability and previous, recent labour market experience) that are most directly relevant for the immigrant selection process. This will shed light on the extent to which, by altering returns, changes in labour market conditions and income-support policy might have influenced outcomes for new arrivals to Australia.

The immigration process

Eighteen months into the settlement process, women entering Australia between 1999 and 2000 had a participation rate that was 3.4 percentage points higher than otherwise similar women who had migrated five years earlier. This inter-cohort differential in women's participation is much smaller when one controls for individual characteristics (see Table 2.3) than when one does not (see Table 2.1), suggesting that cohort differences in women's

Table 2.3a Determinants[a] of labour market participation by gender and cohort: Probit marginal effects and standard errors (in brackets)

Women

	Total		Cohort 1		Cohort 2		
Cohort 2	0.035	(2.11)	-	-	-	-	
PA status	0.168	(7.44)	0.181	(6.34)	0.151	(3.85)	p=0.526
Visa status							p=0.000
Family	-0.137	(-4.30)	-0.132	(-3.20)	-0.129	(-2.45)	
Skilled – Australian Sponsored	0.071	(2.30)	0.101	(2.65)	0.058	(0.98)	
Independent	0.058	(1.88)	0.078	(2.01)	0.053	(0.97)	
Humanitarian	-0.110	(-3.4)	-0.003	(-.07)	-0.249	(-4.91)	
Education							p=0.450
University	0.066	(2.69)	0.083	(2.67)	0.039	(0.96)	
10–11 years	-0.032	(-1.01)	-0.017	(-0.41)	-0.050	(-0.92)	
<10 years	-0.050	(-1.65)	-0.051	(-1.32)	-0.034	(-0.65)	
Trade	0.017	(0.73)	0.023	(0.78)	0.017	(0.42)	
Enrolled	-0.108	(-5.54)	-0.136	(-5.54)	-0.061	(-1.83)	
English ability							p=0.830
Speaks it well	-0.072	(-2.66)	-0.081	(-2.29)	-0.047	(-1.06)	
Speaks it badly	-0.193	(-6.22)	-0.203	(-5.10)	-0.178	(-3.41)	
Pre-migration experience							p=0.006
Professional	0.141	(6.16)	0.074	(2.63)	0.234	(5.90)	
Skilled	0.178	(7.89)	0.141	(5.03)	0.215	(5.48)	
Unskilled	0.247	(5.90)	0.189	(3.75)	0.365	(4.71)	
Time unemployed	0.009	(2.89)	0.011	(2.66)	0.006	(1.12)	
N	4,992		3,105		1,887		
R-squared	0.281		0.247		0.370		

Notes:
a Model also includes: marital status, a quadratic in age, the presence of children by age categories, state dummies, time since migration, and English proficiency group. Omitted categories are BS/ENS immigrants, high school degree, native English speakers, and not employed in home country.

Source: Longitudinal Survey of Immigrants to Australia.

Table 2.3b Determinants[a] of labour market participation by gender and cohort: Probit marginal effects and standard errors (in brackets)

Men

	Total		Cohort 1		Cohort 2		
Cohort 2	-0.030	(-2.19)	-	-	-	-	
PA status	0.077	(3.66)	0.071	(2.8)	0.101	(2.55)	p=0.823
Visa status							p=0.000
Family	-0.119	(-4.12)	-0.107	(-3.13)	-0.116	(-2.19)	
Skilled – Australian Sponsored	-0.087	(-2.9)	-0.064	(-1.95)	-0.022	(-0.34)	
Independent	-0.097	(-3.13)	-0.050	(-1.49)	-0.120	(-1.97)	
Humanitarian	-0.258	(-7.98)	-0.146	(-4.09)	-0.519	(-8.13)	
Education							p=0.002
University	0.023	(1.11)	0.032	(1.31)	0.008	(0.21)	
10–11 years	-0.018	(-0.62)	-0.007	(-0.21)	-0.046	(-0.79)	
<10 years	0.006	(0.24)	0.032	(1.09)	-0.049	(-0.92)	
Trade	-0.017	(-0.85)	-0.007	(-0.28)	-0.015	(-0.41)	
Enrolled	-0.218	(-11.96)	-0.261	(-11.85)	-0.124	(-3.71)	
English ability							p=0.042
Speaks it well	-0.035	(-1.48)	-0.077	(-2.58)	0.044	(1.01)	
Speaks it badly	-0.087	(-2.96)	-0.131	(-3.48)	0.003	(.07)	
Pre-migration experience							p=0.414
Professional	0.041	(2.03)	0.031	(1.33)	0.050	(1.24)	
Skilled	0.094	(5.04)	0.075	(3.48)	0.113	(3.04)	
Unskilled	0.077	(3.34)	0.075	(2.88)	0.067	(1.41)	
Time unemployed	0.001	(0.48)	0.005	(1.76)	-0.001	(-.41)	
N	4,451		2,817		1,634		
R-squared	0.315		0.276		0.422		

Table 2.4a Determinants[a,b] of unemployment rate since migration: OLS coefficients and standard errors (in brackets)

Women

	Total		Cohort 1		Cohort 2		
Cohort 2	-0.107	(-6.76)	-	-	-	-	
PA status	-0.017	(-0.77)	-0.054	(-1.61)	0.023	(1.04)	p=0.086
Visa status							p=0.250
Family	0.215	(4.94)	0.242	(3.80)	0.172	(2.70)	
Skilled – Australian Sponsored	0.252	(5.25)	0.267	(4.28)	0.224	(2.36)	
Independent	0.181	(3.95)	0.163	(2.68)	0.224	(2.52)	
Humanitarian	0.385	(6.27)	0.355	(4.66)	0.566	(3.96)	
Education							p=0.407
University	0.000	(0.00)	-0.020	(-0.56)	0.034	(1.22)	
10–11 years	0.080	(2.13)	0.138	(2.44)	0.011	(0.27)	
<10 years	0.042	(1.19)	0.045	(0.88)	0.067	(1.48)	
Trade	-0.032	(-1.37)	-0.057	(-1.68)	0.003	(0.12)	
Enrolled	0.033	(1.72)	0.041	(1.40)	0.016	(0.85)	
English ability							p=0.146
Speaks it well	0.012	(0.51)	0.035	(0.96)	-0.015	(-0.65)	
Speaks it badly	0.036	(1.10)	0.085	(1.68)	-0.034	(-1.25)	
Pre-migration experience							p=0.942
Professional	-0.043	(-1.91)	-0.051	(-1.53)	-0.027	(-1.04)	
Skilled	-0.050	(-2.42)	-0.065	(-2.10)	-0.026	(-1.16)	
Unskilled	-0.053	(-1.71)	-0.086	(-1.91)	-0.008	(-0.22)	
Time unemployed	-0.002	(-0.52)	-0.003	(-0.68)	-0.001	(-0.42)	
N	2,066		1,256		810		
R-squared	0.162		0.157		0.144		

Notes:

a Model also includes: marital status, a quadratic in age, the presence of children by age categories, state dummies, time since migration, and English proficiency group. Omitted categories are BS/ENS immigrants, high school degree, native English speakers, and not employed in home country.

b Chi-square tests were used to test the significance of the difference in marginal effects between cohorts. Individual tests were performed for Principal Applicant (PA) status, and time since migration. Joint tests were performed for the remaining subsets of variables.

Source: Longitudinal Survey of Immigrants to Australia.

Table 2.4b Determinants[a,b] of unemployment rate since migration: OLS coefficients and standard errors (in brackets)

Men

	Total		Cohort 1		Cohort 2		
Cohort 2	-0.080	(-6.33)	-	-	-	-	
PA status	-0.005	(-0.27)	0.001	(0.04)	-0.011	(-0.55)	p=0.629
Visa status							p=0.276
Family	0.231	(6.61)	0.234	(5.05)	0.211	(3.51)	
Skilled – Australian Sponsored	0.238	(6.64)	0.258	(5.80)	0.157	(2.26)	
Independent	0.216	(5.98)	0.226	(4.96)	0.189	(2.71)	
Humanitarian	0.517	(11.5)	0.508	(9.45)	0.542	(5.25)	
Education							p=0.097
University	0.031	(1.45)	0.052	(1.67)	-0.004	(-0.20)	
10–11 years	0.059	(1.91)	0.048	(1.13)	0.097	(2.29)	
<10 years	0.075	(2.59)	0.100	(2.46)	0.022	(0.72)	
Trade	0.005	(0.25)	0.012	(0.42)	-0.007	(-0.35)	
Enrolled	0.065	(3.94)	0.111	(4.57)	0.008	(0.46)	
English ability							p=0.103
Speaks it well	0.032	(1.51)	0.066	(2.14)	-0.020	(-0.96)	
Speaks it badly	0.100	(3.52)	0.141	(3.46)	0.030	(0.99)	
Pre-migration experience							p=0.827
Professional	-0.038	(-1.79)	-0.039	(-1.27)	-0.032	(-1.41)	
Skilled	-0.014	(-0.71)	-0.009	(-0.29)	-0.015	(-0.75)	
Unskilled	-0.034	(-1.46)	-0.022	(-0.64)	-0.031	(-1.45)	
Time unemployed	0.003	(1.46)	0.006	(1.76)	0.000	(-0.02)	
N	3,425		2,248		1,177		
R-squared	0.233		0.211		0.298		

Table 2.5a Determinants[a,b] of employment-to-population ratio by gender and cohort: Probit marginal effects and standard errors (in brackets)

Women

	Total		Cohort 1		Cohort 2		
Cohort 2	0.098	(6.37)	-	-	-	-	
PA status	0.135	(6.65)	0.149	(6.06)	0.103	(2.81)	p=0.148
Visa status							p=0.001
Family	-0.160	(-5.73)	-0.160	(-4.60)	-0.148	(-3.07)	
Skilled – Australian Sponsored	-0.021	(-0.78)	-0.015	(-0.48)	0.003	(0.06)	
Independent	-0.002	(-0.08)	0.012	(0.36)	-0.016	(-0.32)	
Humanitarian	-0.173	(-6.38)	-0.103	(-2.92)	-0.275	(-6.15)	
Education							p=0.513
University	0.048	(2.16)	0.065	(2.37)	0.013	(0.35)	
10–11 years	-0.052	(-1.81)	-0.055	(-1.55)	-0.043	(-0.85)	
<10 years	-0.051	(-1.80)	-0.048	(-1.37)	-0.055	(-1.10)	
Trade	0.031	(1.43)	0.044	(1.65)	0.014	(0.37)	
Enrolled	-0.089	(-5.25)	-0.103	(-5.06)	-0.059	(-1.96)	
English ability							p=0.521
Speaks it well	-0.053	(-2.24)	-0.061	(-2.06)	-0.024	(-0.60)	
Speaks it badly	-0.158	(-5.78)	-0.168	(-4.99)	-0.123	(-2.54)	
Pre-migration experience							p=0.038
Professional	0.136	(6.39)	0.079	(3.11)	0.223	(5.87)	
Skilled	0.172	(8.03)	0.139	(5.36)	0.208	(5.53)	
Unskilled	0.245	(5.91)	0.202	(4.13)	0.335	(4.30)	
Time unemployed	0.007	(2.37)	0.008	(2.22)	0.004	(0.86)	
N	4,992		3,105		1,887		
R-squared	0.291		0.264		0.352		

Notes:

[a] Model also includes: marital status, a quadratic in age, the presence of children by age categories, state dummies, time since migration, and English proficiency group. Omitted categories are BS/ENS immigrants, high school degree, native English speakers, and not employed in home country.

[b] Chi-square tests were used to test the significance of the difference in marginal effects between cohorts. Individual tests were performed for PA status, and time since migration. Joint tests were performed for the remaining subsets of variables.

Source: Longitudinal Survey of Immigrants to Australia.

Table 2.5b Determinants[a,b] of employment-to-population ratio by gender and cohort: Probit marginal effects and standard errors (in brackets)

Men

	Total		Cohort 1		Cohort 2		
Cohort 2	0.077	(4.26)	-	-	-	-	
PA status	0.073	(2.66)	0.055	(1.56)	0.121	(2.59)	p=0.259
Visa status							p=0.000
Family	-0.281	(-7.79)	-0.277	(-6.03)	-0.272	(-4.45)	
Skilled – Australian Sponsored	-0.254	(-6.90)	-0.262	(-5.92)	-0.121	(-1.65)	
Independent	-0.242	(-6.39)	-0.221	(-4.77)	-0.219	(-3.19)	
Humanitarian	-0.539	(-14.72)	-0.484	(-10.47)	-0.654	(-10.43)	
Education							p=0.011
University	-0.005	(-0.18)	-0.022	(-0.59)	0.022	(0.45)	
10–11 years	-0.073	(-1.82)	-0.048	(-0.96)	-0.149	(-2.04)	
<10 years	-0.068	(-1.79)	-0.071	(-1.51)	-0.056	(-0.86)	
Trade	-0.014	(-0.51)	-0.017	(-0.48)	0.009	(0.19)	
Enrolled	-0.245	(-11.36)	-0.301	(-11.2)	-0.142	(-3.77)	
English ability							p=0.007
Speaks it well	-0.062	(-2.10)	-0.133	(-3.43)	0.065	(1.34)	
Speaks it badly	-0.167	(-4.58)	-0.231	(-4.93)	-0.043	(-0.69)	
Pre-migration experience							p=0.971
Professional	0.078	(2.68)	0.068	(1.85)	0.089	(1.81)	
Skilled	0.104	(3.72)	0.080	(2.26)	0.118	(2.49)	
Unskilled	0.113	(3.26)	0.095	(2.17)	0.119	(2.01)	
Time unemployed	-0.002	(-0.59)	-0.002	(-0.53)	0.000	(-0.10)	
N	4,451		2,817		1,634		
R-squared	0.315		0.273		0.425		

characteristics are an important part of the process leading to higher participation rates. Men in Cohort 2, on the other hand, had a significantly lower participation rate (3.0 percentage points) than men in Cohort 1, a disadvantage that is larger at 18 months than at six months (see Cobb-Clark 2003). This implies that improvements in participation between six and 18 months after migration were faster for men in Cohort 1. At the same time, both men and women entering Australia at the end of the 1990s had a much lower propensity to be unemployed relative to immigrants who entered earlier.[17]

Together these changes resulted in large increases in the proportion of new arrivals to Australia who had found employment a year and a half into the settlement process. The employment-to-population ratio was 9.8 percentage points higher for women in Cohort 2 and 7.7 percentage points higher for Cohort 2 men, even after differences in productivity-related skills were taken into account.

Not surprisingly, Principal Applicants (who were subject to selection criteria) generally had higher participation and lower unemployment rates than spouses (who were not) (see Tables 2.3 and 2.4). Overall, women entering as Principal Applicants are 13.5 percentage points more likely to be employed 18 months after migration, while men were 7.7 percentage points more likely to be employed. Given that in 1999 additional points began to be awarded to those Principal Applicants whose spouses also met the minimum age, language, and skill requirements, it is also useful to focus on the inter-cohort difference in the employment advantage enjoyed by Principal Applicants relative to spouses. This advantage fell over time for women – as might be expected, given the policy change – but increased over time for men, although these inter-cohort differences are not statistically significant (see Table 2.5).

Diversity in labour market experiences across visa categories is particularly informative about the role of selection criteria in facilitating labour market entry. The following discussion will focus on the employment-to-population ratio in order to illustrate the key results (see Table 2.5). The omitted category in each of the models is individuals holding an Employer Nomination Scheme or Business Skills (ENS/BS) visa and all of the results are interpreted relative to this group. It is striking that 18 months into the settlement process there are no significant differences in the propensity for skills-based women (that is, ENS/BS, Skilled – Australia Sponsored (SAS), or Independent migrants) in either Cohort 1 or Cohort 2 to be employed, though both family-based and refugee women have significantly lower employment-to-population ratios.

The lack of variation in outcomes across women holding a range of immigrant visas may not be particularly surprising given that the points test is generally used to select men rather than women, who disproportionately enter as accompanying family members for whom no selection criteria apply.[18] At the same time, the results clearly point to a deterioration in the relative position of women holding a Humanitarian visa across the two cohorts. Women entering Australia on a Humanitarian visa between 1993 and 1995 were 10.3 percentage points less likely to be employed 18 months after migration. This disadvantage more than doubled to 27.5 percentage points amongst women entering five years later.

Differences in the employment experiences of men holding ENS/BS visas and other men are much sharper. Men entering Australia in the first half of the 1990s on the basis of prearranged employment (ENS) or their business skills (BS) had more than a 20 percentage point employment advantage over other skills-based and family immigrants and an almost 50 percentage point advantage over men selected out of humanitarian concerns. This advantage relative to SAS immigrants fell over time (though the change was not quite significant), but widened significantly (to 65.4 percentage points) relative to Humanitarian immigrants. This widening gap was not the result of large improvements in the outcomes of ENS/BS immigrants – their employment-to-population ratio increased only slightly (see Table 2.1) – but rather to the worsening position of Humanitarian category immigrants.[19]

Human capital endowments

Focusing on the cohorts' returns to labour market skills informs us about the extent to which changes in Australian labour market conditions and income-support policy over the 1990s may have affected new immigrants' labour market outcomes. Let us begin by considering changes in the return to formal education. In each of the cases, those individuals who have completed 12 years of schooling, but who have not continued on to university, are the omitted category and all results are interpreted relative to this group. There is no evidence that the returns to education changed for women over the 1990s. Inter-cohort differences in female returns to education are neither individually nor jointly significant for any of the three outcomes under consideration.[20] There are, however, significant changes in the returns to education for male immigrants. The labour market advantage enjoyed by relatively educated men increased, while the penalties associated with currently being enrolled in formal education decreased. It is not possible to separately identify the effects of labour market conditions themselves from the effects of income-support policy – which most likely affects the incentives to find employment – in producing these changing returns to education. Still, tighter access to a range of income-support options would be expected to have a direct effect on students' incentive to find employment while studying.

While the penalty for having relatively little education increased over the 1990s, the employment penalty for not speaking English well actually decreased so that there were fewer differences in outcomes for individuals with differing levels of English language ability.[21] As with changes in the returns to education, changes in the returns to English language ability were more evident for men. Men who entered Australia in 1993–1995 and were not native English speakers faced substantial penalties in terms of lower participation and higher unemployment 18 months after migration (see Tables 2.3–2.5). These penalties disappeared for men who entered Australia five years later. For example, men in Cohort 1 who reported speaking English badly had an unemployment rate that was 13.1 percentage points higher than native English speakers. In contrast, Cohort 2 men who spoke English badly had the same propensity to be unemployed as men who were native English speakers. In fact, there is no evidence that language ability is significantly related to either the participation or unemployment experiences of men entering Australia at the end of the 1990s.[22]

While education and English language ability dominate the story for men, it is pre-migration labour market experiences that are particularly salient for women. There was a dramatic increase over the 1990s in the extent to which a woman's labour market attachment immediately prior to migration was useful in predicting whether she had chosen to enter the Australian labour market a year and a half later. Cohort 2 women who were employed as professionals in the year before migration were 23.4 percentage points more likely to be labour market participants than women who were not employed at all prior to migration. Amongst Cohort 1 women this difference was only 7.4 percentage points. Interestingly, the stronger link over time between pre- and post-migration outcomes is apparent for participation – and hence employment – but not unemployment outcomes. It is also apparent only for women, leaving the relationship between previous and current employment outcomes much the same for men irrespective of when they entered Australia.

DECOMPOSING THE DIFFERENCES IN COHORT OUTCOMES

To what extent are changes in immigrant selection policy the source of Cohort 2's improved labour market outcomes? What role do labour market conditions and income-support policy have in facilitating immigrants' entry into the Australian labour market? To address these questions it is first necessary to decompose relative improvements in the participation, unemployment, and employment-to-population rates of new arrivals in Australia into characteristics-related and returns-to-characteristics-related components. Generally speaking, the influence of changes in immigration policy is expected to have its most direct effect on changes in characteristics themselves, while labour market conditions and income-support policy work most directly to alter the Australian labour market returns to labour market skills such as education, English language ability, etc.

The discrete (yes/no) nature of the participation, unemployment, and employment outcomes that interest this study leads to the use of probit estimation (see section on labour market participation). However, the non-linearity of the cumulative normal distribution, upon which the probit model is based, implies that standard linear decompositions are not possible. Given this, the next step is to follow a decomposition procedure based upon a linear approximation that has been suggested by Doiron and Riddell (1994) and is outlined in detail in Cobb-Clark (2003).[23] This decomposition is not unique and it always depends on which returns (Cohort 1's or Cohort 2's) are chosen to weight the differences in average characteristics. Results based on both sets of weights are presented in Table 2.6.

Eighteen months into the settlement process men and women entering Australia in 1999–2000 (Cohort 2) had labour market participation rates that were higher (3.4 and 9.9 percentage points respectively) than immigrants entering in 1993–1995. Most, if not all, of this difference is due to differences in the demographic and productivity-related characteristics underlying the participation decision itself. Between 75.0 and 94.5 per cent of the inter-cohort difference for women is due to differences in the average characteristics of cohort members. Moreover, differences in cohort characteristics more than explain the disparity in the participation rates of men, implying that if Cohort 2 men had faced the same labour market returns that Cohort 1 men did their participation advantage would have been even greater.

In contrast, inter-cohort differentials in the propensity to be unemployed 18 months after migration – given that one has chosen to seek work – are largely driven by the returns to productive characteristics. Differences in returns completely explain the 12.5 percentage point decline in the unemployment rate of women and explain between 57.4 and 65.0 per cent of the 12.9 percentage point fall in the unemployment rate of men. As was the case for changes in participation rates over the 1990s, disparities in human capital endowments play a larger role (between 43.8 and 51.4 per cent) in explaining the fall in men's as opposed to women's unemployment rates. This is not particularly surprising given that men are disproportionately more likely to be subject to the selection criteria (see Table 2.2).

Overall, the fact that approximately two-thirds of the gap in the proportion of men who have found employment one and a half years into the settlement process stems from inter-cohort differences in their demographic and human capital characteristics. For women, characteristics account for between half and two-thirds of the gap.

Table 2.6 Decomposition of cohort gap in labour market status and unemployment experience

	Decomposition 1		Decomposition 2	
	Level	Per cent	Level	Per cent
Women				
Labour market participation				
Difference (Cohort 2 – Cohort 1)	0.099	-	0.099	-
Characteristics	0.093	94.5	0.074	75.0
Returns	0.005	5.3	0.024	24.8
Approximation	0.001	0.2	0.001	0.2
		100.0		100.0
Unemployment rate				
Difference (Cohort 2 – Cohort 1)	-0.125	-	-0.125	-
Characteristics	-0.009	7.5	0.010	-8.1
Returns	-0.123	98.4	-0.143	114.0
Approximation	0.007	-5.9	0.007	-5.9
		100.0		100.0
Employment-to-population ratio				
Difference (Cohort 2 – Cohort 1)	0.139	-	0.139	-
Characteristics	0.091	65.8	0.072	52.0
Returns	0.046	33.2	0.065	47.0
Approximation	0.002	1.0	0.002	1.0
		100.0		100.0
Men				
Labour market participation				
Difference (Cohort 2 – Cohort 1)	0.034	-	0.034	-
Characteristics	0.043	125.1	0.048	139.6
Returns	-0.008	-23.7	-0.013	-38.1
Approximation	-0.001	-1.4	-0.001	-1.4
		100.0		100.0
Unemployment rate				
Difference (Cohort 2 – Cohort 1)	-0.129	-	-0.129	-
Characteristics	-0.056	43.8	-0.075	51.4
Returns	-0.084	65.0	-0.104	57.4
Approximation	0.011	-8.8	0.013	-8.8
		100.0		100.0
Employment-to-population ratio				
Difference (Cohort 2 – Cohort 1)	0.133	-	0.133	-
Characteristics	0.086	64.5	0.090	68.0
Returns	0.051	38.2	1.046	34.7
Approximation	-0.004	-2.7	-0.004	-2.7
		100.0		100.0

DISCUSSION AND CONCLUSION

The increased emphasis on productive skills in the procedures Australia used to select new immigrants in the late 1990s led to striking differences in the human capital endowments of new arrivals. Though the demographic composition (that is, average age, gender ratio and marital status) of immigrants remained much the same, individuals entering Australia in 1999–2000 had more education, better English language skills and more pre-migration labour market experience than did their predecessors. These improvements in human capital endowments completely explain the higher participation rates amongst immigrants arriving in Australia at the end of the 1990s. Moreover, approximately half of the fall in men's unemployment rates also stems from more productive skills, though the substantial decline in women's unemployment rates is driven solely by changes in the returns to skills rather than the skills level itself.

These results indicate that there is a large potential for immigrant selection policy to influence immigrant outcomes not just immediately after migration but in the medium term. Changes in immigrant skills are consistent with those policy changes that give greater emphasis to educational qualifications, language ability and recent labour market experience. Moreover, men are much more likely than women to be assessed under the prevailing selection criteria and so it is perhaps not surprising that changes in characteristics are more directly responsible for improvements in male than in female labour market outcomes.

At the same time, it is also clear that income-support policy and the overall state of the Australian labour market had a hand in the improved labour market position of those arriving between 1999 and 2000. It is true that women in the second LSIA cohort were more attached to the Australian labour market than their predecessors. In particular, women in Cohort 2 were much more likely to have recent, pre-migration labour market experience in a profession – an effect which is most likely attributable to changes in selection policy. At the same time – conditional on having pre-migration experience – they were also substantially more likely to have entered the Australian labour market a year and a half into the settlement process. This latter effect results from changes in the returns to (rather than in the level of) pre-migration experience. Unfortunately, it is difficult to know whether it arises because an inability to access the income-support system pushed more women into the Australian labour market in order to support their families, or whether increased wage returns for previous experience encouraged more women to seek employment.

The changing rewards resulting from skills are an important part of the story for men as well. These changes seem to have opened up employment opportunities for men who do not speak English well. In particular, there is no evidence that language ability is significantly related to either the participation or unemployment experiences of men entering Australia at the end of the 1990s. Moreover, men in Cohort 2 who were enrolled in formal education 18 months after migration were much more likely to be combining that education with employment. Again, it is unclear whether this stems from changes in employment conditions that opened up employment opportunities for these men or is due to the disappearance of the income-support safety net.

In the context of the broader story it is important to take special note of the worsening position of Humanitarian immigrants. Though their numbers declined proportionately (from 16.6 to 8.8 per cent of the total inflow), their story is a striking exception to the overall positive picture painted here. Humanitarian immigrants entering as part of the second cohort were simply much less likely to have entered the Australian labour market 18 months after migration. Although the probability of being unemployed – conditional on labour market entry – is also substantially lower, the fall in participation dominates, leading the employment-to-population ratio for Humanitarian migrants to be lower in Cohort 2 than in Cohort 1. These changes occurred despite the fact that Australian immigration policy with respect to refugees remained largely unchanged. It seems likely that push factors – which may have altered the characteristics of the Humanitarian stream – are also important in understanding outcomes for refugees.

Overall Australian selection policy was largely successful in selecting immigrants whose skills led them to be more inclined to seek out employment, while changes in labour market conditions and income-support policy over the intervening period contributed to making them more likely to get it. Eighteen months into the settlement process these patterns largely, though not completely, confirm those observed immediately after migration. Six months after migration, inter-cohort differentials in human capital characteristics accounted for the majority of the difference in unemployment experiences between the two cohorts. Twelve months on, variation in labour market returns play a much larger role in generating inter-cohort disparities in unemployment (though not participation). These differences in returns are the result of a complex interaction between changes in income-support policies that affected individuals' incentives to search for jobs, and changes in labour market conditions which affected their ability to find them. Unfortunately, it is not possible to definitively isolate the two effects.

NOTES

1 In particular, Stalker (2000) estimates that the number of people worldwide living outside their country of birth now exceeds 120 million and more countries than ever are being classified as major suppliers or receivers of international migrants.

2 See, for example, Vialet and Eig (1990) for a discussion of the United States and Green and Green (1999) for a discussion of Canada.

3 For example, a great deal of debate has centred on the extent to which immigration can be used to compensate for the effects of population aging (see for example, Straubhaar and Zimmermann 1993, McDonald and Kippen 2001, Withers 2002) while Lazear (1998) considers the extent to which US selection policy is successful in enhancing population diversity. A large literature also ties the formation of attitudes towards immigrants to

immigration policy and the extent to which immigrants are seen to successfully integrate into the host country (see for example, Chiswick and Miller 1999, Bauer et al. 2000, Dustmann and Preston 2000).

4 In effect, immigrants entering Canada in the 'independent class' (who are points tested) are a residual category and are increasingly outnumbered by immigrants in other classes (Green and Green 1995, Green 1999).

5 See Cobb-Clark (2003) for a description of the LSIA cohorts. Unfortunately Cohort 2, unlike Cohort 1, was only interviewed twice, giving us no direct comparison between the cohorts later in the settlement process. For a similar analysis of outcomes six months after migration see Cobb-Clark (2003).

6 Note that the LSIA measures of participation, employment, and unemployment differ from standard Australian Bureau of Statistics definitions. As such, it is difficult to make comparisons between these results, in particular the unemployment rate, and those based on more standard definitions. This is not such a particular problem for this analysis as it will be the determinants of relative outcomes for different individuals that concern us.

7 This occurred even though Cohort 2 immigrants had been in Australia somewhat longer on average at the interview date than Cohort 1 immigrants (see Table 2.2).

8 When measured six months after migration the participation rate of ENS/BS immigrants fell from Cohort 1 to Cohort 2 while unemployment rates were relatively constant across cohorts (see Cobb-Clark 2003). Eighteen months after migration these differences have been reversed with unemployment substantially lower and participation somewhat higher amongst those immigrants entering in the second half of the 1990s.

9 LSIA respondents were asked to report about their ability to speak English. Those who reported speaking English 'only' or 'best' are classified as 'native' English speakers. Non-native speakers who reported speaking English 'very well' or 'well' are combined to form the 'English well' category. Non-native speakers who reported speaking English 'badly' or 'not at all' form the 'English badly' category. See Chapter 1 for more details.

10 Although LSIA data do not contain direct measures of labour market experience, LSIA respondents were asked about their labour market experiences in their former home country in the year prior to migration. Individuals employed at some point in the year prior to migration reported their occupation. These occupations have been coded into three major categories: professional, skilled, and unskilled. Individuals not employed in the 12 months before migration are coded as 'not employed'. Finally, 'time unemployed' measures the number of months in the year prior to migration that an individual reported being unemployed and looking for work.

11 In this analysis source countries are divided into English proficiency groups based on the English-speaking ability of recent immigrants to Australia (see DIMA 1996). Group 1 includes the mainly English speaking countries (Canada, New Zealand, United Kingdom, Ireland, United States, and South Africa). Immigrants from these countries rate 98 per cent or higher on the English proficiency index. Group 2 includes those countries with a rating of 80 per cent or higher, while Group 3 includes countries with a rating between 50 per cent and 80 per cent. Countries with a rating of less than 50 per cent make up Group 4.

12 The employment-to-population ratio is in effect the product of the participation rate and one minus the unemployment rate.

13 All estimation was done in STATA 8.0. Results based on a random effects probit model are similar and are available from the author.

14 These outcomes are defined in the section in this chapter on data sample and variables.

15 Note that for continuous variables such as age, the probit marginal effect represents the effect of an infinitesimal change in the independent variable on the probability that an immigrant was in a specific labour market state. For discrete variables, such as marital status, the marginal effect represents the effect of a one-unit change in the independent variable. See the STATA manual for more details. Probit coefficients and robust standard errors are available upon request.

16 These tests were conducted by estimating a fully interacted version of each of the equations. Coefficients on the interactions then reflect the difference in the determinants of the two cohorts. The results reported in Tables 2.3–2.5 are the p values from the Chi-square tests of

the significance of the interaction terms. Individual tests were performed for Principal Applicant status and time since migration. Joint tests were performed for other subsets of variables.

17 The magnitude of these differences 18 months after migration are much the same as those at six months after migration for women, but considerably larger for men. In proportionate terms, however, these relative differences in unemployment are much more important 18 months after migration because the overall level of unemployment (the base) is much smaller.

18 Only 5.4 per cent of all female immigrants to Australia in 1990–1991 entered as Principal Applicants in one of the skill-based programs (Madden and Young 1993). Women also tend to be over-represented in family classes and under-represented in skill classes in Canada and the United States (Houstoun et al. 1984, UN 1995).

18 It is important to note that this relative deterioration occurs despite accounting for a range of productive skills in the regression model. At the same time, other factors omitted from the regression model may contribute to producing this effect. In particular, although more than a third (35.9 per cent) of Humanitarian migrants in Cohort 1 came from Europe and the former Soviet Union, this was true of less than 1 per cent of Humanitarian migrants in Cohort 2. Humanitarian migrants entering Australia in the late 1990s were more than twice as likely (44.2 versus 20.5 per cent) to come from the Middle East or Africa.

20 Results of the joint significance tests are given in Tables 2.3–2.5.

21 Here native English speakers are the omitted category.

22 Similar trends are observed for women, though there is evidence that poor English skills continued to be a barrier to women's labour market participation – and hence employment probability – throughout the 1990s. Conditional on labour market entry, however, language ability is not significantly related to the unemployment experiences 18 months after migration of women in the second LSIA cohort.

23 Unlike the standard linear case, a proportion of the difference in average outcomes will be attributable to the approximation itself.

3. Finding Employment After Migration: How Long Does It Take?

Prem Jung Thapa and Tue Gørgens

INTRODUCTION

Australia has one of the highest proportions of people born overseas among major developed countries,[1] and so there is an enduring research interest in the process through which immigrants are assimilated into the Australian labour market. The key indicators of the labour market outcomes of migrants previously studied have been their participation in the labour force (Ackland and Williams 1992), current employment status and unemployment (Miller and Neo 1997, Thapa 2004), earnings and wage adjustments (Beggs and Chapman 1988), expected earnings profile with duration of residence (Miller and Neo 2003), the match between migrants' jobs and their skills and qualifications (Evans and Kelley 1986), and occupational status (Borooah and Mangan 2002). But these previous studies, using mainly census data, provided only a static perspective on immigrant labour market outcomes.

The research discussed in this chapter extends the traditional static focus by analysing the dynamics of migrants' job search and the time they take to find their first job after arrival in Australia. It uses data from the Longitudinal Survey of Immigrants to Australia (LSIA) that followed two different cohorts of recent migrants and focuses on a key measure of labour market success in a dynamic perspective – the time taken since arrival in Australia for migrants to be employed in their first job.

Comparative analyses of the labour market outcomes of migrants can be either in reference to the native-born population, or to migrant groups themselves distinguished along several characteristics. Most Australian research has been of the former kind because, until the recent release of the LSIA, there were few large-scale representative surveys of the migrant population. There are now several studies that look at the labour market outcomes of migrants during the early settlement period based on the LSIA data set – for instance, Cobb-Clark (2000, 2003), VandenHeuevel and Wooden (2000), Richardson et al. (2001, 2004), Junankar, Paul and Yasmeen (2004), and Junankar and

Mahuteau (2005). These previous studies, however, do not fully exploit the richness and the longitudinal nature of LSIA, captured in the various wave interviews. Most are limited to being either cross-sectional comparisons across waves of a given cohort, or inter-cohort comparisons for a given wave. Such comparisons, though valuable, offer a restricted perspective on migrant labour market outcomes.

This chapter uses a duration model framework to assess the relative success of the two LSIA cohorts on their initial labour market entry. The measure of labour market outcome that is of interest is the time interval between the date of the migrant's arrival and the date of starting the first job in Australia. Such a duration perspective is often blurred in previous studies using LSIA that have focused mainly on inter-wave comparisons of labour market and other outcomes.

LSIA is a very valuable resource for analysing the changing labour market experience of recent migrants to Australia. In addition to being one of a few longitudinal surveys focusing on migrants, a special feature of LSIA is the inherent differences between the Cohort 1 and Cohort 2 samples which were induced partly by the different immigration policy settings at these two time periods (see Chapter 1). One promising line of inquiry that exploits this special feature of LSIA has been to analyse the sources of the overall differences in the early labour market outcomes for the two cohorts (as in Cobb-Clark 2003 and Chapter 2). In this approach a conventional decomposition method is used to assess the relative importance of differences in immigrant selection criteria (which lead to differences in immigrant characteristics) compared to the differences in the initial labour market and income-support eligibility conditions at the time of arrival (which lead to differences in immigrant behavioral responses and in the labour market returns to immigrant characteristics) when explaining the overall differences observed for the two cohorts.

This is the approach pursued in this chapter. Using a proportional hazards duration model framework, it first tests for systematic differences in the time taken by migrants in the two cohorts to find their first job after arrival in Australia. It then uses the estimated model to simulate the differences in the cumulative distribution of the time taken to find the first job for each cohort. Finally, it decomposes these differences into a contribution of varying individual characteristics and a contribution of varying time-specific factors captured in the duration model parameters in order to explain the total inter-cohort gap.

DATA LIMITATIONS AND METHODOLOGY

Although the LSIA is an extremely valuable dataset, it has certain limitations which constrain the methodological approaches that are feasible for the duration analyses carried out in this chapter and which must be highlighted at the outset. The LSIA interviews did not canvass a job calendar where employment status could be continuously monitored over the observation window of the various waves. Instead, in each wave interview questions were asked about current labour market status and current jobs, and previous jobs where relevant. A continuous time perspective on the labour market outcomes and job search activities of a particular individual was not directly recorded, nor can it be easily inferred from the available LSIA data. The main implication of this limitation is the inability to determine whether a person who reported not having a job at successive wave interviews was continuously looking for a job in the entire intervening period. The measurement of 'time to first job' is most relevant for individuals who are continuously looking for a job, but unfortunately they cannot be easily identified in the LSIA dataset.[2]

This problem was mitigated to some extent by restricting the duration model analysis to the sample of Principal Applicants who were in the working-age group of 18 to 59 years at the time of the first wave interview. This is the subgroup of migrants for whom it was most reasonable to assume would have been actively and continuously looking for a job since their arrival in Australia.[3]

Cohort 1 of LSIA has a total sample of 5,192 Principal Applicants which represents about 7 per cent of the total in-scope population of Principal Applicants who arrived in the specified two-year period; and Cohort 2 has a sample size of 3,124 Principal Applicants representing about 10 per cent of the in-scope population. The final estimation sample for this chapter, which includes only Principal Applicants aged 18 to 59 years at Wave 1, consists of 4,898 individuals in Cohort 1 and 2,804 individuals in Cohort 2.[4]

A second shortcoming of the LSIA data is that many of the post-immigration changes in the characteristics of migrants after arrival cannot be precisely timed. Changes such as having undertaken further training or gained qualifications in Australia, or having completed English language courses, or having moved interstate to improve job prospects could be very important in determining labour market success.[5] The inability to precisely time these events means a simple specification must be adopted for the duration models estimated, where all explanatory variables are taken to be time invariant – that is, migrant characteristics are fixed at the pre-immigration level or as defined at the time of the first interview (which normally occurred six months after arrival). The main explanatory variables used in the analysis are discussed below in the section on model specification.

INTER-WAVE LABOUR MARKET OUTCOMES AND TRANSITIONS

Table 3.1 presents a summary of the static labour market outcomes for the two cohorts of Principal Applicants aged 18 to 59 at each wave interviews.

The outcomes are summarised by gender for the proportion who were employed, the proportion in the labour force (the participation rate) and the proportion reporting being unemployed.[6] In Table 3.1 the general pattern for Cohort 1 is that employment rates increased significantly (and unemployment rates fell) between Waves 1 and 2; but smaller changes were observed for the longer time period between Waves 2 and 3. In fact, between Waves 2 and 3 employment rates appeared to have leveled off. The further decrease in unemployment rates in Wave 3 for Cohort 1 coincides with the decline in the participation rate in Wave 3 for both male and female Principal Applicants. This decline in participation in Wave 3 (by as much as 10 percentage points for men) is a surprising outcome. It could possibly reflect a 'discouraged worker' effect for those new migrants who had not been able to find an appropriate job before the Wave 3 interview (which, on average, was 42 months after arrival in Australia).

Table 3.1 Summary labour market outcomes at time of interview: Principal Applicants (aged 18–59 years at Wave 1) (%)

		All PAs		Male PAs		Female PAs	
		Cohort 1	Cohort 2	Cohort 1	Cohort 2	Cohort 1	Cohort 2
Employment rate	Wave 1	38.1	53.4	49.6	65.0	25.5	40.5
	Wave 2	44.8	55.4	56.8	66.1	31.7	43.5
	Wave 3	42.0	-	53.5	-	29.4	-
Participation rate	Wave 1	62.1	65.0	79.5	80.0	42.9	48.9
	Wave 2	57.3	61.8	72.9	73.5	40.2	49.2
	Wave 3	49.8	-	62.8	-	35.6	-
Unemployment rate	Wave 1	24.0	11.6	29.9	15.0	17.5	8.0
	Wave 2	12.5	6.4	16.1	7.5	8.5	5.3
	Wave 3	7.8	-	9.3	-	6.2	-
Sample size		4,898	2,804	2,814	1,514	2,084	1,290

Note:
PA – Principal Applicant.

Source: Longitudinal Survey of Immigrants to Australia.

Comparing across cohorts, Cohort 2 showed substantially higher employment and lower unemployment rates at Wave 1, and these differences generally narrowed by Wave 2. Since Cohort 2 started out with substantially more favourable outcomes in Wave 1, the changes observed in Wave 2 for Cohort 2 were smaller, as expected.

Table 3.1 also shows significant gender differences. Both participation and employment rates were substantially lower for female Principal Applicants in both cohorts, and the lower labour force participation rate led to a lower unemployment rate for women than for men. For both cohorts there were also significant differences on employment status associated with English language ability and visa categories for each gender (although these results are not shown in Table 3.1).[7] Men and women with lower English language ability had substantially lower employment rates compared to those with better English ability. Better labour market skills were also mirrored in the visa categories, where the Humanitarian visa group stood out as having uniformly low employment outcomes and very low levels of labour force participation. Even by Wave 3 in Cohort 1 – which was some 42 months after arrival on average – only 33 per cent of female Principal Applicants on Humanitarian visas were participating in the labour market. Employment transitions between the successive waves are indicated in Table 3.2. Current labour market status in each wave is measured in three categories: employed, unemployed and 'not in labour force'. These tables indicate that while there were significant transitions for those initially in the unemployed and 'not in labour force' categories, those who were employed at Wave 1 were very likely to remain employed in subsequent waves. For instance, in Cohort 1 among those employed at Wave 1, about 87 per cent remained employed at both Waves 2 and 3. While employment status changed to some degree over the time period between interviews, the stable employment patterns of those who were initially employed at Wave 1 highlights the importance of being able to quickly find that first job after arrival in Australia.

Table 3.2 Employment status transitions across waves: All Principal Applicants (%)

	Cohort 1			Cohort 2		
	Wave 1 employment status			Wave 1 employment status		
	Employed	Unemployed	Not in labour force	Employed	Unemployed	Not in labour force
Wave 2 employment status						
Employed	87.3	44.4	22.2	80.0	47.3	20.6
Unemployed	3.9	31.4	15.2	2.0	19.6	8.8
Not in labour force	8.8	24.3	62.6	18.1	33.1	70.7
Wave 3 employment status						
Employed	86.7	56.3	32.8	-	-	-
Unemployed	3.7	19.0	13.6	-	-	-
Not in labour force	9.7	24.7	53.5	-	-	-

Source: Longitudinal Survey of Immigrants to Australia.

FINDING THE FIRST JOB

Definitions and data summary

The LSIA survey forms do not contain a detailed job calendar from which the starting date of a migrant's first job after arrival in Australia can be derived. However, such a date can be readily inferred from the starting dates attached to one of potentially six different jobs that can be distinguished in the Cohort 1 interviews, and to one of eight jobs that can be distinguished in the Cohort 2 interviews. The first job is designated as the one with the earliest starting date among the set of current or previous jobs identified in any of the interviews.

This imputation appears quite robust for the Cohort 2 sample, which has a shorter follow-up period and where the jobs are more clearly distinguished by sequential order – that is, current, most recent previous, next recent previous, and so on. For Cohort 1 there is a longer gap in the observation period between the Wave 2 and Wave 3 interviews. Furthermore, the job starting dates are compiled only for the current job and the previous job that lasted for the longest period of time. This means that the scenario under which the derived job starting date is most likely to be misidentified is Cohort 1 Principal Applicants who began their first job after the Wave 2 interview but had changed jobs more than twice by the time of the Wave 3 interview. For such persons the assigned starting date of the first job can lead to an overestimation of the length of the initial non-working spell. The number of people possibly affected, however, is likely to be small. For many migrants the starting date of the first job was already assigned on the basis of the information about current and previous jobs reported in the Wave 1 and Wave 2 interviews.

Summary data on the inter-wave timing of the first job, as well as the average time taken (in months) to find the first job for those migrants who reported having at least one job, are indicated in Table 3.3. Figures 3.1 and 3.2 show the full frequency distribution of time taken to find the first job respectively for Cohorts 1 and 2 migrants.[8]

In Cohort 1 only about 28 per cent of Principal Applicants aged 18 to 59 years reported not having any job in Australia at the time of their last (Wave 3) interview. The largest number of migrants (42 per cent) found their first job within six months of arrival. About 20 per cent of these started their first job between six and 18 months after arrival, and another 10 per cent started their first job during the period between the Wave 2 and Wave 3 interviews. A very small percentage (1 per cent) reported starting their first job before arrival. Most of these could be foreign residents in Australia who were already working and changed their visa status to permanent migrant.[9] Also, among Cohort 1 migrants who reported having at least one job, the mean time taken to find their first job was 8.3 months after arrival.[10]

In Cohort 2, the corresponding proportion of migrants without a job by the last interview (18 months after arrival) was also about 28 per cent. However, this actually represents a lower proportion in comparison with Cohort 1. In Cohort 1, the 27.9 per cent without a job by the last interview took account of the 9.6 per cent who found a job between the Wave 2 and 3 interviews, a period not observed for Cohort 2. Looking only at the time period between the Waves 1 and 2 interviews for both cohorts, it is interesting to note that a higher proportion of Cohort 1 was employed by Wave 1; whereas for Cohort 2 the largest percentage of people started their first job between Waves 1 and 2. The average time to starting the first job for all ever-employed migrants was less for Cohort 2 at 4.1 months, than for Cohort 1 at 5.5 months (evaluated only for those who had a job by Wave 2 as indicated in the last column of Table 3.3).

The other panels in Table 3.3 show how the three indicators – the proportion without a job, the inter-wave timing of the first job, and the average time taken to find the first job – vary by gender, English language ability and visa class. The mean time taken to obtain the first job among the ever-employed reached a high of 15 to 17 months after arrival for migrants on Humanitarian visas, and for those with poor English ability. Almost 60 per cent of Cohort 1 women who spoke English badly had not found a job by Wave 3.

Figures 3.1 and 3.2, which show the full histogram of 'time to first job' among those ever-employed, reveal similar patterns, even though the time period covered is shorter for Cohort 2. There is a high frequency of success in finding a job within the first few months after arrival, after which the frequency trails off quickly. The largest number of migrants in both cohorts found their first job in the second month after arrival.

Main source used to find a job

Migrants who were employed were asked to identify the main source used to find their current job. While there was no direct information on the source used to find the very first job, the data noted above could be used to derive the source cited for the earliest recorded job. Presenting the data in this format focuses attention on the sources used by migrants to find the jobs they held soon after arrival. For the majority of people, these early job sources can be taken as a reasonable proxy for the main source used to find the very first job after arrival.

Figure 3.3 shows the frequency distribution of the main sources cited for the earliest job held by the sample of all ever-employed migrants. In each cohort the most frequently cited main source for finding the current job was 'friends'. The importance of this source also increased with length of stay in Australia, as is to be expected. Figure 3.3 shows that in Cohort 2 about 17 per cent of employed migrants at Wave 1 cited 'friends' as the main source, while for newly employed migrants in Wave 2 this proportion increased to 28 per

Table 3.3 Summary outcomes on timing of first job by wave and main characteristics of migrants

	Proportion without a job by last interview	Timing of first job (%)				Among ever-employed			Cohort 1 mean at Wave 2[b]
						Months to first job			
		Before arrival	Before Wave 1	Before Wave 2	Before Wave 3	mean	s.d.[a]	Sample N	
All Principal Applicants									
Cohort 1	27.9	1.0	41.6	19.9	9.6	8.3	9.3	3,579	(5.5)
Cohort 2	27.7	4.9	32.1	35.3	-	4.1	4.1	1,889	-
Male PAs									
Cohort 1	16.7	1.6	52.8	21.1	7.8	7.2	8.5	2,343	(5.9)
Cohort 2	16.7	6.5	37.9	38.9	-	3.6	3.6	1,154	-
Female PAs									
Cohort 1	40.2	0.4	29.2	18.6	11.6	10.1	10.1	1,236	(7.6)
Cohort 2	39.4	3.2	25.9	31.5	-	4.9	4.6	735	-
Male by English ability									
Cohort 1									
English only	5.2	2.4	79.4	12.1	0.9	3.6	4.2	735	(3.4)
English well	14.1	2.1	52.8	24.8	6.1	6.9	7.5	915	(5.9)
English badly	31.2	0.2	25.3	26.6	16.7	12.7	11.0	693	(9.5)
Cohort 2									
English only	6.2	7.0	46.4	40.4	-	3.1	3.0	449	-
English well	10.3	9.1	38.7	41.9	-	3.4	3.6	478	-
English badly	46.6	1.6	20.7	31.1	-	5.8	4.9	227	-
Female by English ability									
Cohort 1									
English only	20.0	0.5	58.0	17.6	3.9	5.4	5.7	342	(5.0)
English well	30.1	0.9	32.3	24.6	12.1	10.0	10.2	537	(7.7)
English badly	59.5	0.0	10.5	14.5	15.5	15.4	11.2	357	(10.6)
Cohort 2									
English only	16.7	5.6	39.4	38.3	-	3.6	3.1	257	-
English well	31.0	4.1	27.9	37.0	-	5.6	5.3	330	-
English badly	68.3	0.3	11.6	19.9	-	6.5	5.0	148	-

Table 3.3 (continued)

Men by visa type									
Cohort 1									
Family	15.0	0.8	57.0	21.6	5.6	6.4	7.5	616	(5.5)
Skilled – Australian Sponsored	11.5	1.2	58.5	20.7	8.1	7.0	8.6	496	(5.7)
BS/ENS	8.2	3.4	76.9	8.2	3.3	3.1	5.1	400	(2.7)
Independent	9.1	3.6	66.1	17.8	3.4	5.2	6.1	535	(4.8)
Humanitarian	37.5	0.0	12.3	29.8	20.4	15.9	11.0	296	(11.4)
Cohort 2									
Family	16.5	0.7	31.4	51.4	-	4.3	3.7	412	-
Skilled – Australian Sponsored	9.4	4.6	37.7	48.3	-	3.2	2.7	162	
BS/ENS	19.9	16.4	39.6	24.2	-	8.0	5.0	233	-
Independent	6.0	12.0	51.5	30.5	-	2.6	2.7	242	-
Humanitarian	67.1	0.0	8.9	24.0	-	9.0	5.0	105	-
Women by visa type									
Cohort 1									
Family	43.5	0.2	25.4	18.9	12.1	10.8	10.3	657	(8.0)
Skilled – Australian Sponsored	19.1	0.5	46.2	21.3	13.0	8.6	8.9	159	(7.0)
BS/ENS	8.4	1.1	79.5	8.1	3.0	3.0	5.0	87	(2.7)
Independent	9.6	2.8	67.6	16.0	4.1	5.1	6.6	224	(4.5)
Humanitarian	60.1	0.0	5.6	19.0	15.3	17.2	10.7	109	(12.6)
Cohort 2									
Family	44.2	0.6	21.8	33.4	-	5.6	4.9	456	-
Skilled – Australian Sponsored	21.5	2.7	36.3	39.5	-	4.3	3.9	90	-
BS/ENS	37.7	6.7	30.6	25.0	-	4.1	4.4	52	-
Independent	12.3	14.6	45.1	28.1	-	3.1	3.1	112	-
Humanitarian	89.4	0.0	0.2	10.3	-	10.6	4.6	25	-

Notes:
a s.d. – Standard deviation
b Figures in parentheses in the last column are the mean time to first job for Cohort 1 migrants using information only up to their Wave 2 interview. This figure is more directly comparable to the mean time to first job reported for Cohort 2 since the latter migrants were only interviewed up to Wave 2.

Source: Longitudinal Survey of Immigrants to Australia.

Figure 3.1 Frequency of time to first job: Cohort 1

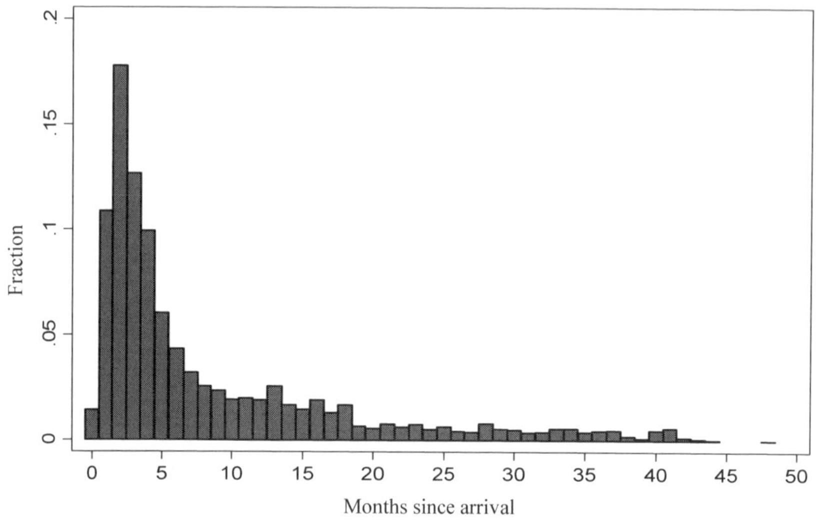

Figure 3.2 Frequency of time to first job: Cohort 2

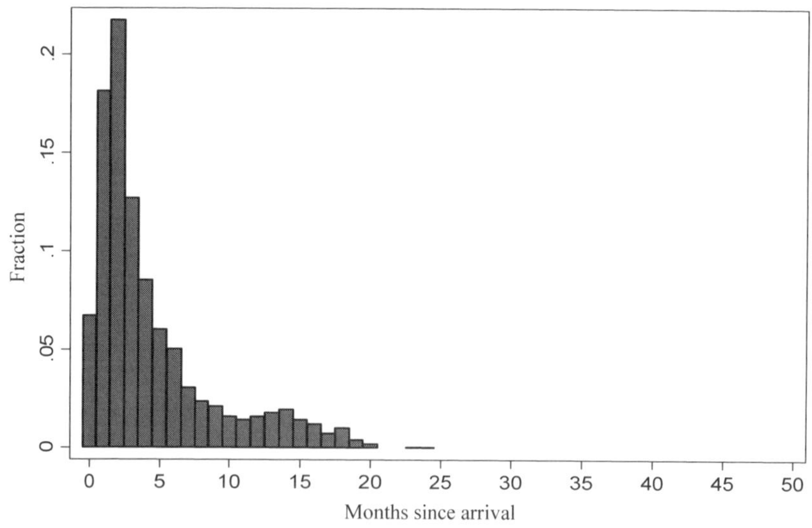

Note:
Cohort 1 and Cohort 2 frequency distributions are not comparable since the time periods over which a first job is found are very different. Cohort 2 data extend only up to the Wave 2 interview and show a maximum observation period of 27 months since arrival, while in Cohort 1 the maximum observation period is 57 months since arrival.

Source: Longitudinal Survey of Immigrants to Australia.

Figure 3.3 Main source used to find (new) current job: Percentage of employed Principal Applicants (in Cohort 1 and Cohort 2)

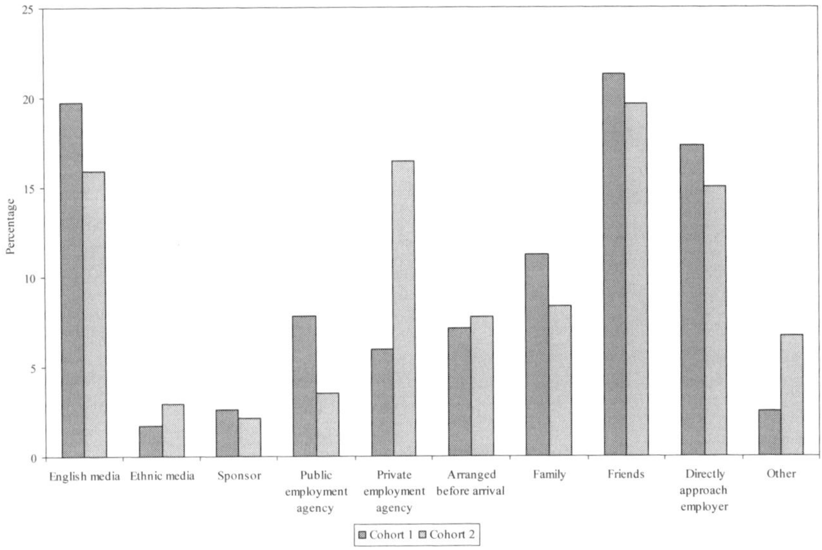

Source: Longitudinal Survey of Immigrants to Australia.

cent. The informal channels of friends, family, sponsor and even direct personal approach to the employer accounted in total for almost 50 per cent of the main sources for migrants in Cohort 1, and about 45 per cent for migrants in Cohort 2.

Government and other employment agencies played a limited role, even though there was a significant increase in the role played by other private employment agencies in Cohort 2. This increase (to 16 per cent) was partly due to the privatisation of the public sector Commonwealth Employment Service (CES) which operated during the interview period for Cohort 1.

In both cohorts about 10 per cent of the respondents with a job at Wave 1 reported that their jobs were arranged before arrival in Australia. This sub-group was larger than the sample of migrants in the Employer Nomination Scheme visa category, and possibly included individuals who were already working in Australia but had subsequently changed their visa status to become permanent migrants and had continued with the same job.[11]

Time plots on proportion without a first job

A fuller perspective on the time taken to find the first job can be obtained by plotting the proportion of migrants who had not found their first job at each

Figure 3.4 Kaplan-Meier survival estimates by cohort

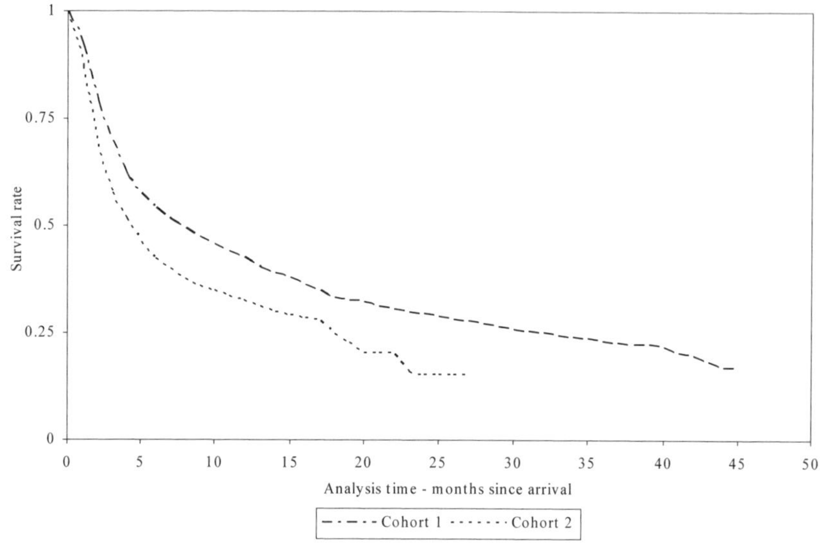

Figure 3.5 Kaplan-Meier survival estimates by cohort and gender

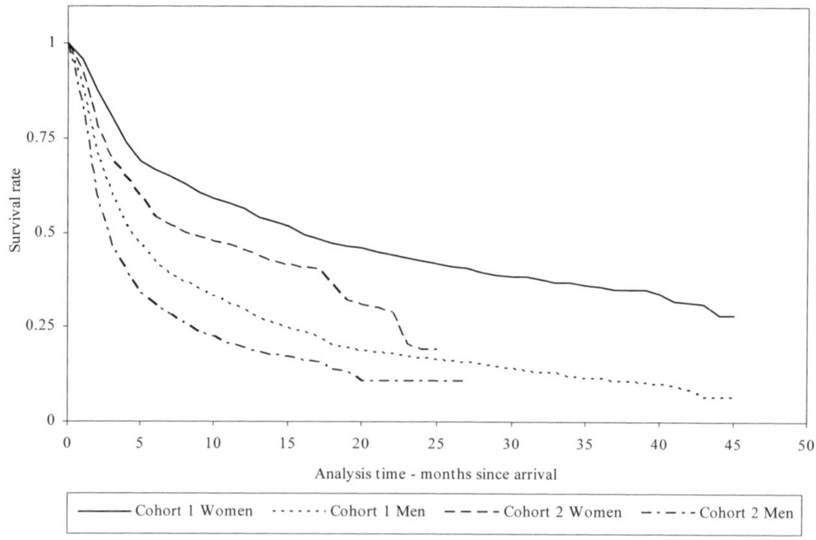

Source: Longitudinal Survey of Immigrants to Australia.

Figure 3.6 Kaplan-Meier survival estimates: Cohort 1 by major visa class

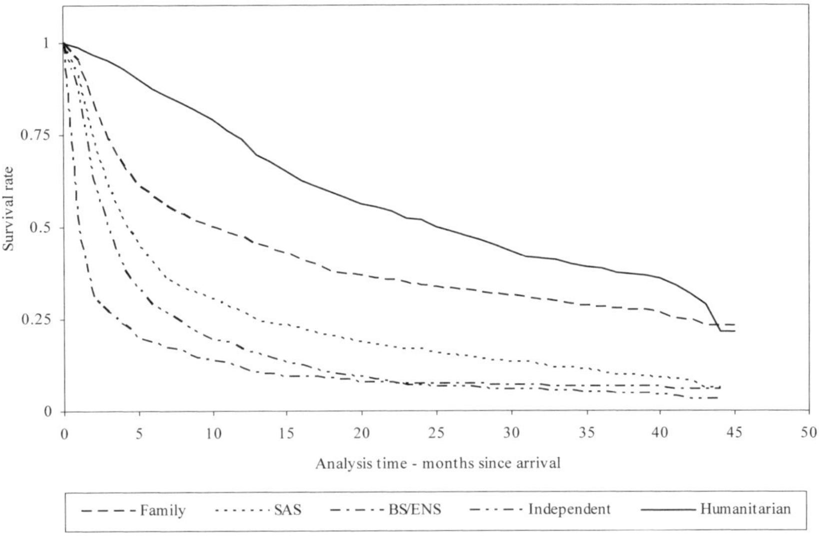

Figure 3.7 Kaplan-Meier survival estimates: Cohort 2 by major visa class

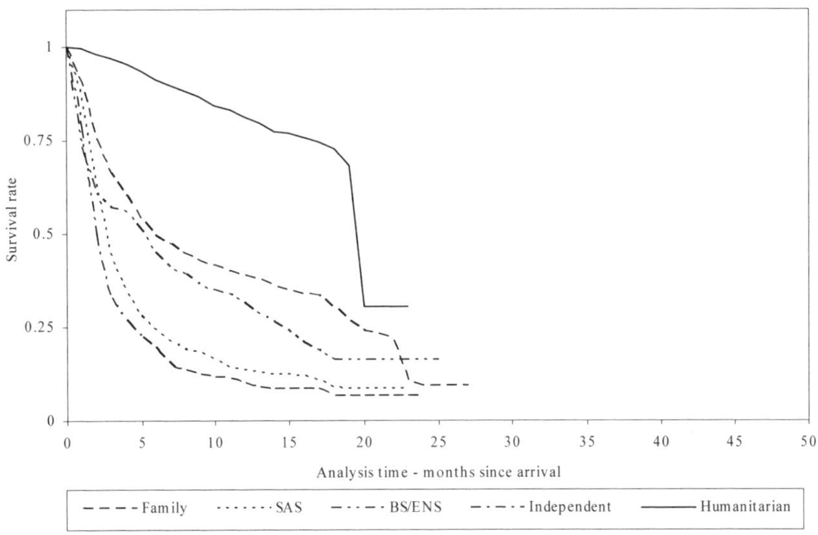

Source: Longitudinal Survey of Immigrants to Australia.

month after arrival in Australia. This relationship is referred to as the 'survival function'. Figures 3.4 to 3.7 show the survival functions for different sub-groups of the sample of migrants.[12]

Figure 3.4, which compares migrants in Cohorts 1 and 2, shows uniformly higher proportions without a first job for Cohort 1. However, the time pattern of the survival function, including a steep fall during the early period of settlement up to the first 20 months after arrival, is quite similar for both cohorts. Figure 3.5 plots the survival ratios by cohort and gender, and it demonstrates clearly that women in both cohorts took much longer than men to find their first job. The rate of decline of these survival functions is quite similar for the men in the two cohorts; but for women the slope of the Cohort 1 survival function is flatter, indicating slower rates of finding the first job compared to Cohort 2 for the period up to the Wave 2 interview.

Figures 3.6 and 3.7 present survival functions classified by the five main visa categories for each cohort.[13] The differences are quite stark. The Business and Skilled Independent visa classes had dramatically lower survival function profiles, indicating that more migrants in these visa classes were employed at any given time compared to migrants in other visa classes. The slowest rates of finding the first job are observed for migrants in the Humanitarian visa category. The size of the relative gaps in the plots of Figures 3.6 and 3.7 demonstrate clearly just how significantly lower is the propensity of the Humanitarian visa holders to find their first job at any given time since arrival, compared to the other four major visa classes.

DETERMINANTS OF THE TIME TAKEN TO FIND THE FIRST JOB

This section presents the main estimation results on the characteristics of the migrants that are important in determining the rate at which they find their first job. The analysis technique used in these estimations follows the conventional proportional hazards (PH) framework for duration models. PH models formulate an underlying baseline 'hazard function' for assessing the probability of observing an event (that is, finding the first job, in this case) at time t, and assumes that the effect of a dependent variable included in the regression model is to alter the baseline hazard in a proportional manner (that is, by a multiplicative factor) for all t.

Two specific functional forms were selected for these estimations – the semi-parametric Cox model and the fully parameterised Weibull model.[14] While the Cox specification is a robust workhorse for PH models, the Cox model in itself is insufficient for the purpose of this chapter. A fully specified parametric model is required to test for inter-cohort differences and to carry out simulations to decompose the sources of these inter-cohort differences.[15]

Model specification

The main regression variables used in the estimated PH models are summarised in Table 3.4. As noted in the section of this chapter on inter-wave labour market outcomes, the specification of these models is limited to explanatory variables that are time invariant because changes in the characteristics of migrants after arrival cannot be timed precisely. Therefore, potentially important determinants of labour market success that depend on changed characteristics of the migrant after arrival in Australia, such as acquiring a subsequent educational qualification in Australia or having completed English language training, cannot be included in this analysis. The hazards model framework with only time invariant variables is, however, not overly restrictive in the present setting since the focus is on the time to starting the first job. There is a high incidence of starting the first job within the first few months of arrival (when, presumably, migrants' characteristics changed very little).

In addition to visa category and English language ability, which are expected to be important determinants of the time to first job, other explanatory variables included in these analyses are the source region of the migrants; their educational levels; occupation and recent employment history prior to immigration; the region of initial residence in Australia; presence of relatives in, and having visited, Australia before migration; whether information on job prospects in Australia was received prior to arrival; the amount of funds brought into Australia; and the existence of long term health conditions prior to arrival.

Table 3.4 highlights some clear differences in the characteristics of the LSIA sample of migrants by cohort and gender. Female migrants were overwhelmingly in the non-points-tested Family visa category (more than two-thirds in both cohorts). Cohort 2 migrants, both men and women, had more favourable labour market characteristics. They had higher levels of education; better English language ability; higher incidence of full-time work in the home country prior to immigration; higher incidence of managerial and professional occupations; and a higher incidence of having visited Australia prior to migration.

Table 3.4 also shows the distribution of Cohort 2 migrants whose visa applications were assessed under the post-July 1999 points test. These changes in the points test affect Cohort 2 migrants in the Independent and Skilled – Australian Sponsored visa classes only.[16] In the Independent visa category of Cohort 2, about 17 per cent were assessed under the revised points system. A relatively smaller proportion (about 4 per cent) of the Skilled – Australian Sponsored migrants were assessed under the post-July 1999 points test.

Table 3.4 Summary characteristics on regression variables by cohort: All Principal Applicants aged 18–59 at Wave 1 interview (%)

	Men		Women		All	
	Cohort 1	Cohort 2	Cohort 1	Cohort 2	Cohort 1	Cohort 2
Marital status and age						
Currently married[a]	71.7	72.6	74.6	77.1	73.1	74.8
Previously married	2.5	2.6	8.4	4.7	5.3	3.6
Never married	25.8	24.8	16.9	18.1	21.6	21.6
Age at Wave 1 (in years)	33.0	34.4	31.2	31.3	32.1	32.9
Source regions						
English speaking countries	23.8	27.7	16.3	17.5	20.2	22.8
Asia[a]	39.4	38.2	52.5	52.8	45.6	45.3
Northwest Europe	3.9	3.7	4.2	3.4	4.0	3.6
Southeast & East Europe	13.6	8.8	12.0	8.5	12.8	8.6
Other	19.3	21.6	15.0	17.8	17.3	19.7
Visa type						
Family[a]	38.1	35.3	73.8	66.5	55.1	50.4
Skilled – Australian Sponsored (all)	11.5	12.1	5.0	8.9	8.4	10.5
BS/ENS[b]	6.1	9.7	1.1	2.0	3.7	6.0
Independent (all)	26.4	34.3	10.0	16.6	18.6	25.8
Humanitarian	17.9	8.6	10.1	6.0	14.2	7.3
SAS – Cohort 2 post-July 1999 points	-	0.5	-	0.4	-	0.5
Independent – Cohort 2 post-July 1999 points	-	5.8	-	2.8	-	4.4
Pre-arrival employment status						
Not working	15.8	11.2	31.6	31.1	23.3	20.8
Working part time	6.9	7.6	13.2	10.6	9.9	9.1
Working full time[a]	77.3	81.1	55.2	58.2	66.8	70.1
Pre-arrival Occupation						
Manager	12.0	14.3	5.6	5.9	8.9	10.2
Professional	26.4	29.4	24.2	30.0	25.3	29.7
Para-professional[a]	4.4	12.0	4.9	8.3	4.6	10.2
Tradesperson[a]	22.0	18.0	5.6	2.1	14.2	10.3
Clerks[a]	3.1	4.0	13.4	11.3	8.0	7.5
Sales and service workers[a]	8.0	5.9	8.8	8.8	8.4	7.3
Machine operators[a]	3.5	3.6	2.9	1.1	3.2	2.4
Labourers[a]	4.7	1.6	3.2	1.5	4.0	1.5
Education level						
Post graduate or higher	15.5	23.9	8.8	16.2	12.3	20.2
Bachelor's degree[a]	21.6	22.9	22.7	25.1	22.1	24.0
Technical or professional degree	22.2	19.8	21.8	21.8	22.0	20.7
Trade qualification	12.2	11.3	2.0	2.0	7.3	6.8
Year 12	13.5	12.8	20.0	17.9	16.6	15.3
Year 10 or 11 only	6.4	4.3	9.9	6.9	8.1	5.6
Year 9 or less	8.2	4.5	14.3	9.8	11.1	7.1
English ability						
Native English speaker	33.7	42.4	24.2	31.3	29.2	37.1
Non-native but speaks English well	33.7	35.1	33.2	34.1	33.4	34.6
Non-native and speaks English badly[a]	32.6	22.5	42.6	34.6	37.3	28.3

Table 3.4 (continued)

	Men		Women		All	
	Cohort 1	Cohort 2	Cohort 1	Cohort 2	Cohort 1	Cohort 2
Residence regions (at Wave 1)						
New South Wales[a]	43.3	41.6	44.8	45.7	44.0	43.6
Victoria	24.0	24.4	26.9	25.3	25.3	24.8
Queensland	11.6	11.6	11.2	11.4	11.4	11.5
South Australia	5.6	4.7	4.9	4.5	5.3	4.6
Western Australia	12.5	14.7	8.8	10.6	10.7	12.7
ACT, Northern Territory or Tasmania	3.1	3.0	3.5	2.6	3.3	2.8
Visited Australia before	43.2	55.1	40.0	46.9	41.6	51.1
Has relatives in Australia	61.2	59.5	63.8	71.3	62.5	65.2
Received job information pre-arrival	38.4	39.6	25.7	28.2	32.3	34.1
Was sponsored or nominated	57.8	42.6	82.4	71.7	69.5	56.6
Funds available on arrival ($ '000)	20.9	43.3	7.2	16.2	14.4	30.2
Highest qualification received in Australia	3.9	6.5	3.4	6.1	3.7	6.3
Qualifications assessed pre-arrival	24.1	29.4	9.3	12.8	17.0	21.4
Has long term health condition pre-arrival	3.3	7.0	5.2	5.8	4.2	6.4
Intends to stay permanently (Wave 1)	96.1	99.6	94.2	99.7	95.2	99.6
Sample N	2,814	1,514	2,084	1,290	4,898	2,804
Percentage reporting a job by last interview	83.3	83.3	59.8	60.6	72.1	72.3

Notes:

a Excluded category in all regression model results. The English-speaking source countries are Canada, Ireland, New Zealand, South Africa, United Kingdom and United States.

b BS/ENS – Business Skills/Employer Nomination Scheme.

Source: Longitudinal Survey of Immigrants to Australia.

Estimation results

The full results of the duration model using the Weibull functional form are reported in Tables 3.5 and 3.6.[17] This model is estimated separately for male and female Principal Applicants in each cohort,[18] resulting in four sets of estimates.

The coefficient estimates shown in Tables 3.5 and 3.6 are in the form of hazard ratios, and not the original hazard function coefficients. Hazard ratios are easier to interpret when most of the variables represent specific categories, as is the case here. Hazard ratios greater than one correspond to positive regression coefficients in the duration model and they have the effect of increasing the probability of finding the first job, relative to the baseline hazard, at any time interval after arrival. Conversely, hazard ratios of less than one imply that the variable reduces the probability of finding the first job, relative to the baseline hazard. A hazard ratio equal to one implies that the variable has no additional effect on the probability of the event occurring beyond that already specified in the baseline function.[19]

Table 3.5 Estimates of proportional hazards: Women aged 18–59 years by cohort

	Cohort 1 women (Sample N=2074)			Cohort 2 women (Sample N=1254)		
	Hazard Ratio	Std. Err.	P>|z|	Hazard Ratio	Std. Err.	P>|z|
Marital status and age						
Previously married	1.27	0.14	0.04	1.51	0.24	0.01
Never married	1.69	0.13	0.00	1.48	0.14	0.00
Age at Wave 1	1.11	0.03	0.00	1.02	0.04	0.64
Age at Wave 1 squared	1.00	0.00	0.00	1.00	0.00	0.24
Source regions						
English-speaking countries	1.75	0.21	0.00	1.71	0.24	0.00
Northwest Europe	1.88	0.23	0.00	1.11	0.19	0.55
Southeast & East Europe	1.34	0.12	0.00	1.44	0.19	0.00
Other	0.78	0.07	0.01	0.94	0.12	0.63
Visa type						
Skilled – Australian Sponsored (all)	1.24	0.14	0.05	1.09	0.18	0.62
BS/ENS	5.35	0.82	0.00	2.05	0.52	0.01
Independent (all)	1.28	0.18	0.08	1.07	0.26	0.79
Humanitarian	0.75	0.09	0.02	0.32	0.09	0.00
Independent – Cohort 2 post-July 1999 points	-	-	-	1.99	0.48	0.01
SAS – Cohort 2 post-July 1999 points	-	-	-	1.47	0.45	0.21
Pre-arrival employment status						
Not working	0.65	0.06	0.00	0.45	0.05	0.00
Working part time	0.84	0.08	0.05	1.01	0.12	0.92
Pre-arrival occupation						
Manager or professional	0.92	0.07	0.28	0.94	0.09	0.52
Education level						
Post graduate	0.95	0.09	0.58	1.16	0.14	0.21
Technical or professional degree	0.92	0.08	0.35	1.08	0.13	0.54
Trade qualification	0.81	0.16	0.29	0.94	0.27	0.84
Year 12	0.85	0.09	0.12	0.78	0.11	0.08
Year 10 or 11 only	0.76	0.12	0.08	0.80	0.15	0.24
Year 9 or less	0.77	0.11	0.07	0.89	0.18	0.54
Highest qualification received in Australia	1.79	0.26	0.00	1.01	0.20	0.95
Non-Australian qualifications assessed pre-arrival	1.19	0.12	0.08	1.33	0.19	0.04
English ability						
Native English speaker	2.40	0.27	0.00	2.29	0.34	0.00
Non-native but speaks English well	1.62	0.13	0.00	1.81	0.21	0.00

Table 3.5 (continued)

	Cohort 1 women (Sample N=2074)			Cohort 2 women (Sample N=1254)		
	Hazard Ratio	Std. Err.	P>|z|	Hazard Ratio	Std. Err.	P>|z|
Visited Australia before	1.34	0.10	0.00	1.60	0.16	0.00
Has relatives in Australia	0.91	0.06	0.16	0.90	0.08	0.24
Received job information pre-arrival	1.07	0.07	0.32	1.13	0.10	0.17
Was sponsored or nominated	0.96	0.09	0.67	1.06	0.19	0.75
Funds available on arrival ($ '000)	1.00	0.00	0.01	1.00	0.00	0.03
Has a long term health condition pre-arrival	0.95	0.17	0.76	0.77	0.17	0.22
Constant	-4.83	0.52	0.00	-3.40	0.69	0.00
Weibull parameter *(ρ)*	0.97#	0.02	0.00	1.11*	0.03	0.00

Notes:
Other regression variables included are regional dummies for place of residence at Wave 1 interview.
The estimated Weibull parameter for Cohort 2 (indicated by *) is significantly different from one; but the estimated parameter for Cohort 1 (indicated by #) is not significantly different from one.
(When $\rho=1$ the Weibull reduces to the exponential distribution which has a constant baseline hazard).

BS/ENS – Business Skills/Emploer Nomination Scheme.

Source: Longitudinal Survey of Immigrants to Australia.

The hazard ratios for categorical variables, such as marital status and visa class, are defined in relation to a reference category that is excluded from the set of variables specified in the estimated model. For instance, as indicated in Table 3.4, marital status is defined in terms of three categories – being currently married, previously married and never married. The duration model results in Tables 3.5 and 3.6 show estimated hazard ratios only for the latter two of these three categories. The excluded category is being currently married; hence the estimated hazard ratio for the previously and never married variables indicate the proportional effect of being in these marital status categories relative to being currently married. In Table 3.4 the categories indicated with a footnote mark ([a]) represent the reference category in the interpretation of the estimated hazard ratios.

The estimated hazard ratios in Tables 3.5 and 3.6 show some common and some divergent effects for men and women. Significant common effects are observed for migrants' region of origin and English language ability. Better English language ability clearly increases the probability of getting the first job quickly. A female migrant in Cohort 1 who was a native English speaker had a 2.4 times higher probability of finding the first job at any given time compared to the reference category of someone who spoke English badly. The equivalent probability in Cohort 2 was 2.3 times higher. For male migrants (Table 3.6) a native English speaker had an even higher probability of finding a first job (2.8 times in Cohort 1 and 2.4 times in Cohort 2) compared to someone who spoke English badly. Non-native English speakers who nevertheless spoke English well also had a significantly higher probability of finding their first job.

Table 3.6 Estimates of proportional hazards: Men aged 18–59 years by cohort

	Cohort 1 men (Sample N=2764)			Cohort 2 men (Sample N=1423)		
	Hazard Ratio	Std. Err.	P>|z|	Hazard Ratio	Std. Err.	P>|z|
Marital status and age						
Previously married	1.16	0.16	0.27	1.04	0.22	0.84
Never married	0.94	0.05	0.29	1.18	0.10	0.04
Age at Wave 1	1.08	0.02	0.00	1.11	0.04	0.00
Age at Wave 1 squared	1.00	0.00	0.00	1.00	0.00	0.00
Source regions						
English-speaking countries	1.83	0.16	0.00	1.67	0.19	0.00
Northwest Europe	2.08	0.23	0.00	1.19	0.17	0.24
Southeast & East Europe	1.25	0.09	0.00	1.12	0.13	0.31
Other	0.89	0.05	0.04	0.94	0.09	0.49
Visa type						
Skilled – Australian Sponsored (all)	1.06	0.08	0.44	1.07	0.14	0.62
BS/ENS	2.93	0.29	0.00	1.89	0.33	0.00
Independent (all)	1.13	0.11	0.20	1.05	0.19	0.78
Humanitarian	0.55	0.04	0.00	0.30	0.05	0.00
Independent – Cohort 2 post-July 1999 points	-	-	-	1.22	0.21	0.23
SAS – Cohort 2 post-July 1999 points	-	-	-	1.65	0.36	0.02
Pre-arrival employment status						
Not working	1.00	0.08	0.95	0.70	0.08	0.00
Working part time	0.83	0.08	0.04	0.81	0.11	0.12
Pre-arrival occupation						
Manager or professional	0.94	0.05	0.30	0.91	0.08	0.23
Education level						
Post graduate	0.96	0.06	0.54	1.30	0.12	0.01
Technical or professional degree	1.10	0.07	0.13	1.34	0.14	0.00
Trade qualification	1.27	0.11	0.01	1.94	0.26	0.00
Year 12	1.06	0.09	0.50	0.91	0.11	0.42
Year 10 or 11 only	1.15	0.13	0.21	1.01	0.18	0.95
Year 9 or less	0.99	0.11	0.95	1.03	0.20	0.90
Highest qualification received in Australia	0.99	0.12	0.96	1.16	0.19	0.37
Non-Australian qualifications assessed pre-arrival	1.00	0.06	0.96	1.13	0.11	0.21
English ability						
Native English speaker	2.81	0.23	0.00	2.42	0.30	0.00
Non-native but speaks English well	1.65	0.10	0.00	2.04	0.21	0.00

Table 3.6 (continued)

	Cohort 1 men (Sample N=2764)			Cohort 2 men (Sample N=1423)		
	Hazard Ratio	Std. Err.	P>|z|	Hazard Ratio	Std. Err.	P>|z|
Visited Australia before	1.12	0.06	0.03	0.94	0.08	0.46
Has relatives in Australia	0.88	0.04	0.01	0.89	0.06	0.10
Received job information pre-arrival	1.04	0.05	0.40	1.04	0.07	0.55
Was sponsored or nominated	1.16	0.08	0.03	1.14	0.15	0.33
Funds available on arrival ($ '000)	1.00	0.00	0.00	1.00	0.00	0.00
Has a long term health condition pre-arrival	0.89	0.13	0.44	0.62	0.10	0.00
Constant	-3.83	0.41	0.00	-4.34	0.61	0.00
Weibull parameter *(ρ)*	1.04*	0.02	0.00	1.21*	0.03	0.00

Notes:
Other regression variables included are regional dummies for place of residence at Wave 1 interview.
The estimated Weibull parameter is significantly different from one (*) for male Principal Applicants in both cohorts.

There is consistency in the effects of the source regions as well. Migrants from the mainly English speaking countries[20] and European regions had significantly higher probabilities of finding the first job, relative to migrants from Asia (who formed the reference category). For migrants from the residual 'Other' source region (mainly Latin America and Africa) the hazard ratio was less than one. The effects of source region on time taken to first job was more clearly established in Cohort 1 where all of the source region effects were significant at the 10 per cent level for men and women.

An example of divergent effects for men and women is the effect of marital status. Compared to the reference category of currently married migrants, being never married or previously married (that is, currently divorced/separated) significantly increased the probability of finding the first job for women, but not for men. Marital status had a limited effect for men in the time they took to find their first job; but married women always had a lower probability of finding their first job at any given time interval after arrival in Australia.

With regard to visa category, the reference category is the Family stream visa (which is not points-tested). Relative to this, the Skilled – Australian Sponsored (SAS) and Independent visa categories (both of which are points-tested) and also the Business Skills/Employer Nomination Scheme visa categories had estimated hazard ratios greater than one in all four sets of results; but there was no consistency in whether these visa category effects were statistically significant. Being a points-tested male migrant in either cohort had no significant effect on the time taken to start the first job. For female migrants significant positive effects (leading to a shorter time to the first job) were observed for Cohort 1, but not for Cohort 2 for the two points-tested visa categories. As expected, being a migrant in the Business Skills/Employer Nomination Scheme category significantly increased the probability of finding the first job. On the other hand, the Humanitarian visa category had estimated hazard ratios that were consistently and significantly less than one, indicating a much longer time to the first job for this group. Both male and female Humanitarian visa holders in Cohort 2 seemed to be particularly disadvantaged in terms of finding their first job in Australia, compared to Cohort 1 (even though everybody else in Cohort 2 did relatively better than their counterparts in Cohort 1). This result was consistent with the labour market outcomes observed in Chapter 2.

Tables 3.5 and 3.6 also show mixed results for the time to finding the first job for those migrants in Cohort 2 who were assessed under the post-July 1999 points-tested visa categories. The July 1999 changes to the points test affect only a subset of Cohort 2 migrants in the two major points-tested visa categories, Independent and Skilled – Australian Sponsored. These migrants are grouped as 'Independent – Cohort 2 post-July 1999 points' and 'SAS – Cohort 2 post-July 1999 points'. The hazard ratios for these two groups, as shown in Tables 3.5 and 3.6, represent the additional effect of being assessed under the post-July 1999 points test relative to the pre-July 1999 test for the Independent and SAS categories.[21] The hazard ratios for both of these post-July 1999 groups are estimated to be consistently greater than one in Tables 3.5 and 3.6, but they are not always statistically significant. For female migrants, only the hazard ratio for the Independent post-July 1999 group is significantly greater than one. For male migrants, only the hazard ratio for the SAS post-July 1999 group is significantly greater than one. These estimated hazard ratios for the post-July 1999 points test group, where significantly different from zero, represent quite large effects. For instance, female migrants in the post-July 1999 Independent visa group had nearly twice the probability of finding the first job than their pre-July 1999 points-tested counterparts. This favourable effect of the change in the points test remained even after controlling for migrant's age and English language ability, which were the two criteria that were tightened in the post-July 1999 points test. This suggests that the post-July 1999 points tested migrants possibly had other more favourable labour market characteristics that were not included in the data analysis.

The results for level of education are also mixed. For men, compared to migrants with a Bachelor or equivalent degree (the reference category), the hazard ratios are significantly greater than one for migrants with a trade qualification (in both cohorts), and for migrants with a postgraduate qualification or a technical/professional degree (in Cohort 2 only). Lower levels of education (Year 12, or even lower) do not significantly affect the length of time to find the first job. For women the pattern is reversed. Higher levels of education such as postgraduate, professional and technical degrees do not offer any significant advantages over the reference group with Bachelor or equivalent qualifications. However, women with lower levels of education had hazard ratios that were significantly less than one in many instances in Table 3.5, indicating that they took a longer time to find their first job compared to women with Bachelor degrees, the reference group.

Furthermore, receiving the highest educational qualification in Australia, no matter what that qualification level is, had a significant positive effect on finding the first job only for Cohort 1 women. And for those with non-Australian qualifications, having these qualifications assessed as equivalent to Australian qualifications prior to migration had a positive effect on the hazard ratios, again, for women only. In contrast, the rate at which men found their first job was surprisingly insensitive to these additional characteristics of their educational qualifications.

The effect of pre-immigration employment was also mixed. For women, those not working at all had a hazard ratio significantly less than one compared to those who worked full time just prior to immigration. For men, those not working at all had a hazard ratio significantly less than one only in Cohort 2. For Cohort 1 men, the negative effect on time taken to find the first job was observed only among those who worked part-time in comparison to those who worked full-time.

The effect of being sponsored for migration significantly increased the probability of finding the first job only for Cohort 1 men. Other divergent results of some interest are that having visited Australia prior to immigration tended to increase the rate of finding the first job; while having relatives in Australia worked in the other direction. These effects are as expected, with the latter result possibly arising because migrants with relatives already in Australia were able to depend on them for some initial support while taking more time to find an appropriate first job.[22] On the other hand, for both men and women the probability of finding the first job was not increased for those who engaged in some job search behaviour by requesting and receiving information about job prospects prior to migration.

Another significant effect of interest that is consistent for men and women in both cohorts is that those people who brought in a larger amount of funds at the time of migration took a longer time to find their first job. Having a long-term health condition prior to arrival also increased significantly the time it took to find the first job for Cohort 2 men. The effects of initial region of residence in Australia (which are not shown in Tables 3.5 and 3.6) indicate only small differences, with the shortest time to finding the first job observed among migrants who settled initially in the state of New South Wales.

Estimates of the Weibull parameter (ρ) that determines the shape of the baseline hazard function are also reported in Tables 3.5 and 3.6. Estimates of ρ significantly higher than one indicate a monotonically increasing baseline hazard rate of finding the first job as the period of residence in Australia increases, while ρ equal to one signifies a constant hazard over time. A seemingly constant baseline hazard is observed only for Cohort 1 women, while ρ is significantly greater than one for all other migrants.

A restricted version of the Weibull model was also estimated where the Cohort 1 and Cohort 2 migrants are combined, but with separate analyses for men and women. This model permits a test of the null hypothesis that a common set of hazard coefficients apply to both Cohorts 1 and 2; that is, all migrants, regardless of when they arrived, were affected by the various characteristics considered in the analyses in the same way. The likelihood ratio tests from comparing the unrestricted cohort-specific model with the restricted pooled model strongly reject the hypothesis of a common set of hazard model parameters for the two cohorts, indicating that the various characteristics affect the two cohorts of migrants differently.

Table 3.7 Estimates of the proportional hazards of cohort status by gender

	Women			Men		
	Hazard Ratio	Std. Err.	P>|z|	Hazard Ratio	Std. Err	P>|z|
Cohort 1 indicator	0.69	0.036	0.000	0.78	0.033	0.002

Note:
Selected regression results from a Weibull model estimated over the pooled sample of Cohort 1 and Cohort 2 migrants, with all other regression variables as in Tables 3.5 and 3.6.

This model, based on the combined cohorts, can also be used to measure the proportional effect that membership of a specific cohort has on the time taken to find the first job. Table 3.7 shows that the hazard ratios associated with being in Cohort 1 are significantly less than one for both men and women. This means that all things being equal, migrants in Cohort 1 took more time to find their first job than did migrants in Cohort 2. The relative disadvantage of being in Cohort 1 is greater for women. Cohort 1 women had more than a 30 per cent lower probability of finding the first job (hazard ratio estimate of 0.69) compared to Cohort 2 women. For men the relative disadvantage of being in Cohort 1 was smaller at 22 per cent.

EXPLAINING INTER-COHORT DIFFERENCES: SIMULATION AND DECOMPOSITION RESULTS

This section addresses the question of what are the sources of the relative disadvantage of Cohort 1 migrants in terms of the time taken to find their first job. Using the Weibull parametric regression results from the previous section, simulations are carried out to predict the time taken to find the first job for every individual in the sample of the two cohorts. These predictions are then compared with a hypothetical prediction of the time taken to find the first job that is derived from cross-cohort simulations in which the estimated hazard model parameters of one cohort are applied to the data for the other cohort. This provides a standard method of decomposing the total difference between the cohorts into two components: (i) the effects of changing characteristics of the sample of migrants in the two cohorts, and (ii) the effect of the different labour market environment faced by the two cohorts as reflected in the differences in the hazard model parameters. Isolating effect (ii) through such decompositions helps to shed light on the impact of the immigration policy and other changes that occurred in the time interval between the arrival in Australia of the two cohorts.

The results of these simulations are graphed in Figures 3.8 and 3.9 for male and female migrants respectively. In these figures the original simulated survival functions for each cohort are presented together with the hypothetical survival function that arises when the time to the first job for Cohort 1 individuals is simulated using Cohort 2's estimated returns to their characteristics (that is, the estimated coefficients of Tables 3.5 and 3.6 for Cohort 2). The survival function resulting from this cross-cohort simulation is indicated with the legend 'Coh1 with Coh2 parameters' in Figures 3.8 and 3.9, while the own cohort simulations are denoted, respectively, as 'Coh1 with Coh1 parameters' and 'Coh2 with Coh2 parameters'.

In the interpretation of these figures, the relative horizontal distance between the survival function marked 'Coh1 with Coh2 parameters' (broken line) and the survival function marked 'Coh2 with Coh2 parameters' (dotted line) represents the difference in the time to the first job arising from the different individual characteristics of Cohort 1 and Cohort 2. In both of these simulations the returns to migrant characteristics (that is, the hazard model coefficients used) are the same; hence differences in outcomes are produced solely by differences in the characteristics of the two cohort of migrants. Similarly, the horizontal distance between the broken line of 'Coh1 with Coh2 parameters' and the solid line of 'Coh1 with Coh1 parameters' represents the difference produced by the changed settings of the time periods of arrival of Cohort 1 and Cohort 2.

For male migrants, the middle broken line in Figure 3.8 is only a little bit closer to the broken line than to the solid line. This indicates that the different sample characteristics of the two cohorts were less important than their timing of arrival in explaining overall inter-cohort differences (in which Cohort 2 find the first job much more quickly than Cohort 1 men). For the sample of female migrants, the middle broken line in Figure 3.9 is much closer

Figure 3.8 Inter-cohort simulated survival function: Men

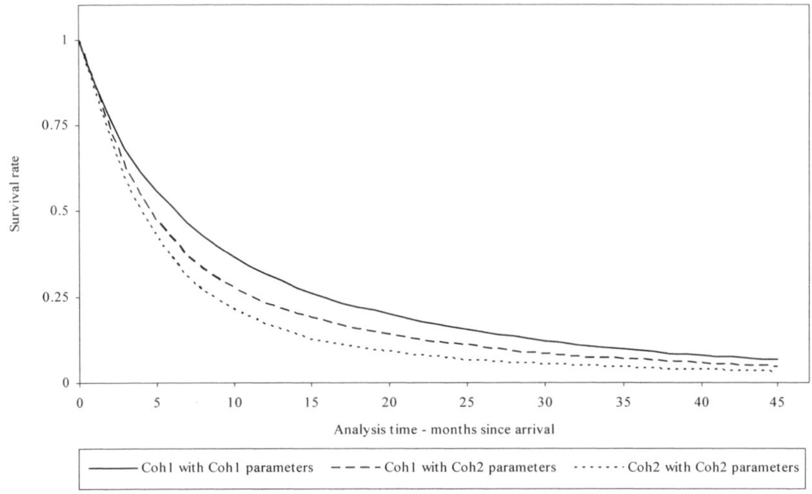

Figure 3.9 Inter-cohort simulated survival function: Women

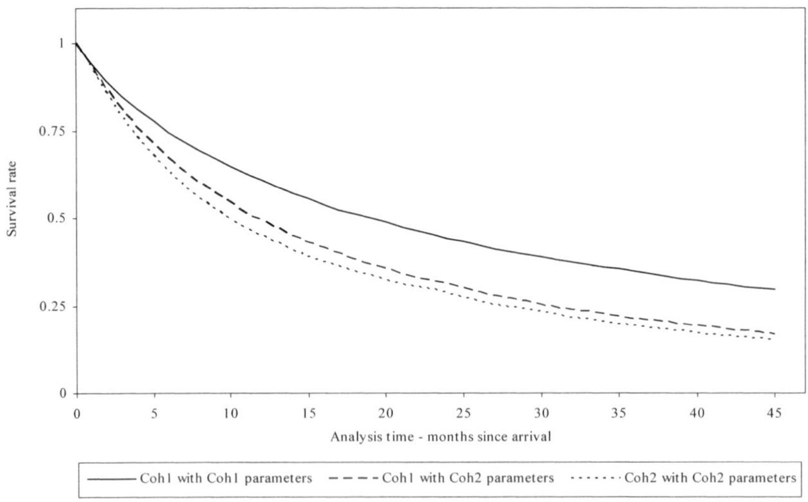

to the dotted line than to the solid line. This indicates that for female migrants the labour market environment in the latter part of the 1990s was much more important than their more favourable individual characteristics in explaining why Cohort 2 women found their first job more quickly. In other words, if the individual female migrants from Cohort 1 had also arrived at the same time as the Cohort 2 women, the time taken to finding their first job would have been much less than was actually observed.

A precise numerical assessment of the relative strengths of these two factors (varying time of arrival and varying characteristics) can be gleaned from the decompositions presented in Table 3.8 for three specific points on the distribution function of the simulated values of the time taken to find the first job. The three points chosen to illustrate the decomposition of the differences between Cohort 1 and Cohort 2 are the 25th percentile, 50th percentile and 75th percentile values of the simulated distribution function. The 25th percentile value of the distribution indicates the time (in months) at which 25 per cent of the sample found their first job (corresponding to the survival rate of 0.75 in the survival function graphed in Figures 3.8 and 3.9). Similarly, the 50th percentile (or median) values in Table 3.7 correspond to the time by which half of all migrants had found a job. Finally, the 75th percentile value indicates the time by which 75 per cent of all migrants had found a job.

For each of these three points on the distribution of the time migrants take to find the first job, the top panel of Table 3.8 shows either the actual sample value or simulated value of the number of months since arrival in Australia. Rows A to D report actual and simulated values for each cohort. Rows E and F report simulated values across cohorts, conditioning on whether one has used Cohort 1 or Cohort 2 regression parameters for the cross-cohort simulation. To illustrate for male migrants, Rows A and B show that 75 per cent of Cohort 1 men had found their first job by 15 months after arrival, and the corresponding figure for Cohort 2 men was 9 months after arrival. Reading down the same columns in Rows C and D, the simulated values for the estimated time by which 75 per cent of male migrants had found their first job were 15.6 and 8.7 months for Cohort 1 and Cohort 2, respectively. Row E then shows that the simulated 75th percentile value for Cohort 1 would have reduced substantially from 15.6 to 11.0 months if these individuals had arrived in the late 1990s as Cohort 2 did (that is, using cross-cohort simulations applying Cohort 2 regression parameters to Cohort 1 characteristics).

The lower panel of Table 3.8 then presents the decomposition of the total difference in the time taken to obtain the first job between these two cohorts. Row G computes this total difference, or cohort gap, for the three points on the distribution. Numerically the value reported in Row G is the extra time in months taken by Cohort 1 to reach the same percentile milestone as that taken by Cohort 2. For instance, the total cohort gap at the 75th percentile value for male migrants is about 7 months. Finally, this total difference reported in Row G is decomposed in two different ways into the relative share of varying characteristics, and the relative share of varying parameters. Decomposition I and II differ on which cohort's parameters are held constant in deriving the intermediate steps of the cross-cohort simulations in Rows E and F, respectively. Decomposition I uses the estimated regression parameters of Cohort 1 applied to Cohort 2 as well; while Decomposition II (which corresponds to the decomposition implicit in Figures 3.8 and 3.9) uses Cohort 2 parameters for the cross-cohort simulation.

The full result of these decompositions (in rows J and K) show some variability in the results along all three dimensions captured in Table 3.8; that is, by gender, by the percentile point of the distribution of time to the first job, and by the base chosen for the regression parameters (Cohort 1 or Cohort 2). The largest difference in the decomposition results is usually observed across gender. Using Decomposition I for men, the relative contribution of varying characteristics accounts for about 40 per cent of the total cohort gap (row J1); and this share does not vary much at the three points of the percentile distribution. Decomposition II for men shows a slightly lower relative contribution from varying characteristics, and this relative share is also more variable across the selected percentile points of the distribution.

The decomposition for women shows, in general, a lower relative contribution from varying characteristics than for the men. For example, using Decomposition II (row K), varying characteristics for male migrants account for between 28 and 40 per cent of the total cohort gap at the three selected percentile points. For female migrants varying characteristics account for only 10 to 22 per cent of the total cohort gap. This shows how Cohort 1 women were particularly disadvantaged in terms of the time taken to find their first job. Had these Cohort 1 women, holding their observable characteristics constant, arrived in 1999–2000 (at the same time as Cohort 2), they would have obtained their first jobs much more quickly.

The decompositions in Table 3.8 of the inter-cohort gap in the time taken to find the first job show that the contribution to this gap of the differences in the individual characteristics of the migrants in the two cohorts is the minor component – at most around 40 per cent of the total gap. However, the remaining component, which is captured by the differences in the hazard model parameters estimated for Cohort 1 and Cohort 2, can represent a combination of different elements. One element in this component is undoubtedly the more favourable overall macroeconomic and employment conditions in Australia at the time of arrival of Cohort 2. This more favourable setting increases the returns to the employment related characteristics of Cohort 2 (as reflected in the different hazard model parameters for Cohort 2 compared to Cohort 1).

Table 3.8 Simulation results on time to first job (in months) and decomposition of the cohort gap

		Male Principal Applicants			Female Principal Applicants		
		Distribution of time to first job			Distribution of time to first job		
		25th percentile	Median value	75th percentile	25th percentile	Median value	75th percentile
Observed sample results							
A	Cohort 1	2.0	5.0	15.0	4.0	16.0	48.0
B	Cohort 2	2.0	3.0	9.0	3.0	8.0	23.0
Simulated results							
C	Cohort 1	2.2	6.2	15.6	5.9	18.9	56.6
D	Cohort 2	1.7	4.0	8.7	3.6	9.8	27.4
E	Cohort 1 using Cohort 2 parameters	1.9	4.6	11.0	4.1	11.6	30.4
F	Cohort 2 using Cohort 1 parameters	2.0	5.4	12.8	5.0	16.2	48.3
Decomposing inter cohort differences							
G	*Total difference in simulated values (C - D)*	0.48	2.20	6.95	2.23	9.03	29.22
	Difference with common parameters:						
H	Cohort 1 – Cohort 2 with Cohort 1 parameters (C – F)	0.20	0.83	2.83	0.88	2.72	8.37
I	Cohort 1 with Cohort 2 parameters – Cohort 2 (E – D)	0.19	0.62	2.33	0.49	1.73	2.96
	Decomposition I (based on H with Cohort 1 parameters)						
J1	% due to varying characteristics (H/G)	41.7%	37.7%	40.7%	39.5%	30.1%	28.6%
J2	% due to time varying parameters	58.3%	62.3%	59.3%	60.5%	69.9%	71.4%
	Decomposition II (based on I with Cohort 2 parameters)						
K1	% due to varying characteristics (I/G)	39.6%	28.2%	33.5%	22.0%	19.2%	10.1%
K2	% due to time varying parameters	60.4%	71.8%	66.5%	78.0%	80.8%	89.9%

Note:
For the sample of female Principal Applicants the 75th percentile values reported in the last column of this table must be interpreted with caution since they involve out of sample predictions. In the actual data the 75th percentile value is not observed, as indicated in the Kaplan-Meier survival estimates of Figure 3.5. Close to 25% of female Principal Applicants in both cohorts were still to find their first job at the time they were last observed in the LSIA data.

Another element is that Cohort 2 may differ markedly from Cohort 1 on some other (unobservable) individual characteristics that are not captured in the hazard model estimations, and which lead to their more favorable labour market outcomes. These unobservable variables could be characteristics such as individual ability and motivation, attitudes towards work and work force attachment. One mechanism that could generate significant differences in the unobservable characteristics between the two cohorts is the different policy regime faced by them, both in terms of selection criteria and the changed rules on welfare eligibility (see Chapter 1). The latter policy change in particular, requiring a two-year waiting period for most welfare payments (the previous requirement was six months) may have served as a screening device making Cohort 2 migrants differ substantially from Cohort 1 on various unobservable factors. These more favourable unobservable factors would then lead to significant differences in the estimated parameters for Cohort 2 relative to Cohort 1. This effect seems likely to be more pronounced for the female migrants in Cohort 2. They appear to be cut from a different cloth than their counterparts in Cohort 1. Further disentangling these direct policy effects, indirect migrant self-selection effects, and macro-economic setting effects is not straightforward with the structure of the LSIA dataset, and is left to future research.

SUMMARY AND CONCLUSIONS

Understanding the determinants of the labour market outcomes of migrants during their early settlement period is of considerable interest for several reasons. In particular there is a strong public policy focus in the design of migrant selection criteria and post-arrival assistance programs that help migrants to find suitable jobs quickly. Using longitudinal data for two cohorts of migrants of working age, this chapter has analysed the determinants of the time they took to find their first job in Australia. It also presented simulations that decomposed the sources of the inter-cohort differences in the time that migrants took to find their first job.

The measure of labour market success used in this analyses – the length of time taken since arrival to obtain the first job – was different from the labour market outcomes analysed in previous studies using the LSIA, which relied mainly on comparisons of employment and participation rates at various times after the migrants' arrival in Australia. However, the results discussed in this chapter were consistent with those earlier studies that have documented the more favourable labour market outcomes for Cohort 2, who arrived in Australia between September 1999 and August 2000, compared to Cohort 1, who arrived some six years earlier.

The important factors determining the length of time migrants took to find their first job as identified in this chapter were conventional migrant characteristics, such as educational qualification, source region, recent work history in the former home country, marital status, the category of Australian migration visa received, and English language proficiency. The positive effects of better English language proficiency and of several source regions were particularly strong. Humanitarian visa migrants took a substantially longer time to find their first job.

There are also significant differential effects for men and women. For women, the points-tested Independent visa migrants took a shorter time to find their first job compared to those who migrated in the Family visa stream. This important visa class distinction had no significant effect on the time that male migrants took to find their first job. The positive effect observed from having visited Australia prior to migration was also significant only for women. Male migrants who were sponsored or nominated by employers took a significantly shorter time to find their first job compared to those who were not sponsored by relatives or nominated, but this difference was not observed for women.

Consistent negative effects on the length of time it took to find the first job were observed for those migrants who brought in a larger amount of funds at the time of migration, and also for those with a long-term health condition. It was also observed that Cohort 1 and Cohort 2 migrants were affected differently by the factors determining the time taken by migrants to find their first job.

The simulation results in Table 3.8 show that 50 per cent of male migrants in Cohort 2 found their first job within four months after arrival, compared to 6.2 months for Cohort 1. For female migrants, the contrast is even stronger: 50 per cent of Cohort 2 migrants found their first job within 9.8 months compared to 18.9 months for those in Cohort 1.

The decomposition results show that the more important reason for the shorter time taken by Cohort 2 was related to the changed macro-economic setting and policy regimes faced by Cohort 2. This component, arising from the varying returns to the characteristics of Cohort 2 and Cohort 1, was more important than the effect due to differences in the characteristics of the two cohorts, particularly for female migrants. The differences in observed cohort characteristics could account for no more than 40 per cent of the cohort gap in the time taken by migrants to find their first job.

The results show the increasing reward to labour market-related skills provided by the Australian labour market to Cohort 2 migrants. This chapter has not looked further into decomposing the likely sources of the increased labour market rewards to migrant skills and characteristics in Cohort 2. These could be related directly or indirectly to the different macro-economic conditions and the different policy regimes faced by the two cohorts with respect to selection criteria and welfare eligibility after arrival in Australia. Further disentangling these policy and macro-economic effects is a useful area to explore in future extensions of this research.

One specific policy effect detected in the results is that the changes to the Australian points test system introduced on 1 July 1999 for Independent and Skilled – Australian Sponsored visa categories had the general effect of reducing the time these migrants take to find their first job, compared to other migrants in Cohort 2 whose visa applications were assessed under the pre-July 1999 points system. This suggests that migration selection criteria play a demonstrably important role in determining initial labour market outcomes after arrival.

Another fruitful line of extension of this research would be to exploit the information in the LSIA about changes in migrant characteristics after arrival that are recorded in the later waves of interviews. As mentioned in the methodology section in this chapter, data limitations in LSIA make it difficult to time precisely any changes in the characteristics of migrants in relation to the starting date of the first job (or other jobs). Nevertheless, it would be useful to check the robustness of the results by specifying, to the extent possible, some approximate time intervals around these changes and using these variables in a more general model to examine the time new migrants take to find their first job.

A related area to explore further would be to refine the measurement of the time taken to find the first job to finer gradations that distinguish various characteristics or quality of the job, such as the first job in which migrants regularly use their educational qualifications, or jobs in the same occupational hierarchy as their last job in their former home country. Australian research on labour market outcomes for migrants has not focused on the quality of the jobs migrants obtain in their initial settlement period; and the notion of 'good' and 'bad' jobs, as introduced by Junankar and Mahuteau (2005) in their analysis of the LSIA dataset, could be usefully applied in extending the duration model framework on the time to finding the first job presented in this chapter.

NOTES

1. For June 2002 this proportion was 23 per cent, which is equal highest with New Zealand among countries with major migration programs. See Australian Bureau of Statistics (ABS), *Migration 2002–03* (Catalogue 3412, pp.85–6).
2. Not knowing if someone is continuously looking for a job leads to a difference between the time taken to find the first job and the length of the initial unemployment spell after arrival. These two duration measures will differ for any individual who has one or more periods of absence from the labour force during the inter-wave periods of the LSIA data. The analysis carried out in this chapter is presented exclusively in the framework of the time taken since

arrival to start the first job; but this framework applies as well for the initial unemployment spell of migrants in those instances where the migrants have been continuously looking for work after arrival.

3 This ignores the potential problem that some Principal Applicants will themselves be spouses of persons who are already settled in Australia, including native-born Australians; and some of these Principal Applicants may have no intention of working in Australia. This possibility is more likely to affect female Principal Applicants in the LSIA sample. While individuals who are spouses coming to join their families in Australia can be identified in LSIA through the detailed visa categories, it is not feasible to clearly infer their work intentions in Australia at the time of arrival. Hence they have not been excluded from the analyses in this chapter.

4 The estimation sample represents only small reductions from the total available sample of Principal Applicants in both cohorts. To be eligible for inclusion in the LSIA sampling frame Principal Applicants had to be over 15 years of age. But there are very few Principal Applicants in the 15 to 17 age group. Almost all of the reduction in the size of the estimation sample comes from dropping Principal Applicants aged 60 and above.

5 For instance, acquiring Australia-specific human capital through post-immigration qualifications has been shown to be an important determinant of labour market outcomes for new migrants. This finding is reported in Chiswick and Miller (1992b) and Cobb-Clark, Connolly and Worswick (2005).

6 The summary statistics in Table 3.1 (and in subsequent tables that summarise the LSIA data) are all based on sampling weights that reflect the relative size of the various sub-groups of immigrants in the in-scope population at the time of their arrival in Australia. The weights are not adjusted for the minor changes in the population of immigrants from these two cohorts who are sill residing in Australia at the time of the later wave interviews.

7 See Chapter 2 in this volume for further details on how employment, participation and measured unemployment rates vary by these important migrant characteristics in the Wave 2 period for each cohort.

8 The mean time interval to find the first job reported in Table 3.3 and the full frequency distribution in Figures 3.1 and 3.2 should be interpreted strictly as a description of patterns within a given cohort. Cross-cohort comparisons are problematic because the time periods over which these data are generated are different for the two cohorts. In particular, the mean and any other moment of the distribution involving ever-employed persons will have a different structure, based on the length of time over which the 'ever employed' status is measured.

9 The LSIA sample normally does not include individuals who change their visa status while they are already in Australia. But such individuals can lodge migration visa applications offshore, and travel offshore to receive the new visa and re-enter Australia. An example of such a case might be an overseas student in Australia who makes an offshore application for a migration visa during the period of study, and who is already working at the time they complete their studies or soon after. When such individuals travel offshore to receive the new visa and re-enter Australia as migrants and continue with the same job, they will have a job start date that precedes their arrival date in Australia as a migrant.

10 This mean time includes cases where a resident jobholder has changed visa status to become a migrant. Such cases have the 'time to first job' coded as 0 months. These cases, however, are excluded from the duration model analyses in the subsequent sections of this chapter.

11 For instance, in Cohort 2 some 11 per cent of Independent Principal Applicants who were employed at Wave 1 also said that their job was arranged prior to arrival in Australia.

12 The Kaplan-Meier survival function is a non-parametric plot that tracks the proportion of the Principal Applicants who 'survive' into the next time period (month) without finding their first job. See Kalbfleisch and Prentice (2002) for details on the interpretation and derivation of the Kaplan-Meier survival function.

13 See Chapter 1 of this volume for a description of the main visa categories and the specific names applicable at the time of entry of Cohort 1 and Cohort 2.

14 See Kalbfleisch and Prentice (2002) for further details on proportional hazards models and their common functional forms.

15 The Cox model estimation results still play a useful role because they help in determining which specific functional form to choose for the parametric version of the PH model. Alternative parametric models, such as the Exponential and Gompertz, were also considered. The estimation results for the Weibull version are most similar to the more general Cox model estimates; therefore the Weibull model was chosen for the estimations reported in this section.

16 See Chapter 1 of this volume for further details of the July 1999 changes to the points test and other policy changes that came into effect on that date which affect Cohort 2.

17 The estimation results on the determinants of the time taken to find the first job using the semi-parametric Cox model are not reported in this chapter. These results are very similar to the estimates for the Weibull model. Indeed, a primary purpose for the initial investigations using the Cox model was to help determine which specific parametric functional form should be chosen for the final estimations. Since the Cox model, which does not impose a specific functional form for the underlying baseline hazards, is a more general specification, the objective is to choose a parametric version of the duration model whose results are closest to the Cox model. This diagnostic procedure led to the selection of the Weibull functional form for the parametric model.

18 Another important inference drawn from the initial Cox model results was that it would be inappropriate to estimate the duration model jointly for both male and female Principal Applicants in each cohort. The hypothesis that the effect of gender on time taken to first job can be represented simply as a proportional effect to an underlying baseline hazard in a pooled model for both genders was clearly rejected in diagnostic tests from the Cox model results. This is an a priori plausible result as well since the motivations for early labour market entry after arrival in Australia can differ substantially for men and women. Consequently, the final set of the Weibull model estimation is done separately for the male and female Principal Applicants in each cohort.

19 The standard errors reported in Tables 3.5 and 3.6 are also for the hazard ratio. The statistical test for whether a regression variable has a significant effect on the time taken to find the first job is reported in the third column of each set of results in these tables (under the '$P>|z|$' heading). The values in this column indicate the significance level (p-values) of the test statistic for the null hypothesis that the hazard ratio for that variable is equal to one. Using conventional statistical significance levels of 10 per cent and 5 per cent, the null hypothesis that a particular regression variable has no effect on 'time to first job' (that is, has a hazard ratio = 1) is rejected if the computed '$P>|z|$' value is less than 0.1, or less than 0.05, respectively.

20 The mainly-English-speaking source countries are Canada, Ireland, New Zealand, South Africa, the United Kingdom, United States and Canada.

21 The visa category variables specified in Tables 3.5 and 3.6 have been defined such that the variables labeled 'SAS (all)' and 'Independent (all)' apply to all Cohort 1 individuals in these visa categories, and also to Cohort 2 individuals assessed with the pre-July 1999 points test. Hence the additional effect of being in the relevant sub-class of the post July-1999 points tested category is captured by the hazard ratio associated with the variables labeled 'Independent – Cohort 2 post-July 1999 points' and 'SAS – Cohort 2 post-July 1999 points', respectively. If these hazard ratios are significantly greater than one then individuals with the post-July 1999 points test had an even higher rate to finding their first job within their specific visa sub-categories.

22 Surprisingly, there is little direct connection between the two variables of 'visiting Australia prior to immigration' and 'having Australian relatives'. In both cohorts a majority of the Principal Applicants (more than 60 per cent) report having Australian relatives. But this is not closely correlated with them having visited Australia prior to immigration. In Cohort 1 about 42 per cent of the Principal Applicants had visited Australia before and this ratio is almost the same among those with, and without, Australian relatives. Similarly in Cohort 2 the proportion having visited Australia prior to immigration is 50 per cent among those without Australian relatives and 52 per cent among those with Australian relatives.

4. Female Migrants' Participation in the Australian Labour Market

Anh Tram Le

INTRODUCTION

The number of migrants entering Australia has been increasing steadily over time. For example, in 1999–2000 a total of 70,200 migrants arrived in Australia; this had increased to 108,070 by 2002–2003. In 2002–2003, 52 per cent of all settler arrivals in Australia were female (Department of Immigration and Multicultural and Indigenous Affairs 2004). Female migrants' adjustment and labour market outcomes in the host country have been widely researched (see, for example, Duleep and Sanders 1993, Baker and Benjamin 1997, Cobb-Clark and Connolly 2001, Cobb-Clark and Crossley 2004). Of particular interest to this chapter are the labour market outcomes of women who were not the primary decision-makers but had migrated as accompanying family members (referred to in this chapter as tied movers). The chapter compares, over time and across cohorts, the labour market supply of female migrants who are primary migrants and those are tied movers, using the Longitudinal Survey of Immigrants to Australia (LSIA).

The first part of the chapter involves within-cohort analysis of the differences in labour market participation between primary and tied movers over time. The aim is to determine the factors that contribute to the difference in labour market participation of primary and tied movers and to assess whether these factors can explain long-term labour market choices. The next section involves across-cohort analysis. The impact of changes in migration selection criteria in the late 1990s on female migrants' labour market participation is examined. Of interest is whether the changes in the selection criteria for skilled migrants during this time have affected the gap in the labour market participation of female primary and tied movers across cohorts.

This research adds to the limited Australian literature on tied movers' labour market choices and is important for a number of reasons. First, Australian migration policy changed during the late 1990s, to place a greater focus on recruiting immigrants who were skilled and who could contribute to the development and well-being of the Australian community. Therefore, analysis of the factors that influence female migrants' labour market choices provides useful information on the type of migrants who are likely to contribute most to the economic well-being of Australia. Second, the welfare of migrant women is different from the welfare of migrant men. Migrant women are concerned not only with their primary nurturing role in the family but also their role in the Australian community. They have to consider their role in the home and the workplace (Wooden et al. 1994). These analyses will provide useful information about the relative importance of family responsibilities and pecuniary benefits in relation to female migrants' decision to enter the labour market. Third, little is known about the labour market choices of female primary and secondary movers. The difference in labour market choices between the two groups can inform on the importance of the motive for migrating to a woman's choices in the labour market. The LSIA data set used in this chapter (see Technical Appendix) provides a unique opportunity to compare directly the labour market choices of both female primary and tied movers. We can also examine the impact of the changes in migration policy during the 1990s on the labour market participation of female migrants using both cohorts interviewed in the LSIA.

The results show that there is a difference in the inter-temporal preference for work or family responsibilities between primary and tied female migrants. The presence of very young children (0–2 years) explains tied movers' long-term absence from the labour market. For primary movers the substitution between work and family responsibilities remains unchanged over time. In addition, while pecuniary benefits have a positive influence on the labour market entry of both primary and tied movers, wage elasticities for primary movers are, in the long run, greater than for tied movers. This can be linked to the motive or motives for migration: primary movers who migrated for economic reasons will place greater importance on pecuniary benefits than tied movers – who are assumed to migrate for their spouses' employment prospects. Primary movers' labour force participation is greatly enhanced if their spouses are employed. A comparison across cohorts of the labour force participation rate of those who migrated on points-tested visas reveals that while the change (six months after migration) for primary movers has been modest, nearly half resulted from changes in characteristics of these women. In comparison, while the variation in the predicted participation rate of tied movers (who arrived under points-tested visas) has been larger, the proportion due to changes in characteristics is similar to that of primary movers. Given that changes in characteristics are likely to arise from the modifications made to migration selection policy, the results suggest that migration policy has played an important role in enhancing labour market participation of migrant women.

LITERATURE REVIEW

The decision to migrate may not have been initiated by both partners in a family acting together. Mincer (1978), for example, suggests that in a family unit the prospects of the partner who is the major contributor to the total income may be weighted more heavily in the decision to migrate. From this perspective, women may often move more for their partners' employment prospects than for their own well-being. Migration can have a negative impact on their employment status.

The importance of this tied migration behaviour has been widely recognised, although the impact of family migration on the wife's labour market choices has been examined predominantly from an internal migration perspective (see, for example, Spitze 1984, Morrison and Lichter 1988, Cooke and Bailey 1996, Bielby and Bielby 1992, Boyle et al. 2001) where families migrate from one region/state to another. The general consensus among these studies is that married women are disadvantaged in the labour market after migration.

The concept of family migration has been extended to international migration (see, for example, MacPherson and Stewart (1989) and Duleep and Sanders (1993) on the United States labour market, Wooden and VandenHeuvel (1997), Cobb-Clark and Connolly (2001) and Cobb-Clark and Crossley (2004) on the Australian labour market). These studies have applied variants of the 'family utility-family budget constraint' model of labour supply and have developed a wider set of implications for female migrants' post-migration labour market activity than that associated with the Mincer (1978) formulation. For example, the labour market supply of migrant women may be high soon after migration because migrant women have to assume the role of financial providers while their spouse invests in human capital (see Baker and Benjamin (1997) on the Canadian labour market). However, female migrants may be forced to take low paid jobs offering little opportunity for advancement. In this regard female migrants are disadvantaged in the labour market after migration. The 'family utility-family budget constraint' model assumes that the family maximises its total utility subject to the total family income (non-wage and wage income of each family member). The estimating equations for females derived from this model are distinguished by the inclusion of wage variables for both the wife and the husband.

The results of empirical studies that adopt this type of framework (for example, MacPherson and Stewart 1989, Duleep and Sanders 1993, LeClere and McLaughlin 1997, Wooden and VandenHeuvel 1997, Cobb-Clark and Connolly 2001, Cobb-Clark and Crossley 2004) centre on four main themes: variations in female migrant labour supply across migrant groups; the importance of family formation; the role of economic incentives (for example, wage rates, husbands' earnings); and institutional influences.

A number of studies report pronounced variations in labour market participation rates across migrant groups (see, for example, Evans 1984, Reimers 1985, MacPherson and Stewart 1989, Wooden and VandenHeuvel 1997). Evans (1984) shows that while the husband's presence has little effect on the labour market participation of Mediterranean and Eastern European women in Australia, it is important for women from Northwest Europe, Third World and English-speaking countries. Similarly, migrant women other than those from Mediterranean and Eastern European countries were less likely to participate in the labour market if they had children. Wooden and VandenHeuvel (1997) show that there is a significant difference in labour market participation between English-speaking (ES) and non-English-speaking (NES) migrants with pre-school age children. NES migrants whose youngest child is aged two or three years old have a higher probability of participating in the labour force on a full-time basis than ES migrant women.

Much of the recent research into the links between family formation and female labour supply has been aimed at informing on the relevance of the 'family investment' model. However, these studies provide only mixed support for this explanation of female migrants' labour supply. Duleep and Sanders (1993) show that in the United States migrant groups with the largest expected growth in male earnings (Filipinos, Koreans and Chinese) are those with the highest labour force participation of married migrant women, while the groups with the smallest expected growth in male earnings (non-Hispanic whites and Japanese) are those with the lowest female participation rates. This suggests that wives help to finance their husbands' post-migration investment in skills. Consistent with this hypothesis, the wife's labour market participation is inversely related to the husband's years spent in the country of destination. Cobb-Clark and Crossley (2004) find empirical support for the 'family investment' hypothesis in immigrant households in Australia where the male partner has a comparative advantage.[1] However, there is no support for the 'family investment' hypothesis among households where the female partner holds the comparative advantage in the labour market.[2] In contrast, MacPherson and Stewart (1989) find only weak support for the 'family investment' strategy hypothesis, with significant effects being reported only for migrants from Canada and the West Indies.[3]

The mixed findings in relation to the 'family investment' hypothesis may reflect its narrow focus: not all migrant women can be expected to assume the role of family financial provider after migration. In particular, some will exit the labour market or delay entry as a result of increased family responsibilities in the new country. There is some evidence to suggest that some migrant women withdraw from the labour market after migration – but this is only a short-term phenomenon. LeClere and McLaughlin (1997), for example, show that in the United States family migration causes migrant women to leave the labour force in the short term. Consequently, this imposes a large earnings penalty on the family in their first year after migration. This penalty dissipates with years spent in the United States.

The main economic incentive variable that has been considered in empirical work is husbands' wage/income. MacPherson and Stewart (1989), LeClere and McLaughlin (1997) and Cobb-Clark and Connolly (2001) show that an increase in the husband's income has a negative impact on the wife's labour market participation. Wooden and VandenHeuvel (1997) find an inverse U-shaped relationship between full-time participation of English-speaking (ES) migrant women in Australia and their husbands' income. For non-English-speaking (NES) migrant women, the relationship between full-time participation and husbands' income is relatively flat. The wife's labour market participation starts to fall only if the husbands' income is in the upper income category (greater than $50,000). Wooden and VandenHeuvel (1997) suggest that the cost of wives not working in low income families is relatively small for NES migrants.

The main institutional influence on female participation rates that has been examined is visa class. Cobb-Clark (2000), for example, shows that the initial participation rates of migrant women differ across visa categories. For example, female migrants arriving in Australia in the Family, Skilled – Australian Sponsored, Independent or Humanitarian visa category are less likely to participate in the labour market compared to those who arrived in the Business Skills and Employer Nomination category. Cobb-Clark (2000) suggests that these differences may reflect unobserved factors that are correlated with visa category and are also related to participation (for example, preferences for work).

Other factors that also influence the labour market choices of migrant women include the presence of children in the family, proficiency in English, the presence of adult relatives in the same household and employment in the home country before migration (see, for example, MacPherson and Stewart 1989, Duleep and Sanders 1993, Wooden and VandenHeuvel 1997, Cobb-Clark and Connolly 2001).

The studies reviewed above record strong associations between family and individual related characteristics and female labour market participation. However, comparatively little is known about the labour market participation of female primary and tied movers. In addition, the effect of changes in migration selection policies on the labour market choices of primary and tied movers has not been extensively researched.

DEFINITION AND CHARACTERISTICS OF PRIMARY AND TIED MOVERS

Two categories of primary movers are defined, namely strict and weak. These categories are identified using visa class, reasons for migration and information on who made the decision to migrate. The strict definition of primary movers is based on one of the following criteria:

1. The migrant gave at least one economic reason for migrating, held a skilled visa and participated in the decision to migrate;
2. The migrant gave at least one economic reason for migrating and held a skilled visa;
3. The migrant gave at least one economic reason for migrating and participated in the decision to migrate;
4. The migrant gave at least one economic reason for migrating; or
5. The migrant held a skilled visa and participated in the decision to migrate.

Female Principal Applicants who do not satisfy one of the above criteria are defined as weak primary movers.

The economic reasons for migrating include:

1. Better employment opportunities in Australia;
2. Undertake studies;
3. Lack of employment in former country; and
4. Dislike of economic conditions in former country.

Skilled visa categories include: Independent, Skilled – Australian Sponsored visa and Business Skills and Employer Nomination visa. Participation in the decision to migrate includes: making the decision oneself to migrate independently; making the decision to migrate jointly with a spouse or partner; and making the decision to migrate with other relatives.

The distinction between the two categories of primary movers is important for a number of reasons. First, it enables Mincer's (1978) definition of primary movers to be studied. Second, the two definitions of primary movers allow for the identification of female migrants who were the Principal Applicant as identified in the data set but whose husbands have initiated the migration decision. That is, the family migrated to benefit the employment opportunities of the husband, but its chances of gaining entry into Australia were higher if the wife applied for the visa. Although the wife was identified in the data set as the Principal Applicant, she did not fit the strict definition of primary mover as suggested by Mincer (1978).

This chapter examines female primary and tied movers who were 15–64 years old at the time of migration. Table 4.1 presents the characteristics of female primary movers (classified under strict and weak definitions) and tied movers in the two migration cohorts interviewed in the LSIA.

Table 4.1 Characteristics of primary and tied movers in Cohorts 1 and 2 at the Wave 1 interview (six months after arrival)

Characteristics	Cohort 1			Cohort 2		
	Primary movers (Strict definition)	Primary movers (Weak definition)	Tied movers	Primary movers (Strict definition)	Primary movers (Weak definition)	Tied movers
Birthplace (%)						
Oceania	2.7	2.7	1.9	4.0	2.6	3.1
Europe & former USSR	31.6	24.1	34.4	19.6	22.7	26.4
Middle East & North Africa	6.5	9.4	8.9	7.6	10.2	8.0
Southeast Asia	27.8	32.8	13.1	28.1	23.6	12.7
Northeast Asia	15.0	13.5	14.3	15.7	22.0	12.3
Southern Asia	7.2	8.4	16.6	9.5	9.0	19.8
North America	2.6	4.4	1.6	2.5	4.3	0.6
South/Central America	2.1	1.7	1.6	2.1	1.7	0.4
Other Africa	4.7	3.0	7.5	10.9	4.0	16.6
Age (years)	30.6	31.7	35.4	31.5	31.3	35.7
Years of education	14.4	13.0	13.4	14.9	13.9	14.5
% with good English	68.2	49.7	53.9	75.4	54.8	63.1
% with poor health	10.1	14.8	11.1	6.2	11.7	8.5
Family characteristics (%)						
Married	60.3	80.5	n.a.	67.9	85.2	n.a.
Children 0–2 years	13.8	9.1	34.2	13.5	9.4	24.5
Children 3–5 years	13.2	6.1	34.9	16.2	5.6	32.1
Children 6–12 years	18.4	12.5	48.9	21.8	13.5	53.4
Visa category (%)						
Family stream	51.2	88.7	7.4	42.1	91.1	1.8
Skilled – Australian Sponsored	12.7	0.6	20.5	17.8	1.6	15.6
BS/ENS	2.1	0.2	11.3	3.6	0.4	20.1
Independent	23.4	0.9	35.0	30.6	1.3	48.6
Humanitarian	10.6	9.7	25.9	5.9	5.7	13.9
Labour market history before migration						
% unemployed/not in labour force	29.9	35.8	47.2	25.0	38.0	40.8
% employed in high skilled jobs	44.3	27.2	24.3	53.8	33.0	30.4
Sample size	**816**	**1,223**	**1,208**	**569**	**701**	**586**

Note:
The figures are weighted means.

Source: Longitudinal Survey of Immigrants to Australia.

There were a number of differences between primary movers under the strict definition (those who migrated for economic reasons) and the weak definition (those who migrated for non-economic reasons). First, primary movers who migrated for economic reasons were more highly skilled than those who migrated for non-economic reasons. For example, those in Cohort 1 who migrated for economic reasons had 18 more months of education than those who migrated for non-economic reasons. As well, a higher percentage of female migrants who migrated for economic reasons had good English skills (68 per cent) than did female migrants who came for non-economic reasons (50 per cent). The former were also less likely to be unemployed or out of the labour market and were more likely to have been employed in highly skilled jobs prior to migration. Second, a higher percentage of primary movers who migrated for non-economic reasons had poor health (15 per cent in Cohort 1) compared to those who migrated for economic reasons (10 per cent). Third, 60 per cent of migrants who migrated for economic reasons were married, compared to 80 per cent of those who migrated for non-economic reasons. Fourth, a higher percentage of female migrants who migrated for economic reasons had children under 13 years old.[4]

There were also a number of differences between primary movers who migrated for economic reasons and tied movers. First, birthplace distribution differed for primary and tied movers. For example, 28 per cent of primary movers in Cohort 1 were from Southeast Asia while only 13 per cent of tied movers were from this region. In addition, 7 per cent of primary movers were from Southern Asia, compared to 17 per cent of the tied movers. The second difference between primary and tied movers was their age. On average, tied movers in Cohort 1 were four years older than primary movers. Third, a higher percentage of female primary movers, as compared to tied movers, had good English skills. Fourth, because tied movers were older on average, a higher percentage of them had children than did primary movers. The difference (31 percentage points) was most pronounced for women with children aged 6–12 years. Finally, there were differences between these two categories with regard to employment before migration. A higher percentage of primary movers worked in highly skilled jobs prior to migrating than did tied movers. In contrast, a higher percentage of tied movers were either unemployed, or not in the labour force, prior to migrating.

There were a number of differences between female migrants from the first and second cohorts. With regard to female primary movers (under the strict definition), those from the second cohort appeared to be more highly skilled. For example, more (75 per cent) female primary movers from the second cohort had good English-speaking skills compared to those from the first cohort. This is to be expected, given the emphasis on English skills in the migration selection criteria applicable to the second cohort but not the first cohort.[5] In addition, a higher percentage of female migrants in the second cohort had been employed in highly skilled occupations before migration (54 per cent) compared to those from the first cohort.

The distribution by visa category also differed between cohorts. For example, a smaller percentage of women from Cohort 2 arrived in Australia in the Family, Skilled – Australian Sponsored and Humanitarian visa categories compared to those from Cohort 1.

Table 4.2 Labour market participation rate (%) of female primary and tied movers in Cohorts 1 and 2 at the time of each wave interview

	Primary movers:		Tied movers
	Strict definition	Weak definition	
Cohort 1			
Wave 1	49.8	36.6	26.7
Wave 2	55.4	40.4	31.0
Wave 3	58.9	43.0	40.6
Cohort 2			
Wave 1	58.3	37.1	32.1
Wave 2	65.5	44.4	38.5

Source: Longitudinal Survey of Immigrants to Australia.

Table 4.2 shows the labour force participation rate of primary and tied movers at six months, 1.5 years and 3.5 years after arrival for Cohort 1 and at six months and 1.5 years after arrival for Cohort 2. Female migrants in Cohort 1 who migrated for economic reasons had a labour force participation rate of 50 per cent at six months after arrival compared to only 36 per cent for those who migrated for non-economic reasons. These results indicate the importance of distinguishing between the two groups of primary movers. The percentage of primary movers who participated in the Australian labour market six months after arrival was 23 points higher than that of tied movers. This difference remains over time. The table also shows that female migrants from Cohort 2 who had moved for economic reasons had a higher participation rate six months after arrival (58 per cent) than their counterparts from Cohort 1.

METHODOLOGY

In this chapter a variant of the 'family utility-family budget constraint' model is applied. This model is used because, compared to the competing models, it provides a more comprehensive representation of the labour market supply of females in a family unit. This advantage follows from the fact that this model allows both the spouse's wage and the primary migrant's own wage to have a direct impact on female labour supply. This is similar to the approach used by Baker and Benjamin (1997).

A number of steps are involved in the estimation of migrant women's labour market participation. First, in order to obtain predicted own and spouse's wages, the respective hourly wage equations are estimated separately for each partner by wave.[6] The coefficients from the hourly wage equations are then used to construct the predicted wage. Second, the predicted wage variables are included in the labour market participation models as explanatory variables. The labour market participation models are estimated separately for primary and tied movers for each wave. It should be noted that labour market participation is defined at each wave as either currently employed or currently unemployed and looking for work.

The labour market participation model includes individual characteristics (for example, age, birthplace, English proficiency) and family characteristics (for example, children), visa category, employment history, predicted own wage and spouse's details (where appropriate). See the Appendix to this chapter for a description of these variables and the model. The model is estimated using logistic regression.

RESULTS

Within-cohort analysis: Cohort 1

In order to investigate whether the motive for migration influences female migrants' labour market participation on arrival in Australia and whether their employment pattern changes over time, separate models of labour market participation are estimated for each sample of female primary and tied movers. These analyses provide insights into the links between the motives for migration and labour market choice.[7]

A number of points need to be addressed with regard to the results. First, in principle, information on the spouses of female primary movers (spouses' earnings, whether spouses are studying) should be included in the model. While there were data on whether the spouses were studying, fewer than 8 per cent of female primary movers' spouses were in this category. Second, data on earnings were available for accompanying spouses, however the number of male accompanying spouses aged 15–64 years was relatively small (19 per cent of the sample, or 350 individuals). Due to the small sample size, detailed analyses of these variables could not be undertaken and only information concerning the employment status of spouses of female primary movers has been included in the analyses.

Tables 4.3 and 4.4 present the marginal effects of the explanatory variables on the probability of participating in the labour market for female primary movers who migrated for economic reasons, and for tied movers, respectively.[8,9] In column (i) the dependent variable is the probability of participating in the labour market six months after arrival (Wave 1) in Australia. The dependent variable in column (ii) is the probability of participating in the labour market 18 months after arrival (Wave 2). The dependent variable in column (iii) is the probability of participating in the labour market 3.5 years after migration (Wave 3).

There are differences with regard to the decision to participate in the labour market among female primary movers over time. First, the advantage of speaking English well dissipated six months after immigration. The marginal effect of English proficiency on labour market participation at six months after arrival was 25 percentage points and it became insignificant thereafter. Second, poor health affected the labour force participation of female primary movers only at 3.5 years in Australia. Compared to female primary movers who had good or very good health, those who had fair, poor or very poor health were 22 percentage points less likely to be in the labour market 3.5 years after arrival. The insignificant difference in labour force participation between female primary movers who had poor health and those who had good health in the early period after arrival in Australia might reflect financial considerations, where individuals in poor health needed to work in the immediate post-arrival period to finance their treatment.[10] Alternatively, this might reflect changing attitudes toward health and work over time.

Married female primary movers were less likely to enter the labour market compared to unmarried female primary movers, and the negative impact of marital status on labour force entry increased over time. Being married reduced labour force participation by 23 percentage points six months after migration and by 30 percentage points 3.5 years after migration. This finding is consistent with Mincer's (1978) hypothesis that single female migrants are more likely to enter the labour market after migration than married female migrants.

Having young children affected the labour force participation of female primary movers and the constraint varied by children's age. For example, compared to mothers who did not have children or those who had children older than 12 years, mothers who had children aged 0–2 years were 28 percentage points less likely to be in the labour force six months after migration, 23 per cent less likely 18 months after migration and 27 percentage points less likely at 3.5 years after migration. Having children in the age group 3–5 years enhanced the likelihood of a mother's participation at six and 18 months after migration. However, mothers with children 3–5 years old were less likely to be in the labour force 3.5 years after migration.

Table 4.3 Marginal effects of migrant characteristics on the probability of participating in the labour market, female primary movers who migrated for economic reasons, Cohort 1

	Wave 1 (i)		Wave 2 (ii)		Wave 3 (iii)	
Variable	**Coeff.**	***t*-ratio**	**Coeff.**	***t*-ratio**	**Coeff.**	***t*-ratio**
Constant	-0.010	-0.01	-2.310	-3.01	-1.751	-1.84
Birthplace						
Oceania & Antarctica	0.147	1.16	0.259	1.87	0.155	0.89
Middle East & North Africa	0.131	1.26	0.261	2.54	0.137	1.12
Southeast Asia	0.052	0.72	0.286	4.14	0.343	4.23
Northeast Asia	-0.348	-4.24	-0.104	-1.26	0.037	0.37
Southern Asia	0.256	3.09	0.143	1.44	0.199	2.11
North America	-0.414	-2.38	-0.030	-0.16	0.193	1.07
South/Central America & Caribbean	-0.202	-1.09	-0.100	-0.52	0.120	0.62
Other Africa	0.237	2.35	0.243	2.31	0.095	0.83
Age	0.008	2.61	0.005	1.54	-0.003	-0.86
Good English	0.254	3.37	-0.015	-0.19	0.056	0.59
Poor health	-0.072	-0.90	-0.026	-0.37	-0.223	-2.68
Family characteristics						
Married	-0.227	-3.88	-0.251	-4.80	-0.297	-4.95
Children 0–2 years	-0.278	-3.29	-0.227	-3.30	-0.265	-3.97
Children 3–5 years	0.177	2.49	0.115	1.68	-0.194	-2.36
Children 6–12 years	-0.042	-0.62	0.069	1.08	0.155	2.49
Made decision to migrate	0.005	0.09	0.013	0.23	-0.134	-2.14
Unemployed/not in labour market	-0.152	-2.11	-0.123	-1.83	-0.204	-2.49
Employed in highly skilled jobs	0.017	0.26	0.011	0.16	-0.166	-1.91
Visa category						
Preferential family	0.107	1.25	0.113	1.38	-0.243	-2.65
Skilled – Australan Sponsored	0.392	4.95	0.261	2.67	0.251	2.44
BS/ENS	0.412	4.35	0.343	2.07	0.147	0.70
Independent	0.517	5.62	0.336	2.93	0.078	0.52
Spouse's details						
Working	0.616	5.10	0.491	8.50	0.578	9.25
Predicted own wage	-0.237	-1.05	0.567	2.19	0.821	2.60
Unemployment rate	-0.011	-0.25	0.076	1.81	0.021	0.40
χ^2 (25)	**461.64**		**311.14**		**383.39**	
MacFadden R^2	**0.30**		**0.28**		**0.29**	
Sample size	**816**		**710**		**593**	

Note:
BS/ENS – denotes Business Skills/Employer Nomination Scheme.

Table 4.4 Marginal effects on the probability of participating in the labour market, female tied movers, Cohort 1

	Wave 1 (i)		Wave 2 (ii)		Wave 3 (iii)	
Variable	**Coeff.**	***t*-ratio**	**Coeff.**	***t*-ratio**	**Coeff.**	***t*-ratio**
Constant	-0.742	-2.13	-1.056	-2.38	-1.369	-2.41
Birthplace						
Oceania & Antarctica	0.099	0.99	0.124	1.06	-0.051	-0.43
Middle East & North Africa	-0.159	-2.79	-0.091	-1.31	-0.134	-1.64
Southeast Asia	0.022	0.41	0.048	0.74	-0.030	-0.41
Northeast Asia	-0.065	-1.53	-0.064	-1.30	-0.053	-0.81
Southern Asia	0.046	1.05	0.112	2.16	0.050	0.84
North America	0.111	1.02	0.117	0.89	-0.259	-2.17
South/Central America & Caribbean	-0.169	-1.80	-0.146	-1.43	-0.132	-1.11
Other Africa	-0.067	-1.37	-0.454	-0.77	-0.168	-2.56
Age	0.002	1.03	0.0002	0.08	-0.006	-1.84
Good English	0.076	2.08	0.038	0.86	0.048	0.86
Poor health	-0.068	-1.58	-0.090	-1.96	-0.092	-1.84
Family characteristics						
Children 0–2 years	-0.073	-2.56	-0.202	-6.31	-0.299	-7.45
Children 3–5 years	0.030	1.06	0.046	1.43	-0.143	-3.52
Children 6–12 years	-0.017	-0.68	0.018	0.61	0.039	1.04
Made decision to migrate	-0.017	-0.67	-0.026	-0.88	-0.031	-0.85
Unemployed in home country	-0.210	-6.78	-0.186	-5.23	-0.144	-3.36
Employed in high skilled jobs	-0.045	-1.43	-0.019	-0.49	-0.015	-0.31
Visa category						
Preferential family	-0.130	-2.13	-0.171	-2.33	0.198	1.91
Skilled – Australan Sponsored	-0.018	-0.36	-0.016	-0.29	-0.004	-0.06
BS/ENS	-0.138	-2.01	-0.213	-3.21	-0.201	-2.06
Independent	-0.070	-1.20	-0.169	-2.73	-0.136	-1.76
Spouse's details						
Working	0.019	0.63	0.202	5.87	0.114	2.51
Studying	0.106	2.14	0.068	1.69	-0.017	-0.39
Predicted wage	0.012	0.13	-0.022	-0.20	-0.062	-0.48
Predicted own wage	0.130	1.00	0.279	1.81	0.405	2.25
Unemployment rate	0.036	1.77	0.049	2.05	0.119	3.60
χ^2 (26)	**175.21**		**251.59**		**194.60**	
MacFadden R^2	**0.12**		**0.14**		**0.11**	
Sample size	**1,208**		**1,084**		**969**	

Note:
BS/ENS – denotes Business Skills/Employer Nomination Scheme.

With regard to employment history, when compared to female primary movers who were employed, those who were either unemployed or not in the labour market in their home country were 15 percentage points less likely to participate in the Australian labour market six months after migration. This increased to 20 percentage points after 3.5 years in Australia, suggesting that women who did not work prior to migration were likely to be non-participants in the labour market.

The impact of visa category on the labour market participation of female primary movers was strongest at six months after arrival.[11] This suggests that any unobserved individual characteristics associated with visa category which affected labour force participation dissipated with residence in Australia. Compared to female primary movers who entered Australia on a Humanitarian visa, those who arrived on a Skilled – Australian Sponsored, Business Skills/Employer Nomination Scheme or Independent visa were 39 percentage points, 41 percentage points and 52 percentage points, respectively, more likely to participate in the labour market six months after arrival. After 3.5 years in Australia, only those arriving on the Skilled – Australian Sponsored visa were significantly more likely to be in the labour force and the advantage was reduced to 25 percentage points.

The results also show that their spouse's employment status had a strong influence on the primary mover's labour market participation. Compared to primary movers whose spouse did not work, those whose spouse was employed were 62 percentage points more likely to enter the labour market.

Finally, predicted wages had a positive impact on the decision of female primary movers to enter the labour force and the effect was significant at six months in Australia.[12] For example, a 1 per cent increase in the predicted hourly wage of primary movers enhanced their participation by 1.04 per cent at 18 months and 1.54 per cent at 3.5 years after migration.[13,14]

A comparison of the results in Tables 4.3 and 4.4 shows a number of differences between female primary and tied movers in their labour market participation. First, the impact of English proficiency in the immediate period after migration was much larger among primary movers. Second, poor health reduced labour force participation for tied movers 18 months and 3.5 years after migration, but had no significant effect on primary movers until 3.5 years after migration. This might reflect different attitudes toward work and health between primary and tied movers. Since tied movers migrated for their spouses' employment prospects, they were less likely to work or look for work if they had poor health. Third, family constraints affected primary and tied movers' labour market participation in a number of ways. The presence of children aged 0–2 years had a strong negative impact on primary movers' labour market participation and this remained relatively unchanged over time. In comparison, having children in this age group increased tied movers' lack of labour force participation over time. This suggests that the inter-temporal preference for work and family responsibilities is observed more strongly among tied movers. Among primary movers, the substitution between work and family responsibilities is unchanged over time. The relationship between having children aged 3–5 years and labour force participation differed between primary and tied movers, particularly in the period up to 18 months after arrival. Female primary movers with children in this age group were more likely to work. Tied movers' labour market choices, on the other hand, were not affected by having children in this age group. These results suggest that the lower labour force participation of tied movers in the immediate period after migration cannot be attributed to the presence of children age 3–5 years. However, tied movers' longer term absence from the labour market can be explained by the presence of very young children (0–2 years).

Visa category is a less important influence on tied movers' labour market participation than it is for primary movers. The reason may be that tied movers entered Australia on their husbands' visas. Therefore, any unobserved factors which might affect labour market choices captured through visa category would not directly affect tied movers.

Predicted own wage has a stronger impact on the primary mover's decision to enter the labour market 3.5 years after migration than on tied movers' decisions. Wage elasticity for tied movers 3.5 years after migration was 1.02 per cent compared to 1.54 per cent for primary movers. Under Mincer's (1978) hypothesis, the husband's gains from migration are offset by his wife's losses. It follows that the husband's gains induce a reduction in the wife's labour supply (for tied movers) as well as earnings losses for her. Given that tied movers are assumed to be migrating to enhance their spouses' employment prospects, their labour market choice may not be strongly dictated by their own potential earnings. These results lend support to Mincer's (1978) hypothesis.

Two variables were included in the model to capture the complementarity of time use between spouses and the role of tied movers in the family unit: namely, whether the spouse worked, and whether the spouse was studying. The results show that if the spouse of a tied mover was studying the probability of her participation in the labour market increased by 11 percentage points six months after migration. This suggests that tied movers might have assumed the role of the family's financial provider in the immediate period after migration while their spouse invested in country-specific skills. If the spouse worked, the tied mover's participation in the labour market might be associated with a greater likelihood that the tied mover would also enter the labour market. Such a positive association might arise where there was assortative mating on the basis of factors that resulted in relatively high labour market attachment. Alternatively, the optimal allocation of time within the household might result in a tied mover choosing home duties when her partner worked. In this study the 'spouse works' coefficient is positive and significant. However, a comparison between primary and tied movers shows that the spouse's employment status had a stronger positive influence on the primary mover's decision to enter the labour market than it did on the tied mover's decision.

The unemployment rate can affect labour market choice in two ways. First, under the discouraged worker argument, an increase in the unemployment rate reduces the labour force participation rate. Alternatively, the discouraged worker effect suggests that an increase in the rate of unemployment may increase labour force participation. This occurs where the husband's unemployment induces the wife's labour force participation. The results in Table 4.4 show a positive and significant relationship between the unemployment rate and the labour force participation of tied movers. Given that the model controls for the husband's current employment status, the increased labour force participation of tied movers may reflect the uncertainty of their husbands' future employment.

Comparison of Cohorts 1 and 2

A useful way to analyse differences in labour market participation between primary and tied movers across cohorts is to consider the predicted labour market participation rates of women with particular characteristics.[15] The predicted labour force participation rates of three groups of primary movers (strict and weak definitions) and tied movers – those with young children, with good English-speaking skills and who worked before migration – are presented in Table 4.5. The predicted values are computed from the sample mean of each group. For example, the predicted labour force participation rate for migrants with infants is computed using the coefficients from the labour force participation model and the sample mean of each variable for this group of migrants.

A comparison between primary and tied movers across cohorts shows that labour market choice differs between these two groups with young children. In Cohort 1 the difference in the labour force participation rate six months after migration between primary and tied movers was 15 percentage points and this increased to 17 percentage points 18 months after migration. This finding provides support for Mincer's (1978) hypothesis that low labour force participation after migration reflects at least a temporary increase in family demand for non-market activities.

The difference in the labour force participation rate six months after migration between primary and tied movers in Cohort 2 is 13 percentage points. This difference is reduced to 7 percentage points 18 months after migration. It appears that the difference in inter-temporal preference between family responsibilities and work for both primary and tied movers is more pronounced for migrants in Cohort 2.

Table 4.5 Predicted labour market participation rates (%) of migrant women by cohort, wave and type of mover

	Primary movers		Tied movers
	Strict definition	Weak definition	
Cohort 1			
Women with young children			
Wave 1 (6 months)	37.9	17.1	22.9
Wave 2 (18 months)	40.1	20.6	22.9
Wave 3 (3.5 years)	43.7	28.4	23.2
Women who spoke good English			
Wave 1 (6 months)	64.8	53.7	34.3
Wave 2 (18 months)	66.1	54.3	40.9
Wave 3 (3.5 years)	67.7	48.2	47.3
Women who worked before migration			
Wave 1 (6 months)	63.4	45.8	37.4
Wave 2 (18 months)	64.4	50.4	40.5
Wave 3 (3.5 years)	69.7	49.5	47.9
Cohort 2			
Women with young children			
Wave 1 (6 months)	45.5	10.0	32.5
Wave 2 (18 months)	33.1	11.7	26.2
Women who spoke good English			
Wave 1 (6 months)	70.7	54.0	43.3
Wave 2 (18 months)	73.4	57.2	43.2
Women who worked before migration			
Wave 1 (6 months)	70.1	50.6	39.8
Wave 2 (18 months)	74.1	59.1	53.1

With regard to English proficiency, the results show that there is greater variation in the labour force participation rate between primary and tied movers over time for migrants in Cohort 1 than for migrants in Cohort 2. For example, the difference in the labour market participation rates between primary and tied movers in Cohort 1 is 31 percentage points at Wave 1 and 25 percentage points at Wave 3. For Cohort 2, the difference in the labour force participation rate between primary and tied movers is 28 percentage points at Wave 1 and 30 percentage points at Wave 2.

Table 4.5 shows that there is only a modest change in the labour market participation rate between primary and tied movers over time for Cohort 1 but a larger change for Cohort 2. For example, the difference in the labour market participation rate between primary and tied movers in Cohort 1 is 26 percentage points at Wave 1 and 23 percentage points at Wave 2. For Cohort 2 migrants the labour market participation differentials between primary and tied movers are 30 percentage points and 21 percentage points at Wave 1 and Wave 2, respectively.

There is also variation in the predicted labour market participation rate across cohorts with regard to English proficiency and labour market participation before migration. For example, among primary movers the difference between the two cohorts with regard to English proficiency is 6 percentage points six months after migration and 6 percentage points 18 months after arrival. Among tied movers, the labour market participation rate difference for those with good English skills between the two cohorts is largest at 18 months after migration (15 percentage points).

A comparison of the labour market participation rates across cohorts for those who worked prior to migration reveals large differences over time for tied movers, but minor changes for primary movers. Among primary movers the difference in the predicted labour force participation rate between Cohort 1 and Cohort 2 six months after migration is 7 percentage points and this increases to 10 percentage points 18 months after arrival. The participation rate differentials of tied movers across cohorts six months and 18 months after migration are 3 percentage points and 13 percentage points, respectively. A further comparison of the labour force participation rate between primary and tied movers from the two cohorts suggests that employment prior to migration results in higher labour market participation for primary movers in Cohort 2.

In order to examine whether changes in migration selection criteria affect labour market participation of migrant women across cohorts, a predicted rate of labour market participation is computed for migrants from each of the cohorts who arrived on points-tested visas (Independent and Skilled – Australian Sponsored). The predicted values are computed using the coefficients from the labour market participation model and the sample mean of the variable from each visa group. A within-cohort comparison of the predicted participation rate, between female migrants who arrived on points-tested visas and those who arrived on non-points-tested visas, informs on the different skills of migrants and their different preferences with regard to labour force participation. A comparison of the participation rate between female migrants who arrived on points-tested visas across cohorts will reveal the impact of policy changes on the labour force participation of female skilled migrants.[16] This comparison can also inform on whether tied movers are indirectly affected by the change in policy through their husband's visas.

Table 4.6 presents the results for the predicted labour force participation rates and the average labour force participation rate for primary migrants who migrated for economic reasons and tied movers.[17] With regard to within-cohort changes, the predicted labour force participation rates of female migrants who arrived on points-tested visas exceeded those who arrived on non-points-tested visas. For example, among female primary movers, those who arrived on points-tested visas had a labour force participation rate of 77 per cent six months after arrival and this increased to 79 per cent 18 months after arrival. In comparison the predicted labour force participation rates of those who arrived on non-points-tested visas were considerably lower. Among female tied movers the predicted labour market participation rates six months and 18 months after arrival were 19 percentage points and 21 percentage points, respectively.

Table 4.6 Average and predicted labour force participation rates for female primary and tied movers by visa category (%)

	Primary movers			Tied movers		
	Sample average	Points tested visas	Non-points tested visas	Sample average	Points tested visas	Non-points tested visas
Cohort 1						
Wave 1	49.8	76.5	36.6	26.7	33.3	19.3
Wave 2	55.4	79.2	45.9	31.0	37.3	21.4
Wave 3	58.9	79.1	48.3	40.6	52.0	33.4
Cohort 2						
Wave 1	58.3	77.9	39.9	32.1	42.3	13.8
Wave 2	65.5	78.3	53.2	38.5	44.1	27.8

Source: Longitudinal Survey of Immigrants to Australia.

A comparison across cohorts for female migrants arriving on points-tested visas shows that there is a small increase in the predicted labour force participation rate six months and 18 months after arrival for primary movers (one percentage point). However, using six months after migration as an example, 47 per cent of the change is due to changes in characteristics.[18] In contrast, there is a larger increase in the predicted labour force participation rate of tied movers across cohorts. The difference in the labour force participation rate across cohorts is 9 percentage points six months after arrival and 54 per cent of this is due to changes in their characteristics.[19] The results suggest that modifications in migration selection policy have important implications for the labour force participation of both primary and tied movers through their impact on the characteristics of these migrant women. The high predicted increase in participation rate and the higher proportion of the actual increase that is due to changes in characteristics of tied movers suggests that there may be an indirect effect arising from the modifications to immigration selection policy on labour market participation for this group. This is because tied movers have a low participation rate, particularly in the immediate period after arrival. It follows that policy changes which improve migrants' skills will increase their labour market choice considerably.

CONCLUSION

This chapter has examined the labour market participation of female migrants who were the primary decision-makers in their own or their family's migration and also those who were accompanying spouses or tied movers. Within-cohort analysis shows that female primary movers had higher participation rates than tied movers and that this difference persisted over time. A number of factors contribute to the difference in labour market participation rate of the two groups of migrants. First, for migrants from Cohort 1 the presence of children aged 0–2 years had an increasing negative effect on a tied mover's decision to enter the labour market. Among primary movers the difference between those with children aged 0–2 years, those with children older than 13 years and those with no children remained relatively unchanged over time. Second, the labour force participation of female primary movers with good English skills was considerably higher than those of tied movers in the immediate period after migration. Third, work experience in the home country provided an advantage to migrants in the immediate post-migration period. This advantage dissipated over time for tied movers, but it increased for primary movers. Fourth, poor health had a stronger effect on the labour force entry of tied movers than primary movers. With regard to predicted earnings, pecuniary benefits were important to primary movers' labour market choice, but it had a smaller influence on tied movers' labour market participation in the long term. Finally, there appeared to be discouraged and out of worker effects among tied movers.

The predicted labour force participation rates for female primary and tied movers across cohorts show a number of differences. First, the difference in the labour market participation rate between primary and tied movers with children 0–2 years decreased over time for Cohort 2, but increased for women in Cohort 1. Second, there was a modest increase in the labour market participation rate with regard to English proficiency over time for Cohort 2 but a decrease for Cohort 1.

These results suggest that female primary movers had different characteristics and different inter-temporal preference for work and family responsibilities from tied movers. It appears that family constraints discourage female tied movers from entering the labour market some years after migration. However, the labour market choice of primary movers does not seem to change over time, regardless of family constraints. Furthermore, the results suggest that the motive for migrating is important in explaining the differences in the labour market choices of primary and tied movers over time. Associated with this view is the role of pecuniary benefits in the labour market choice of primary and tied movers. The results from Mincer's (1978) study suggest that the economic gains from husbands' employment induce a reduction in the wives' participation in the labour market and a loss in their earnings. Therefore, husbands in immigrant families receive larger economic gains, offsetting the wives' potential losses. Given that tied movers are assumed to migrate for their spouses' employment prospects, their own earnings may not be as important as primary movers' in determining labour market entry.

Within- and across-cohort analyses of female migrants who arrived in Australia on points-tested visas and those who arrived on non-points-tested visas reveal that a large proportion of the differences in labour market participation between the two groups occurs within the cohort. While the variation in predicted participation rates across cohorts is modest, nearly half can be attributed to changes in the characteristics of these women. Given that primary movers are likely to migrate to enhance their own employment prospects, their participation rate would be expected to be high. Despite this, the results suggest that migration policy does play an important role in enhancing labour force participation for this group of migrants.

A larger proportion of the difference in the labour force participation rate for tied movers who arrived on points-tested visas can be explained from across-cohort analysis. Since female tied movers' entry into Australia is based on their husbands' visa application, and as points were introduced for Cohort 2 when the spouse (in this case, it is the wife) met certain core requirements, (as discussed in Chapter 1) changes in migration selection criteria may indirectly affect tied movers' skills acquisition. Indeed, characteristics of tied movers account for over half of the actual change in labour force participation rate across cohorts. As a result tied movers may be more likely to participate in the labour market. In addition, given that tied movers migrate for their husbands' employment prospects, changes in migration selection criteria which result in tied movers with better skills may enhance their participation rate.

Mincer (1978) argues that female accompanying spouses experience reductions in employment and labour force participation after migration. This study departs slightly from Mincer's (1978) model in that primary movers are females rather than male migrants. Despite this divergence, the results obtained generally support Mincer's (1978) hypothesis. In particular, tied movers appear to be more constrained by non-market activities that contribute to at least temporary withdrawals from the labour market after migration.

Finally, the data set is important for research on female migrants' adjustment in Australia because its unique characteristics enable a more detailed distinction to be made between primary and tied movers. Until now, the studies of labour market outcomes of female migrants have not been able to distinguish between primary and tied movers as suggested by Mincer (1978). Analysis of the changes in the labour market outcomes of these two groups of primary and tied movers over time is also possible with this longitudinal data set.

NOTES

1 An individual had a comparative advantage in the labour market if he/she met the migration selection criteria and was granted a visa.

2 Cobb-Clark and Connolly (2001) show that while both male and female spouses work fewer hours if their partners have professional qualifications and have them recognised in Australia, women are not financing their partners' human capital investment by increasing their hours worked if their husbands are studying.

3 Baker and Benjamin (1997) find strong support for the 'family investment' hypothesis. They report that annual hours worked for migrant families exceed those of both native families (where both partners are native-born) and families with mixed marriages (only the husband is native-born).

4 The benchmark group for children are migrants who have no children or those who have children 13 years and older. While it is preferable to have a category for migrants with children age 13-18 years, this is not possible due to small number of migrants in this group.

5 See Chapter 1 for a discussion of the changes in selection criteria for skilled migrants in the interim period between the arrival of the first and second migration cohorts in this study.

6 See Appendix for an outline of the wage model.

7 Both married and unmarried primary movers are included in the estimating sample. Pooling unmarried and married female primary movers provides us with a workable sample and this is particularly important for the second cohort where the sample size is smaller.

8 Marginal effects for continuous variables are calculated as $\frac{\partial P}{\partial X} = \beta(p)(1-p)$ and as differences in predictions for binary variables.

9 Results for female migrants who migrated for non-economic reasons are presented in the tables in this chapter's Appendix.

10 See Chiswick, Lee and Miller (2003b) and Chapter 6 in this book for analyses of immigrant health.

11 Chiswick and Miller in Chapter 5 report a similar, short-lived impact of visa category in their analysis of the determinants of migrants' English-speaking skills.

12 Note that the correlation between 'predicted own wage' and 'employed in high skill jobs' prior to migration is only 50 per cent.

13 Killingsworth (1983) notes that studies that use Heckman's (1979) approach to correct for sample selection bias have relatively large wage elasticities (value ranges from one to 15).

14 The elasticity of labour market participation with respect to predicted own wage is computed as $\beta_{wage} \times \frac{(PART)(1-PART)}{(PART)}$, where β_{wage} is the coefficient on the wage variable and *PART* is the average participation rate.

15 This Chapter's Appendix contains the regression results for primary and tied movers in Cohort 2.

16 Note that only characteristics of migrants are allowed to vary in the across-cohort comparison. Hence, variations in the predicted participation rate across cohorts can be interpreted as changes in characteristics of migrants, which are likely to be the result of modifications in migrant selection policy over time.

17 Data for primary movers who migrated for non-economic reasons have not been presented because the algorithm used included unskilled visa entries for this group of migrants only.

18 The actual change in labour market participation rate (six months after arrival) for this group is three percentage points.

19 The variation in participation rate for this group of migrants is 10 percentage points.

APPENDIX 4A

Description of variables

Dependent variable

Labour market participation: This is a dichotomous variable and is set equal to unity if the individual is a wage/salary earner, self-employed, other-employed or unemployed and looking for work. This variable is defined at each wave.

Independent variables

Birthplace: nine categories of birthplace are distinguished, with binary variables being created for: Oceania and Antarctica; Europe and USSR; Middle East and North Africa; Southeast Asia; Northeast Asia; Southern Asia; North American; South/Central America and Caribbean; and Other Africa. Individuals born in Europe and USSR are used as the benchmark group. This variable is defined at migration.

Age: This is a continuous variable. This variable is defined at each wave.

Years of education: This is a continuous variable. This variable is defined at each wave.

Unemployed in the 12 months prior to migration: This is a dichotomous variable and is set equal to unity if the individual was unemployed or not in the labour force in the 12 months prior to migration. This variable is defined at migration.

Employed in high-skilled jobs: This is a dichotomous variable and is set equal to unity if the individual worked in high-skilled jobs (managers and administrators, professionals and para-professionals) in the 12 months prior to migration. This variable is defined at migration.

Good English: This is a dichotomous variable and is set equal to unity if the individual speaks English only, speaks English best or speaks a language other than English best but speaks English well/very well. This variable is defined at each wave.

Health status: This is a dichotomous variable and is set equal to unity if the individual has fair, poor or very poor health. This variable is defined at each wave.

Married: This is a dichotomous variable and is set equal to unity if the individual is married. This variable is defined at each wave.

Children 0–2 years: This is a dichotomous variable and is set equal to unity if the individual has children age 0–2 years. This variable is defined at each wave.

Children 3–5 years: This is a dichotomous variable and is set equal to unity if the individual has children age 3–5 years. This variable is defined at each wave.

Children 6–12 years: This is a dichotomous variable and is set equal to unity if the individual has children age 6–12 years. This variable is defined at each wave.

Visa category: Five visa groups are distinguished, with binary variables being created for: Family; Skilled – Australian Sponsored; Business Skills and Employer Nomination Scheme; Independent; and Humanitarian. Individuals arriving in Australia on a Humanitarian visa are used as the benchmark group. This variable is defined at migration.

Individual made the decision to migrate: This is a dichotomous variable and is set equal to unity if the individual made the decision to migrate or the decision was made jointly with her spouse/partner or with relatives. This variable is defined at migration.

Spouse/partner working: This is a dichotomous variable and is set equal to unity if the spouse/partner is a wage/salary earner, self-employed or other-employed. This variable is defined at each wave.

Spouse/partner studying: This is a dichotomous variable and is set equal to unity if the spouse/partner is a student. This variable is defined at each wave.

Predicted spouse/partner wage: This is a continuous variable and measures the predicted hourly wage. It is entered into the estimating equation in natural logarithmic form. This variable is computed for each wave.

Predicted own wage: This is a continuous variable and measures the predicted hourly wage. It is entered into the estimating equation in natural logarithmic form. This variable is computed for each wave.

Unemployment rate: This is a continuous variable and measures the average state unemployment rate over the period of interview.

Model

The labour market participation of each cohort of migrants is expressed as:

$$PART_{it}^{*} = \beta X_{it} + \delta Z_{it} + \varepsilon_{it} \tag{1}$$

where $PART_{it}$ is a latent (unobserved) variable that captures the propensity towards entering the labour market of female migrant i in year t (Wave 1–six months after arrival; Wave 2–18 months after arrival; Wave 3–3.5 years after arrival). X is a column vector containing explanatory variables (for example, individual-related characteristics, information on a migrant's family, birthplace, own wage and spouse's wage), Z is a column vector of labour market history variables, β and δ are row vectors of coefficients, ε_{it} is a random error term that varies across individuals and across time. The estimates of β and δ for each cohort of migrants are obtained using a logit procedure. This is similar to the approach used by Dolton and Makepeace (2004) who added previous earnings to their current earnings function. They referred to this as a value-added model.

There are a number of issues to be considered with the estimation of Equation (1). The first issue is the interpretation of the influence of the labour market history variables of migrant women. The coefficients on these variables ($\hat{\delta}$) will record the impact of all the person-fixed effects embedded in lagged labour market activity information. These fixed effects have the same impact on work behaviour year after year. The coefficients on the personal characteristic variables ($\hat{\beta}$) from this model measure the impact of these variables after controlling for work behaviour in the previous period. It should be noted that a true fixed effects procedure is not used here. This is because with a fixed effects logit model the estimates are derived from the portion of a sample where there is a change in labour force status. In the presence of considerable inertia in labour force participation rate, this may only be a small proportion of the sample.

The second issue to consider is the endogeneity of the individual's wage variable and the absence of information on the market wage for individuals who do not work. To account for this problem, a wage equation is estimated and the predicted wage is included in the labour supply equation (see, for example, Shamsuddin 1998, Biswal 1999). The wage equation for each cohort of migrants is expressed as:

$$\ln W_{it} = \gamma A_{it} + \varepsilon_{it} \tag{2}$$

where W_{it} is the hourly wage rate of individual i in period t, A is a column vector containing human capital characteristics (for example, labour market experience, education, English proficiency), birthplace, health status, marital status, children, visa categories and area of residence, γ is a row vector of coefficients and ε is a stochastic disturbance term.

It should be noted that the wage rate is observed only for individuals who are working. Therefore, correction is made for sample selection bias (see Killingsworth 1983) as follows. First, the probability of working is estimated using a probit procedure.† In this case a reduced form variant of Equation (1) is used, namely:

$$I_{it}^{*} = \alpha B_{it} + \varepsilon_{it} \qquad (3)$$

where I_{it}^{*} is a latent variable that captures the propensity to work of individual i in period t, B is a column vector comprising the exogenous variables contained in Equation (1) plus area of residence, α is a row vector of coefficients and ε is a stochastic disturbance term. The coefficients from Equation (3) are used to construct the inverse mills ratio (see Heckman 1979). Second, the inverse mills ratio is included in the wage Equation (2) as an additional variable to correct for sample selection bias arising from estimating the equation using only working individuals.

To avoid problems with identification (that is, the same variables being included in both the labour market participation and wage models), variables on labour market history, the spouses' employment status, unemployment rate and wages are not included in the wage model but these variables are included in the labour market participation model. The exclusion of these variables from the wage model is consistent with previous studies (for example, MacPherson and Stewart 1989, LeClere and McLaughlin 1997, Shamsuddin 1998). Thus it is argued that these variables affect the reservation wage for labour market entry but not the market wage rate. Location variables are included in the wage equation but are not included in the model of labour supply.

† The reduced form probit results and the selectivity corrected estimates of the wage equation can be obtained from the author

Tables

Table 4A1 *Marginal effects on the probability of participating in the labour market, female primary movers who migrated for non-economic reasons, Cohort 1*

	Wave 1 (i)		Wave 2 (ii)		Wave 3 (iii)	
Variable	**Coeff.**	***t*-ratio**	**Coeff.**	***t*-ratio**	**Coeff.**	***t*-ratio**
Constant	-2.332	-4.35	-1.869	-3.17	-1.339	-1.85
Birthplace						
Oceania & Antarctica	0.222	1.79	0.192	1.31	-0.037	-0.22
Middle East & North Africa	0.070	0.77	0.016	0.15	0.140	1.16
Southeast Asia	0.096	1.65	0.157	2.35	0.065	0.84
Northeast Asia	-0.072	-1.12	-0.139	-1.83	-0.121	-1.40
Southern Asia	0.095	1.23	-0.031	-0.36	0.060	0.60
North America	-0.104	-1.15	0.010	0.09	-0.236	-2.03
South/Central America & Caribbean	0.122	0.85	-0.043	-0.23	0.097	0.47
Other Africa	0.174	1.66	0.059	0.47	-0.032	-0.24
Age	-0.002	-1.10	-0.001	-0.51	-0.015	-4.91
Good English	0.138	2.77	-0.040	-0.70	-0.236	-3.21
Poor health	0.152	2.91	0.065	1.10	0.092	1.51
Family characteristics						
Married	-0.036	-0.73	-0.114	-2.07	-0.360	-6.16
Children 0–2 years	-0.262	-4.35	-0.317	-6.44	-0.336	-6.59
Children 3–5 years	-0.054	-0.77	0.215	2.52	-0.120	-2.06
Children 6–12 years	0.032	0.57	-0.006	-0.10	0.256	3.75
Made decision to migrate	0.005	0.13	0.100	2.31	0.171	3.37
Unemployed/not in labour market	-0.123	-2.88	-0.023	-0.47	-0.070	-1.24
Employed in high skilled jobs	0.037	0.80	-0.104	-1.87	-0.033	-0.52
Visa category						
Preferential family	-0.250	-3.58	-0.239	-3.36	-0.066	-0.79
Skilled – Australian Sponsored	-0.065	-0.35	-0.024	-0.11	0.241	0.96
BS/ENS	-0.254	-1.00	-0.179	-0.47	-0.346	-1.01
Independent	0.122	0.57	0.371	1.43	0.167	0.65
Spouse working	0.692	12.42	0.692	14.13	0.694	12.94
Predicted own wage	0.443	2.77	0.624	3.49	0.650	2.90
Unemployment rate	0.148	4.23	0.064	1.66	-0.071	1.41
χ^2 (25)	**532.96**		**567.75**		**496.94**	
MacFadden R^2	**0.31**		**0.38**		**0.35**	
Sample size	**1,223**		**1,042**		**868**	

Note:
BS/ENS – Business Skills/Employer Nomination Scheme.

Table 4A2 Marginal effects on the probability of participating in the labour market, female primary movers who migrated for economic reasons, Cohort 2

	Wave 1		Wave 2	
Variable	**Coeff.**	***t*-ratio**	**Coeff.**	***t*-ratio**
Constant	0.394	0.37	-0.776	-0.88
Birthplace:				
Oceania & Antarctica	0.246	1.71	0.190	1.78
Middle East & North Africa	0.092	0.58	-0.249	-1.53
Southeast Asia	-0.206	-1.55	0.059	0.62
Northeast Asia	-0.355	-1.98	-0.009	-0.06
Southern Asia	-0.283	-1.78	-0.073	-0.58
North America	0.055	0.23	0.068	0.34
South/Central America & Caribbean	-0.143	-0.54	0.100	0.60
Other Africa	0.004	0.03	-0.107	-1.03
Age	-0.007	-1.23	-0.013	-3.01
Good English	0.385	2.96	0.154	1.24
Poor health	0.068	0.54	0.050	0.63
Family characteristics:				
Married	-0.293	-3.17	-0.274	-4.03
Children 0–2 years	-0.165	-1.80	-0.481	-6.09
Children 3–5 years	-0.086	-0.99	0.045	0.67
Children 6–12 years	0.192	2.77	0.024	0.39
Made decision to migrate	0.048	0.58	0.064	0.91
Unemployed in home country	-0.542	-4.90	-0.275	-2.59
Employed in high skilled jobs	-0.127	-1.36	-0.039	-0.52
Visa category:				
Preferential family	0.401	1.71	0.100	0.72
Skilled – Australian Sponsored	0.546	3.82	0.231	2.10
BS/ENS	0.384	3.28	0.206	2.05
Independent	0.685	3.64	0.276	1.87
Spouse working	0.596	7.23	0.430	5.81
Predicted own wage	-0.237	-0.55	0.504	1.43
Unemployment rate	-0.031	-0.81	-0.017	-0.47
χ^2 (25)	**401.84**		**340.38**	
MacFadden R^2	**0.47**		**0.39**	
Sample size	**569**		**501**	

Note:
BS/ENS – Business Skills/Employer Nomination Scheme.

Table 4A3 Marginal effects on the probability of participating in the labour market, female primary movers who migrated for non-economic reasons, Cohort 2

	Wave 1		Wave 2	
Variable	**Coeff.**	***t*-ratio**	**Coeff.**	***t*-ratio**
Constant	-1.945	-1.86	-1.639	-1.78
Birthplace:				
Oceania & Antarctica	-0.267	-1.45	0.534	2.80
Middle East & North Africa	0.238	1.69	-0.386	-3.04
Southeast Asia	0.072	0.53	0.281	2.26
Northeast Asia	-0.121	-0.75	0.275	1.86
Southern Asia	-0.110	-0.76	0.204	1.39
North America	0.101	0.53	-0.039	-0.20
South/Central America & Caribbean	-0.109	-0.43	0.030	0.09
Other Africa	0.083	0.43	-0.171	-1.16
Age	-0.011	-2.17	-0.0004	-0.09
Good English	0.175	1.50	-0.047	-0.42
Poor health	0.208	1.78	-0.089	-0.79
Family characteristics:				
Married	-0.251	-2.04	-0.440	-3.70
Children 0–2 years	-0.239	-2.13	-0.035	-4.32
Children 3–5 years	-0.249	-1.90	-0.104	-0.92
Children 6–12 years	-0.019	-0.17	-0.072	-0.69
Made decision to migrate	0.124	1.56	-0.044	-0.59
Unemployed in home country	-0.221	-2.46	-0.044	-0.47
Employed in high skilled jobs	0.077	0.86	-0.046	-0.50
Visa category:				
Preferential family	0.242	1.41	-0.201	-2.37
Skilled – Australian Sponsored	0.676	3.61	n.a.	n.a.
BS/ENS	0.616	1.73	0.023	0.06
Independent	0.617	2.33	n.a.	n.a.
Spouse working	0.894	10.78	0.778	11.15
Predicted own wage	0.332	0.76	1.101	3.03
Unemployment rate	0.113	2.59	-0.132	-2.54
χ^2 **(25)**	**617.69**			
χ^2 **(23)**			**468.11**	
MacFadden R^2	**0.59**		**0.47**	
Sample size	**701**		**594**	

Notes:
n.a. = not available due to small sample size.

BS/ENS – Business Skills/Employer Nomination Scheme.

Table 4A4 Marginal effects on the probability of participating in the labour market, female tied movers, Cohort 2

	Wave 1		Wave 2	
Variable	**Coeff.**	***t*-ratio**	**Coeff.**	***t*-ratio**
Constant	0.808	1.13	-1.650	-1.78
Birthplace:				
Oceania & Antartica	-0.069	-0.72	0.237	1.47
Middle East & North Africa	0.257	2.11	-0.052	-0.40
Southeast Asia	-0.069	-0.99	0.242	2.16
Northeast Asia	-0.100	-1.18	0.145	1.05
Southern Asia	-0.021	-0.31	0.161	1.66
North America	0.008	0.03	0.265	0.77
South/Central America & Caribbean	0.561	1.58	0.257	0.74
Other Africa	0.064	1.08	0.295	3.52
Age	-0.002	-0.54	-0.0001	-0.03
Good English	0.146	2.18	0.002	0.02
Poor health	-0.108	-1.54	-0.157	-1.83
Family characteristics:				
Children 0–2 years	-0.147	-2.42	-0.233	-4.08
Children 3–5 years	-0.032	-0.74	-0.079	-1.39
Children 6–12 years	-0.026	-0.67	-0.031	-0.59
Made decision to migrate:	-0.014	-0.23	0.034	0.43
Unemployed in home country	-0.123	-2.57	-0.277	-4.52
Employed in high skilled jobs	0.182	3.62	0.233	3.59
Visa category:				
Preferential family	0.720	3.37	0.512	2.15
Skilled – Australian Sponsored	0.492	2.50	-0.101	-0.73
BS/ENS	0.591	2.40	-0.366	-2.48
Independent	0.421	2.55	-0.272	-1.78
Spouse details:				
Working	0.199	4.13	0.258	3.62
Studying	0.132	1.94	-0.077	-1.27
Predicted wage	-0.492	-3.15	0.227	1.03
Predicted own wage	0.230	0.92	0.455	1.27
Unemployment rate	-0.092	-2.48	-0.040	-0.67
χ^2 (26)	**191.73**		**191.80**	
MacFadden R^2	**0.24**		**0.24**	
Sample size	**586**		**517**	

Note:
BS/ENS – Business Skills/Employer Nomination Scheme.

PART THREE

SOCIAL AND ECONOMIC OUTCOMES

5. Language Skills and Immigrant Adjustment: The Role of Immigration Policy

Barry R. Chiswick and Paul W. Miller

INTRODUCTION

Knowledge of the ways destination language skills vary among immigrants is important for understanding the determinants of their economic well-being, as well as other aspects of their economic, political, and social life in the destination. Adult immigrant language skills are also of interest because these influence the language skills and other dimensions of human capital formation of their children. Accordingly, the identification of the groups 'at risk' of lacking proficiency in an official language can provide a basis for the design of more effective public policies regarding immigration, language training, and the labour market. Moreover, the changes in immigrants' language skills with duration of residence in the destination country can inform on economic adjustment and cultural assimilation.

Much of our knowledge in this area has been taken from cross-sectional surveys. Study of such data suggests that immigrants rapidly acquire proficiency in destination language skills with increases in the length of their residence in the new country (see, for example, Chiswick and Miller 1995). However, longitudinal inferences, such as those about immigrants' development of dominant language skills, generally should not be made on the basis of cross-sectional evidence, which rests on comparisons of groups of immigrants who arrived in a country in different time periods. Where possible, longitudinal data should be used for this purpose, if only to test the robustness of cross-sectional estimates.

This study provides an account of the dynamics of the dominant language adjustment process among immigrants, with application to Australia. It is based on longitudinal surveys of two cohorts of immigrants arriving in Australia around five years apart. There are two special features of these data that provide the framework for the analysis. The first is that the visa class under which the immigrants entered Australia is known. There are five major visa categories: [1] Independent; Skilled – Australian Sponsored; Business Skills and Employer Nomination Schemes; Family; and Humanitarian. Both the Independent and Skilled – Australian Sponsored immigrants are points tested for entry into Australia, with the main difference between the categories being that the Skilled – Australian Sponsored immigrants need to be sponsored by an Australian citizen, and additional points are available for aspects of this sponsorship (see Tables 1.1 and 1.2 of Chapter 1). Sponsorship by an Australian plays no role in the Independent visa category. Under points testing, points are awarded for a range of attributes that are held to be important to immigrants' employment prospects and settlement in Australia, and only those immigrants with more points than the administratively determined threshold are eligible to be granted a visa. The pass marks for 1989–1998 are displayed in Table 5.1. One of the attributes that is awarded points is English language ability.

Table 5.1 Points test pass marks for Independent and Skilled – Australian Sponsored immigration categories, 1989–1998

Effective date	Independent	Skilled – Australian Sponsored
19 December 1989	100	85
16 May 1990	95	85
8 January 1992	100	90
15 February 1992	110	100
23 December 1993	100	95
1 December 1995	110	95
1 August 1996	115	95
1 November 1996	115	115
3 March 1998	110	115

Source: Department of Immigration and Multicultural Affairs (1999), Attachment A.

The role of English language ability in immigrant selection was progressively strengthened during the 1990s. A major set of changes was made to the points test in the late 1990s, and these affected immigrants in the Independent and Skilled – Australian Sponsored visa categories (see Department of Immigration and Multicultural Affairs 1999).

The second special feature of the data is that many of those in the second cohort in the Independent and Skilled – Australian Sponsored visa classes were points tested under criteria that gave greater emphasis to English language ability than was the case for the first cohort.[2] Immigrants in the two cohorts entering under the Family, Business Skills and Employer Nomination schemes, and Humanitarian categories were not affected by these changes.[3] Comparisons between cohorts within these visa categories therefore provide information on cohort effects, such as those that might arise from general changes in the Australian economy or in the international market for immigrants, that might lead one cohort of immigrants to be more skilled or less skilled than another. Comparisons between the two cohorts of immigrants with Independent and Skilled – Australian Sponsored visas will provide information on the effects of both cohort differences and policy changes regarding English language proficiency. Finally, comparisons of the changes observed for the groups of immigrants points tested and not points tested for entry into Australia will, assuming that any cohort changes are the same for both groups of immigrants, facilitate estimates of the impacts of the policy changes. This will provide an assessment of what immigration policy can do in this area.

LANGUAGE SKILLS IN THE LSIA: DESCRIPTIVE ANALYSES

As outlined in Chapter 1, there were various changes to the points system used in immigrant selection for the two cohorts of the Longitudinal Survey of Immigration to Australia (LSIA). Some immigrants (Independent, Skilled – Australian Sponsored) were directly affected to varying degrees by the policy changes in relation to English skills, while other immigrants (Family, Business/Employer Nomination Scheme, Humanitarian) were not affected by these policy changes. The availability of the data for the two cohorts in the LSIA collected under different points tests provides a natural experiment into what governments can do in relation to immigrants' initial language skills. Moreover, with the second cohort, there are sufficient Independent visaed immigrants who entered under either the pre- or post-1 July 1999 regulations (where the major change is the introduction of the core criteria) to permit assessment of the impact of this change within a cohort.

Table 5.2 displays the main comparisons possible with these data. While the threshold, or pass, number of points changed over 1993–1999, as the characteristics that could be awarded points also changed, it is unclear if these changes in the pass marks represented a tightening or weakening of quality controls.[4]

A differences between differences approach can then be used to establish the net effect of immigration policy.[5] For example, the comparisons listed in the first row of Table 5.2 can be analysed in conjunction with those listed in the second row of the table to help isolate the effect of the expansion of the Occupations Requiring English (ORE) list. Similarly, the comparisons listed in the first and second rows of Table 5.2 can be analysed in conjunction with those listed in the third row of the table to help isolate the effect of using points for English language ability in the selection of immigrants.

Table 5.2 Role of English language ability in immigrant selection in LSIA Cohort 1 and Cohort 2

Visa category	Cohort 1	Cohort 2: pre-1 July 1999	Main differences between cohorts
Non-points tested (Family, Humanitarian)	No points for English ability; no minimum English threshold.	No points for English ability; no minimum English threshold.	Cohort effects
Independent	Points for English ability; English fluency required if usual occupation on ORE list; no minimum English threshold.	Points for English ability; English fluency required if usual occupation on ORE list; no minimum English threshold.	Impact of changes in ORE list + cohort effects
Skilled – Australian Sponsored	No points for English ability; English fluency required if usual occupation on ORE list; no minimum English threshold.	Points for English ability; English fluency required if usual occupation on ORE list; no minimum English threshold.	Impact of points for English ability + impact of changes in ORE list + cohort effects
Visa Category	Cohort 2: pre-1 July 1999	Cohort 2: post-1 July 1999	Differences between cohorts
Independent	Points for English ability; English fluency required if usual occupation on ORE list; no minimum English threshold.	Points for English ability; English fluency required if usual occupation on ORE list; a minimum English threshold.	Impact of minimum English threshold

Note:
ORE – Occupations Requiring English.

Source: Department of Immigration and Multicultural Affairs (1999).

Table 5.3 lists information on the English language skills of non-English-speaking background immigrants in the two arrival cohorts under investigation.[6] The figures in normal type are for immigrants arriving in 1993–1995 (Cohort 1); those in bold type are for immigrants arriving in 1999–2000 (Cohort 2). In each case the data were collected around six months after arrival in Australia. The information is listed for visa category in approximate descending levels of English language proficiency. The final row of data is for Migrating Unit Spouses (MUS). Owing to the smaller numbers involved, especially for males, the information for MUS is not disaggregated by the visa category of the Principal Applicant.

Table 5.3 shows that immigrants arriving in 1999–2000 in the points tested Independent and Skilled – Australian Sponsored visa categories had English skills superior to those of the earlier arrival cohort. For example, if the categories of 'English only/best', 'English very well' and 'English well' are termed 'proficient in English', as in the studies by Chiswick, Lee and Miller (2003a, 2005b, 2006), then the proficiency rate for male Independent immigrants rose from 91 per cent to 98 per cent among Principal Applicants from non-English-speaking countries arriving in 1993–1995 and 1999–2000, respectively. Or expressed differently, the non-proficiency rate fell from 9 per cent to 2 per cent, a 78 per cent decline in non-proficiency. For female Independent immigrants, the proficiency rate rose slightly, from 96 per cent to 97 per cent. Among Independent immigrants, therefore, English proficiency is almost universal. Among Skilled – Australian Sponsored immigrants, the proficiency rate rose from 68 per cent to 92 per cent for males, and from 77 per cent to 85 per cent for females.

In comparison, among the Family category immigrants, who were not tested for English skills, the proficiency rate declined from 54 per cent to 45 per cent for males, and rose marginally from 47 per cent to 51 per cent for females. These changes could be due to a range of factors, including changes in the birthplace mix of immigrants, and other policy changes, such as the cap on the entry of parents under the Family stream. As noted in Chapter 1, this policy change reduced the average age of immigrants in the Family visa category. Similarly, among Humanitarian category immigrants, the proficiency rates remained around 25 per cent among males, and increased slightly, from 15 to 19 per cent, among females.

These changes in rates of English proficiency for Family and Humanitarian visaed immigrants are thus much more modest than those for Independent and Skilled – Australian Sponsored immigrants, where the English language skill levels jumped appreciably in the more recent cohort.

The English skills of Migrating Unit Spouses are superior among the more recent arrival cohort, with the degree of improvement being in-between that for Independent/Skilled – Australian Sponsored and Family immigrants. The skills of spouses might be expected to have improved over time owing to the interaction of the superior English skills of Principal Applicants and assortative mating, learning English from the more proficient spouse or from children, and the impact of the policy change that introduced points for spouse skills (see Chiswick, Lee and Miller 2005b).

The Table 5.3 data do not distinguish between immigrants in the 1999–2000 arrival cohort who were processed according to the pre- and post-1 July 1999 points tests. For the Skilled – Australian Sponsored category, this omission will not matter, as the weighted sample size for those processed according to the post-1 July 1999 points tests is very small (four per cent of

Table 5.3 English language speaking skills by visa category, non-English-speaking background immigrants arriving in Australia 1993–1995 (Cohort 1) and 1999–2000 (Cohort 2)

Visa category	Unweighted sample size	English only or English best %	English is not the only or best spoken language, speaks English: Very well %	Well %	Not well %	Not at all %	Total %
Men							
Independent							
Cohort 1	473	23.5	27.3	39.8	9.2	0.2	100.0
Cohort 2	**192**	**33.8**	**32.6**	**31.9**	**1.7**	**0.00**	**100.0**
SAS							
Cohort 1	469	18.7	16.4	32.5	27.8	4.6	100.0
Cohort 2	**140**	**35.5**	**21.2**	**35.5**	**7.4**	**0.3**	**100.0**
BS/ENS							
Cohort 1	273	19.1	20.5	28.2	25.4	6.8	100.0
Cohort 2	**182**	**26.1**	**16.2**	**31.9**	**20.4**	**5.3**	**100.0**
Family							
Cohort 1	743	14.5	12.4	27.3	34.4	11.5	100.0
Cohort 2	**509**	**12.3**	**13.7**	**19.3**	**39.5**	**15.2**	**100.0**
Humanitarian							
Cohort 1	505	0.4	4.3	20.2	56.7	18.4	100.0
Cohort 2	**346**	**1.7**	**5.1**	**16.6**	**55.1**	**21.5**	**100.0**
Migrating Unit Spouse							
Cohort 1	285	12.0	11.2	21.7	37.2	17.9	100.0
Cohort 2	**199**	**24.3**	**13.0**	**29.1**	**24.5**	**9.2**	**100.0**
Women							
Independent							
Cohort 1	179	17.5	30.2	48.0	4.3	0.00	100.0
Cohort 2	**96**	**40.2**	**30.6**	**26.5**	**2.7**	**0.00**	**100.0**
SAS							
Cohort 1	171	24.8	19.9	32.2	20.9	2.2	100.0
Cohort 2	**77**	**39.0**	**19.3**	**26.7**	**14.9**	**0.0**	**100.0**
BS/ENS							
Cohort 1	69	18.1	27.2	21.1	22.9	10.8	100.0
Cohort 2	**52**	**9.3**	**18.7**	**26.8**	**33.8**	**11.4**	**100.0**
Family							
Cohort 1	1262	9.7	11.3	25.5	33.2	20.3	100.0
Cohort 2	**803**	**12.4**	**12.2**	**26.0**	**35.7**	**13.7**	**100.0**
Humanitarian							
Cohort 1	326	0.8	3.1	10.7	49.9	35.5	100.0
Cohort 2	**212**	**0.1**	**3.6**	**15.0**	**53.0**	**28.3**	**100.0**
Migrating Unit Spouse							
Cohort 1	1117	11.7	9.8	22.6	36.1	19.9	100.0
Cohort 2	**649**	**20.0**	**11.4**	**19.9**	**36.4**	**12.3**	**100.0**

Notes: (see next page)

Source: Longitudinal Survey of Immigrants to Australia.

Table 5.3 (continued)

Notes:

Figures in normal type are for immigrants arriving in 1993–1995, six months after arrival; Figures in bold type are for immigrants arriving in 1999–2000, six months after arrival.

Data exclude persons born in the English-speaking developed countries (New Zealand, United Kindom, United States and Canada).

Row totals may not sum to 100 due to rounding.

Sample Sizes:

Cohort 1: 2,463 male PAs, weighted sample of 29,547; 285 male MUSs, weighted sample of 2,842; 2,007 female PAs, weighted sample of 29,653; 1,117 female MUSs, weighted sample of 12,349.

Cohort 2: 1,369 male PAs, weighted sample of 12,261; 199 male MUSs, weighted sample of 1,723; 1,240 female PAs, weighted sample of 12,874; 649 female MUSs, weighted sample of 5,344.

the major visa category). For the Independent visa category, however, the post-1 July 1999 group is larger, comprising 17 per cent of the Independent category. Table 5.4 presents information on language skills for the pre- and post-1 July 1999 points tested groups.

Among Independent immigrants, English proficiency is almost universal, given the definition adopted above. Using a more stringent definition, where only the top two English-speaking skills categories are defined as proficient in English, there is a slight improvement in the English proficiency rate for those processed under the post-1 July 1999 points tests compared to Independent male immigrants processed according to the pre-1 July 1999 points tests. Among females, however, those processed under the post-1 July 1999 points tests have lower rates of English language proficiency. This is due to a large difference in representation in the 'English only/English best' category. This difference is likely to be associated with differences in the birthplace mix within the arrival groups. The statistical analyses presented below will control for these effects.

English-speaking skills improved for most, but not all, immigrants between the first and second interviews. Panel A of Table 5.5 presents the English-speaking proficiency rate at the time of the Wave 2 interview as a ratio of the rate at the time of the Wave 1 interview. Values greater than one indicate improvement over time in English-speaking proficiency. Panel B of the table presents similar information from a comparison of the English-speaking proficiency at the time of the Wave 3 interview with that at the time of the Wave 1 interview.

Consider the number in the first cell for male Independent visaed immigrants in Cohort 1. This number, 1.03, indicates that the English proficiency rate at the second interview was 3 per cent higher than that at the time of the first interview (in fact, rising by almost three percentage points, from 90.5 per cent to 93.3 per cent).

Table 5.4 English language speaking skills of Independent, non-English-speaking background immigrants arriving in Australia 1993–1995 (Cohort 1) and 1999–2000 (Cohort 2)

	English only or English best	English is not the only or best spoken language, speaks English:				
	%	Very well %	Well %	Not well	Not at all %	Total %
Men						
Cohort 1	23.5	27.3	39.8	9.2	0.2	100.0
Cohort 2 (pre-1 July 1999)	34.4	31.0	32.9	1.7	0.0	100.0
Cohort 2 (post-1 July 1999)	31.2	39.6	27.5	1.7	0.0	100.0
Women						
Cohort 1	17.5	30.2	48.0	4.3	0.0	100.0
Cohort 2 (pre- 1 July 1999)	45.5	28.9	22.1	3.5	0.0	100.0
Cohort 2 (post-1 July 1999)	21.7	36.6	41.8	0.0	0.0	100.0

Source: Longitudinal Survey of Immigrants to Australia.

Table 5.5, Panel A, has two main features. First, the relative improvement in English-speaking proficiency over time is greater for Humanitarian and Family category immigrants than for other immigrants. This could be termed an initial conditions effect: these immigrants have relatively poor English skills at the time of entry into Australia, and hence large proportional changes are easier for them than for immigrants in the skilled categories where proficiency rates are initially much higher. It might also reflect greater investments in English language proficiency among those who arrived with the lowest proficiency, especially refugees who might not have prepared for the move by investing in English language skills in their country of origin and who were less favourably selected for immigration.[7]

Second, comparing immigrants in Cohort 2 with those in Cohort 1, there are two changes of note. The first of these is the limited improvement between the first and second interviews in English-speaking skills among female Independent visaed immigrants in Cohort 2. It is apparent from Table 5.4 that this group had an unusually high rate of English-speaking proficiency at the time of arrival, and the Table 5.5 findings could again be a reflection of an initial conditions effect. The second feature is the stronger improvement in English-speaking skills in Cohort 2 among immigrants in the Skilled – Australian Sponsored category.

Table 5.5 English-speaking proficiency rate in Wave 2 and Wave 3 as a proportion of English-speaking proficiency rate in Wave 1 by visa class, gender and cohort, immigrants from non-English-speaking countries

A: Wave 2 versus Wave 1

Visa category	Cohort 1		Cohort 2	
	Males	Females	Males	Females
Independent	1.03	1.01	1.02	1.03
Skilled – Australian Sponsored	1.10	1.09	1.07	1.02
BS/ENS	1.02	1.11	1.04	1.07
Family	1.20	1.17	1.38	1.16
Humanitarian	1.65	2.39	2.03	1.74
Migrating Unit Spouse	1.38	1.21	1.08	1.27
Total	1.18	1.19	1.15	1.16

B: Wave 3 versus Wave 1

Visa category	Cohort 1	
	Males	Females
Independent	1.04	1.02
Skilled – Australian Sponsored	1.20	1.16
BS/ENS	1.08	1.09
Family	1.35	1.25
Humanitarian	2.18	2.84
Migrating Unit Spouse	1.53	1.43
Total	1.31	1.32

Note:
BS/ENS – Business Skills/Employer Nomination Scheme.

The information in Panel B of Table 5.5 shows that there were further improvements in the English-speaking proficiency of immigrants in all visa classes by the time of the third interview. The relative improvement, however, was greater for those immigrants with poorer English skills at the time of entry into Australia.

Similar analyses were conducted for English reading and writing skills.[8] The major findings found below in the econometric analyses carry over to these other skills.

ECONOMETRIC ANALYSES

The Model

The multivariate analyses presented below are based on the model of dominant language skills developed by Chiswick and Miller (see, particularly, Chiswick and Miller 1992a, 1995, 1998a). This model has previously been applied to Cohort 1 by Chiswick, Lee and Miller (2003a, 2005a, 2006). In the main model an immigrant's language skills are represented by a binary indicator, defined to be equal to one where the immigrant's only or best spoken language is English, or where another language is the best spoken, the immigrant speaks English very well or well. All other proficiency states are defined to be equal to zero.[9] Estimates are, however, also presented for an ordered probability model that utilizes all categories of English skills available in the data set.

Drawing on Chiswick and Miller (1992a, 1995, 1998a), the immigrant's proficiency in English (speaking, reading or writing) skills (LANG) is modeled as:

$$\text{LANG} = f(\text{economic incentives, efficiency, exposure}) \qquad (1)$$

The empirical counterpart of this general model has typically been developed using institutional information (for example, visa category), demographic characteristics (for example, birthplace, age at migration, educational attainment), known activities of the immigrants (for example, whether they visited Australia prior to migration, whether they expected to leave Australia permanently) and behavioural variables constructed from information on the immigrants' birthplace and mother tongue (for example, geographic distance of the country of origin from Australia, linguistic distance of the mother tongue from English) (see Chiswick, Lee and Miller 2003a, 2005a, 2005b).

The emphasis here is on the comparisons across visa categories of differences in English skills at the time of immigration, and of the development of these skills with increases in the length of the immigrants' stay in Australia. To facilitate this focus, the variables with behavioral interpretations that have been used in place of birthplace are not included in the estimating equation.[10]

Economic incentives for the acquisition of English skills among immigrant arrivals in Australia depend on the benefits (such as higher wages, greater productivity in consumption and more informed participation in social and political life in Australia) expected to be associated with these skills, and the length of time over which these benefits are expected to accrue. Two sets of variables may be used to capture this set of influences. The first of these is information on whether immigrants expected to leave Australia permanently. The second is a set of birthplace variables that serve as a proxy for the probability of return migration, since immigrants of different origins have varying outcomes of permanent and sojourner migration.

Efficiency refers to the extent to which a given amount of exposure to English produces language proficiency. It has been shown in numerous studies that proficiency is enhanced by a higher level of education and by migration while young (see Long 1990, and Service and Craik 1993 on the age effects in language attainment).[11]

Exposure has three dimensions. These are: exposure prior to migration, time units of exposure in the destination country, and the intensity of exposure per unit of time in the destination.

Two measures of exposure prior to migration were considered by Chiswick, Lee and Miller (2003a, 2005a, 2006). The first of these is constructed from information on the extent of cross country/culture contact in the country of origin. Immigrants with cross-cultural contact prior to immigration are more likely to have been exposed to English, or at least have a relatively favourable disposition towards other cultures that may be associated with a greater preparedness to learn English.

A second measure of exposure can be based on the LSIA information on whether the immigrant visited Australia prior to migrating. Such visits would have exposed immigrants to English, and the visits could be indicative of a greater degree of planning for the migration, and with greater knowledge gained through such visits there may be a higher likelihood of staying. It is therefore expected that immigrants who visited Australia prior to migrating would have English skills superior to the skills of those who did not visit Australia.

Time units of exposure in the destination country (or years since migration) play an important role in the studies of language skills based on cross-sectional data (for example Chiswick and Miller 1995). As the current study is based on longitudinal data, this effect is captured by dummy variables for each of the waves of data collection, though in the initial set of estimates where the aim is to mimic the cross-sectional approach, a duration of residence variable (weeks since migration) is used.

The intensity of exposure per unit of time in Australia is more complex. It will depend on the characteristics of the person's home and location, and the institutional support offered for English language training, whether financed privately or subsided by the state or national governments. The home environment is measured in most analyses through variables for the number and ages of children, and for the birthplace or language skills of the spouse. In the Longitudinal Survey of Immigrants to Australia there is information both on the family structure and on whether children live with their parents. Moreover, the survey contains details on whether other people who were part of the 'migrating unit' live with the respondent. Hence, the following variables are included in the language model: whether a spouse who was part of the migrating unit is present in the household (*MUS*); whether a spouse who was not part of the migrating unit is present in the household (*OS*); whether there are children in the household (*KIDS*); whether other relatives who gained approval to migrate to Australia as part of the Principal Applicant's migration application are present in the household (*MUR*); whether other relatives are present in the household (*OR*).

The information on the immigrant's living arrangements can be complemented with information on the main reason the immigrant chose his/her State of initial settlement in Australia. Where 'family/friends' is the main reason for the choice of location, it is expected that the immigrant will have access to an ethnic network. The availability of this ethnic network can reduce the exposure to, and practice in using, English, and hence reduce proficiency.

Finally, consideration needs to be given to the degree of institutional support offered for English language training. Two-thirds of immigrants from non-English-speaking countries in Cohort 1 claimed to have studied or learned English in Australia by the time of the first interview. The most frequently cited way that this was done was through the Adult Migrant Education Service. Family and friends was the second most frequently cited way of learning English after arrival in Australia. Ideally, information on attendance at formal English classes might be incorporated into the estimating equation. However, there are several arguments against such an approach. First, information on post-arrival learning of English is available only for those in English-speaking skills categories other than 'English only or English best'. For some groups the English only and English best comprise more than two-thirds of the 'proficient' group used in the statistical analyses below (see Table 5.3). Second, to the extent that individuals with the weakest English skills are more likely to attend formal English classes, a negative relationship between the measures of English proficiency and the attendance at the English language classes might emerge, even though attendance at the classes has a positive impact on English skills. Moreover, among those who enroll, duration in an English language training program might appear to show a similar negative effect, that is those who became the most proficient sooner might drop out sooner. Thus, one would need to use a predicted rather than an observed measure for both enrolment and duration in an English language training program. This is beyond the scope of this research. These practical considerations give rise to a preference for a specification that does not include information on enrolment in English classes. As a result, to the extent that the included explanatory variables influence participation in an English language training program, these effects are reflected in the coefficients of the explanatory variables.

Thus, the empirical counterpart to equation (1) used in this research is:

LANG = f(cohort, wave, visa category, age at migration, education, gender, birthplace, preparation for migration, expected duration in destination, cross country/culture contact in country of origin, family structure, reasons for choice of state of initial settlement).[12] (2)

This general model is applied in this study to a sample pooled across all waves of the data sets (three waves for Cohort 1, two waves for Cohort 2) and across surveys (that is, both Cohort 1 and Cohort 2). The estimating equation may be described as follows. Denote the explanatory variables other than cohort and wave by the vector *X*, and let *W1* represent the first interview, *W2* the second interview, and *W3* the third interview. Then the actual equation to be estimated is:

$$\begin{aligned} LANG_{it} = {} & \alpha_0 + \beta_1 X_{it} + \gamma_2 W2_{it} + \gamma_3 W3_{it} + \delta_2 W2_{it} X_{it} + \delta_3 W3_{it} X_{it} + \phi_1 LSIA2_{it} + \\ & \phi_2 LSIA2_{it} W2_{it} + \varphi_1 LSIA2_{it} X_{it} + \varphi_2 LSIA2_{it} W2_{it} X_{it} + \varepsilon_{it} \end{aligned} \tag{3}$$

where i is the individual and t is the time of the interview. This equation has a full set of interaction terms between waves of data (*W2, W3*) and surveys (Cohort 2) and the explanatory variables (*X*). In this general representation of the estimation equation, β_1 will capture the impact of the *X* characteristics on the distribution of English language skills for the first cohort of immigrants (Cohort 1) at the time of the first set of interviews, approximately six months after arrival. The γ_j's will capture general shifts in the mean levels of English skills between the first and subsequent interviews for this cohort of immigrants, and as such can be viewed as capturing the impact of duration of residence in Australia. The δ's will capture the changes in English skills for immigrants in Cohort 1 with the *X* characteristics with time in Australia. In other words, these parameters will capture the learning or deterioration of language skills for this cohort with time in the destination country.[13]

As the data are not only pooled across waves of interviews within a survey, but across the two cohorts of immigrants, variables and interaction terms for the second cohort of immigrants need also to be included in the specification. ϕ_1 measures the mean difference in language skills between immigrants in the second cohort and those in the first cohort, ceteris paribus. Hence it will capture cohort effects. ϕ_2 will measure the differential growth in language skills between the first two interviews for immigrants in Cohort 2 compared to immigrants in Cohort 1. Likewise, φ_1 will record the differential for immigrants in Cohort 2 compared to immigrants in Cohort 1 of the impact of the *X* characteristics on the initial distribution of language skills. Finally, φ_2 will measure the differential in learning or deterioration in language skills with the *X* characteristics with time in the destination for immigrants in Cohort 2 in comparison with immigrants in Cohort 1.[14]

The estimates: Principal Applicants

Table 5.6 presents the estimates for three different models, namely an Ordinary Least Squares (OLS) model, a probit model and an ordered probit

Table 5.6 Models of English-speaking skills, 15–64 year old males and females from non-English-speaking countries

Variable	OLS (i)		Probit (ii)		Ordered probit (iii)	
Constant	0.091	(3.07)	-1.214	(9.39)	-0.001	(0.01)
Visa category						
Humanitarian	-0.239	(18.53)	-1.171	(18.56)	-0.691	(18.19)
Family	-0.163	(13.78)	-1.066	(15.35)	-0.466	(11.83)
Skilled – Australian Sponsored	-0.048	(4.31)	-0.507	(7.34)	-0.079	(2.03)
BS/ENS[a]	-0.150	(12.96)	-1.014	(11.57)	-0.384	(6.99)
Age at migration	-0.005	(8.53)	-0.019	(12.88)	-0.016	(14.19)
Education	0.050	(48.61)	0.185	(40.88)	0.163	(53.91)
Female	-0.032	(4.64)	-0.099	(3.42)	-0.104	(5.18)
Cross culture/country contact in former home country	0.089	(12.92)	0.338	(12.59)	0.316	(16.43)
Previously visited Australia	0.194	(27.44)	0.854	(25.73)	0.743	(34.19)
Main reason for choosing state settled was family/friends	-0.042	(5.35)	-0.260	(6.60)	-0.122	(4.85)
Contact with ethnic agencies	-0.029	(2.91)	-0.123	(3.14)	-0.105	(3.80)
Expect to stay in Australia	0.024	(1.43)	0.155	(2.19)	0.154	(3.18)
Family structure						
MUS[b]	-0.036	(3.53)	-0.177	(3.74)	-0.062	(1.99)
OS[c]	0.003	(0.30)	0.074	(1.58)	0.025	(0.77)
KIDS[d]	-0.044	(6.03)	-0.175	(5.87)	-0.141	(6.66)
MURS[e]	-0.003	(0.19)	-0.019	(0.31)	0.095	(2.05)
OR[f]	-0.065	(8.50)	-0.205	(6.82)	-0.237	(10.99)
Weeks in Australia/100	0.089	(17.13)	0.353	(15.92)	0.251	(16.54)
Birthplace						
Oceania/Antarctica	0.329	(22.65)	1.879	(15.31)	1.692	(29.31)
Middle East and North Africa	0.012	(0.96)	0.101	(2.27)	0.069	(2.08)
Southeast Asia	0.049	(5.10)	0.255	(6.61)	0.375	(13.66)
Northeast Asia	-0.133	(12.33)	-0.566	(12.73)	-0.552	(17.86)
Southern and Central Asia	0.165	(15.16)	0.724	(13.62)	0.979	(28.65)
South/Central America and Caribbean	-0.069	(2.88)	-0.306	(3.44)	-0.204	(3.14)
Other Africa (Sub-Saharan Africa)	0.188	(11.94)	0.920	(10.99)	1.221	(22.58)
μ_1	g		g		1.646	(20.52)
μ_2	g		g		2.879	(27.04)
μ_3	g		g		3.656	(231.92)
χ^2	g		7423.35		9799.89	
Prediction success rate (%)	g		79.30		47.81	
Adjusted R^2	0.391		g		g	
F - test	386.35		g		g	
Sample size	15014		15014		15014	

Table 5.6 (continued)

Notes:
Numbers in parentheses are '*t*' statistics; No statistical control for cohort, and with a duration of residence variable (weeks in Australia) in place of wave dummy variables.
[a] Variable not relevant.
[b] BS/ENS – denotes Business Skills/Employer Nomination Scheme.
[c] Whether a spouse who was part of the migrating unit is present in the household.
[d] Whether a spouse who was not part of the migrating unit is present in the household.
[e] Whether there are children in the household.
[f] Whether other relatives who gained approval to migrate to Australia as part of the Principal Applicant's migration application are present in the household.
[g] Whether other relatives are present in the household.

model. The first two models are based on a binary dependent variable, being the measure of proficiency developed earlier.[15] The third model is based on all of the categories of English skills presented in the data.

This initial set of estimates is obtained from a sample pooled across waves of data for each cohort of immigrants, and across the two cohorts. As the purpose of this part of the research is to provide a benchmark set of results that may be compared with the literature (which has largely been based on cross-sectional analyses), the estimating equation does not include a variable recording the cohort of arrival. Moreover, to enhance comparability with past research, a continuous period of residence (weeks in Australia) is used in place of dichotomous variables for the wave of data collection.

Table 5.6 lists the estimates for variables on four classes of visas (Humanitarian, Family, Skilled – Australian Sponsored, and Business Skills/ Employee Nomination Scheme), with the benchmark group for visa category being the Independent visa. The ranking of coefficients (Independent Visa, Skilled – Australian Sponsored Visa, Business Skills/ENS Visa, Family Visa, Humanitarian Visa) is consistent across the three methods of estimation employed. The negative coefficients on the four visa category variables indicate that immigrants who entered Australia using these visas have lower English-speaking skills as compared to those with Independent visas. This is presumably due to the selection criteria used for entry into Australia, where English-speaking skills are essential for applicants entering under an Independent visa. On the other hand, those who entered under Humanitarian visas are the least likely to have English-speaking skills since these skills are not required for visa acquisition, and non-economic motives are strongly influencing their migration decisions.

The estimated coefficient on the variable for age at migration is negative in each column of results. This shows that English-speaking skills decrease with age at migration. The OLS result in Table 5.6, column (i), indicates that the level of English-speaking skills decreases by 0.5 percentage points with each additional year of age at migration, with a similar impact being recorded for the probit model. This suggests that this type of effect is associated with learning skills that decrease with age.

Education level has a positive impact on the immigrants' English-speaking proficiency. That is, immigrants with a higher level of educational attainment have a higher level of English-speaking proficiency, by 5 percentage points per year of schooling in the OLS analysis. This partial effect is particularly strong, as can be seen by comparing the estimated effects associated with age at migration and educational attainment: each additional year of education is the equivalent in impact on English skills to ten fewer years of age at migration. This impact associated with educational attainment is far greater than might be expected on the basis of the points awarded for these attributes in immigrant selection in Australia (see Chapter 1). The relationship between the probability of being proficient in English and educational attainment computed from the probit model is illustrated in Figure 5.1.

Female immigrants had lower English-speaking skills compared to their male counterparts. The estimated coefficient in the OLS model indicates a 3.2 percentage points gender differential in English language proficiency. Compared to some of the other estimated effects (for example, that for education, where the partial effect is 5 percentage points greater English proficiency per year of schooling), this gender effect is small.

Figure 5.1 Standardised relationship between the probability of being proficient in English and educational attainment

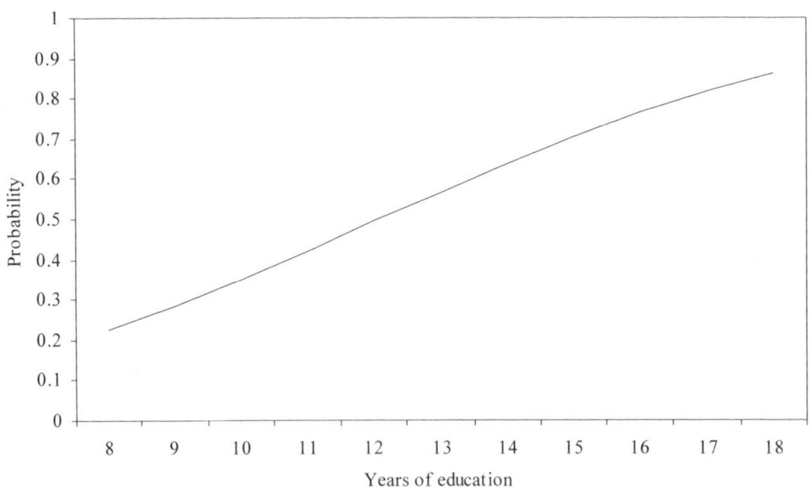

Both the variables for the 'cross country/culture contact in former home country' and 'previously visited Australia' have positive coefficients. This implies that immigrants' exposure to Australia before migration is associated with a higher level of English-speaking skills. Previous exposure to Australia presumably enables the immigrants to adapt more quickly and pick up the language more easily.

The presence of family and friends as the main factor influencing location decisions within Australia has a negative impact on English-speaking proficiency in each of the three models examined. This impact may arise because the presence of these family members and friends facilitates communication in the immigrants' mother tongue and hence reduces the incentive to learn English or the exposure to English. The effect of this variable is similar to that of the variable that records whether immigrants have had contact with ethnic agencies since arrival in Australia. Immigrants who have had such contact appear to have lower English-speaking proficiency, presumably because they have less incentive and possibly fewer chances to speak English when they remain within their ethnic groups.

In comparison to these negative influences on English skills, the variable that captures the immigrants' expectation to stay in Australia is associated with a positive effect, although it is not statistically significant in the OLS model. The expectation of staying is clearly a motivation to develop a better grasp of the English language.

In addition, the coefficient of the variable that records the weeks of residence in Australia is positive; this shows that the English-speaking skills of the immigrants will improve with increases in the duration of their stay in Australia. In these data on recent arrivals, English proficiency improves by 9 percentage points per 100 weeks in Australia, or 4 to 5 percentage points per year.

There are five variables used to capture the effects of different compositions of the immigrants' household.[16] The results show that the presence of a spouse in the household who was part of the migrating unit, the presence of children in the household and the presence of other relatives in the household have negative impacts on the immigrants' English-speaking skills. In contrast, the OLS and ordered probit models show an insignificant positive effect for the presence in the household of other relatives who gained approval to migrate to Australia as part of the Principal Applicant's migration application.

These models also included seven birthplace dichotomous variables, namely 'Oceania/Antarctica', 'Middle East and North Africa', 'Southeast Asia', 'Northeast Asia', 'Southern and Central Asia', 'South/Central America and Caribbean' and 'Other Africa (sub-Saharan Africa)'. The benchmark group for these dichotomous variables is the birthplace group of Europe and the USSR. Controlling for type of visa at entry, all of the coefficients on the dichotomous birthplace variables are positive and statistically significant except those for 'Northeast Asia' and 'South/Central America and Caribbean', where the coefficient is negative and significant.[17] The positive sign on the estimated coefficients shows that immigrants who were born in these birthplace groups will have higher English-speaking skills than those born in Europe and the USSR. On the other hand, those born in 'Northeast Asia' and 'South/Central America and Caribbean' will be less proficient English speakers compared to immigrants born in Europe and the USSR.

The estimated thresholds for the ordered probit model are each statistically significant. This indicates that the underlying language categories recognised in the data are distinct, and as such this is an argument against the use of a binary dependent variable such as that analysed in Table 5.6, columns (i) and (ii). However, tests[18] show that the assumption of equal slope effects across the English proficiency categories does not hold, implying that the parsimony in parameters of this model (compared, for example, to a multinomial probit model) is achieved at a cost. Another possible limitation is that the estimated impacts in the ordered probit are difficult to interpret, as a positive (negative) coefficient can only be unambiguously associated with an increase (decrease) in membership of the highest ranked category and a decrease (increase) in membership of the lowest ranked category. This difficulty can be overcome by computing predicted distributions across the language categories for the values of variables under consideration. The distributions for different values of variables can then be compared, and differences between them attributed to changes in the values of the variables. Table 5.7 presents predictions for the standardised distribution of immigrants across the five English skills categories recognised in the data by level of education.[19]

Table 5.7 Predictions of the standardised distribution of immigrants across English skills categories

Years of education	English only or English best	English is not the only or best spoken language, speaks English:			
		Very well	Well	Not well	Not at all
8	0.006	0.034	0.261	0.569	0.131
10	0.014	0.063	0.345	0.504	0.074
12	0.030	0.105	0.416	0.411	0.038
14	0.060	0.158	0.457	0.307	0.018
16	0.109	0.216	0.457	0.210	0.008
18	0.183	0.267	0.416	0.131	0.003

Note:
Sum of row probabilities may not add to 1.000 due to rounding.

Source: Authors' calculations based on Table 5.6, column 3.

The data in Table 5.7 illustrate clearly the marked improvement in English-speaking skills with educational attainment. Few of the least educated (eight or fewer years of schooling) are predicted to speak English only or have English as their best spoken language, and only four per cent are proficient in English under the 'proficient'/'not proficient' distinction introduced above. Fully 70 per cent have extremely limited English skills ('not well' or 'not at all'). In comparison, among those with 18 years of education, the predictions indicate that 18 per cent speak English only or English best, and a further 27 per cent speak a language other than English at home and speak English 'very well'. Only 13 per cent are in the most limited English skills categories. The improvements in English skills with level of education are shown to be associated with a rapid decline in the 'not at all' category, and an equally pronounced shift away from the 'not well' category. Up to 16 years of education, additional years of schooling are associated with greater representation in the middle of the distribution, the 'speaks English well' category.

The patterns described in Table 5.6 are reasonably well known, being fully consistent with the growing body of literature on the determinants of immigrants' dominant language skills (see Chiswick and Miller 1992a, 1995, 1998a). However, the literature has largely been based on cross-sectional data, and the Table 5.6 analyses have mimicked this approach to facilitate the comparisons made. The remainder of this chapter shows the insights that can be gained from following immigrants through time via a longitudinal study. As noted previously, the panel used is quite short, being three years for the first cohort from the LSIA and only one year for the second cohort. Nevertheless, given the limited availability of longitudinal data sets, the analyses can be instructive, not only for the results obtained but also for the insights that can be offered into future data collection needs. Moreover, the numerous cross-sectional studies for several countries (United States, Canada, Israel, as well as Australia) indicate that the annual improvement in language skills is greatest during the first few years in the destination.

Table 5.8 presents estimates corresponding to Equation (3). These estimates are for a probit model.[20] The estimates listed for Wave 1 of Cohort 1 are main effects: all other estimates are differences in coefficients for the particular wave of data and cohort. For example, consider the figures in the row for the Humanitarian variable. The first figure, -1.390, is the effect on the probit index for English skills among immigrants in Wave 1 of the first cohort associated with arriving in Australia on a Humanitarian visa compared to arrival on an Independent visa, which is the benchmark. This figure shows that those on a Humanitarian visa have significantly poorer English-speaking skills than the benchmark group. The second figure, 0.468, indicates how this effect differs for these immigrants (Humanitarian versus Independent) one year later at the time of their second interview (there is an increase in the relative English-speaking skills of those arriving under a Humanitarian visa, which is statistically significant, '*t*'=2.91). Similarly, the third figure indicates

Table 5.8 Probit model of English-speaking skills, 15–64 year old males and females from non-English-speaking countries

Variable (X_i)	Cohort 1			Cohort 2	
	$\beta_1 X_i$	$\delta_2 W2_i X_i$	$\delta_3 W3_i X_i$	$\varphi_1 LSIA2_i X_i$	$\varphi_2 LSIA2_i W2_i X_i$
Constant/wave/cohort effects	-1.987 (8.91)	1.210 (3.70)	1.781 (4.76)	1.625 (1.95)	2.568 (3.93)
Visa category					
Humanitarian	-1.390 (13.08)	0.468 (2.91)	0.655 (3.69)	-0.439 (1.79)	-0.759 (1.79)
Family	-0.943 (7.58)	0.046 (0.25)	0.174 (0.90)	-1.016 (3.54)	-1.406 (3.14)
SAS	-0.619 (5.34)	0.104 (0.59)	0.280 (1.44)	0.170 (0.65)	-0.307 (0.69)
BS/ENS[a]	-0.985 (6.09)	0.101 (0.41)	0.173 (0.64)	-0.422 (1.52)	-1.095 (2.43)
Age at migration	-0.006 (2.24)	-0.012 (3.02)	-0.027 (6.26)	-0.021 (3.45)	-0.026 (4.08)
Education	0.190 (22.29)	-0.006 (0.47)	0.014 (1.07)	-0.031 (2.00)	0.013 (0.74)
Female	-0.106 (2.04)	0.024 (0.32)	-0.087 (1.04)	0.119 (1.13)	0.107 (0.93)
Cross culture/country contact in former home country	0.304 (6.31)	-0.045 (0.64)	0.001 (0.02)	0.126 (1.26)	0.309 (2.79)
Previously visited Australia	0.494 (3.18)	0.313 (1.85)	0.166 (0.96)	0.329 (2.79)	0.593 (2.99)
Main reason for choosing state settled was family/friends	-0.237 (3.34)	-0.026 (0.24)	-0.065 (0.56)	0.032 (0.24)	-0.047 (0.31)
Contact with ethnic agencies	-0.234 (3.32)	-0.077 (0.75)	0.110 (1.04)	0.540 (3.33)	0.496 (2.66)
Expect to stay in Australia	0.351 (3.15)	-0.324 (1.94)	-0.052 (2.38)	0.012 (0.02)	-0.375 (1.09)
Family structure					
MUS[b]	-0.164 (1.97)	-0.050 (0.41)	-0.051 (0.38)	0.005 (0.03)	-0.190 (0.88)
OS[c]	-0.056 (0.60)	0.095 (0.74)	0.190 (1.47)	0.347 (1.65)	0.005 (0.02)
KIDS[d]	-0.120 (2.08)	-0.136 (1.67)	-0.051 (0.57)	-0.253 (2.20)	-0.126 (1.09)
MUR[e]	0.071 (0.57)	-0.256 (1.48)	0.226 (1.34)	-0.246 (0.98)	-0.326 (1.34)
OR[f]	-0.285 (2.00)	-0.219 (2.01)	0.031 (0.20)	0.079 (0.72)	0.189 (2.08)

Table 5.8 (continued)

Variable (X_i)	Cohort 1			Cohort 2	
	$\beta_1 X_i$	$\delta_2 W2_i X_i$	$\delta_3 W3_i X_i$	$\varphi_1 LSIA2_i X_i$	$\varphi_2 LSIA2_i W2_i X_i$
Birthplace					
Oceania/Antarctica	2.362	-0.391	-0.914	-0.871	-1.083
	(10.07)	(1.10)	(2.59)	(2.25)	(2.41)
Middle East and	0.033	0.113	0.127	-0.146	0.011
North Africa	(0.40)	(0.95)	(0.98)	(0.92)	(0.06)
Southeast Asia	0.495	-0.327	-0.544	-0.111	-0.496
	(7.16)	(3.24)	(1.99)	(0.75)	(2.94)
Northeast Asia	-0.381	-0.034	-0.201	-0.638	-0.656
	(4.88)	(0.29)	(1.55)	(3.98)	(3.67)
Southern and Central	0.807	-0.022	-0.285	-0.040	-0.336
Asia	(8.72)	(0.16)	(1.90)	(0.21)	(1.53)
South/Central America	-0.380	0.027	0.152	0.225	0.201
and Caribbean	(2.45)	(0.23)	(0.59)	(0.70)	(0.58)
Other Africa (Sub-	1.019	-0.023	-0.164	-0.235	-0.287
Saharan Africa)	(6.77)	(0.10)	(0.60)	(0.90)	(0.95)

For notes, see Table 5.6.

how the impact differs for the same group of immigrants a further two years later, at the time of their third interview (a larger improvement in the relative English-speaking skills of those arriving under a Humanitarian visa, which is highly significant, '*t*'=3.69).

The fourth figure of -0.439 shows how the links between Humanitarian visas and English skills differ between immigrants from the second cohort after approximately six months' residence in Australia and their counterparts in the first cohort after a similar length of time. It shows that there is a relatively larger gap between the English-speaking skills of those on Humanitarian visas and the Independent visaed immigrants in the second cohort, but this is statistically significant only at the 10 per cent level ('*t*'=1.79). Finally, the fifth figure records the difference in the links between Humanitarian visas and English skills for immigrants in Cohort 2 at the time of their second interview compared to Cohort 1, Wave 1. This shows a slight worsening of relative position, which is at the margin of statistical significance ('*t*'=1.79). All other entries in this table are to be read and interpreted in this way.

There are six features of results in the Table 5.8.

First, English skills improve with increases in immigrants' duration of residence in Australia, as reflected in the positive coefficients on the wave shift factors (listed in the row for the constant term). Most of this improvement appears to occur during the initial settlement period, with the difference between Wave 3 and Wave 2 being statistically insignificant.

Second, the second cohort of immigrants had, on average, greater proficiency in English than the members of the first cohort at arrival in Australia, but showed less rapid improvement over the interval between the first and second interviews. Given the way the interaction terms are specified in Equation (3), the improvement for the second cohort is given by the difference between the figures in the final two columns. Thus, 2.57 – 1.62 = 0.95, which is smaller than 1.2. A negative relationship between initial levels of English skills and subsequent improvements is the typical finding in the literature.

Third, among the first cohort, immigrants who entered Australia under a Humanitarian visa improved their English skills vis-à-vis Independent-visaed immigrants with increases in their length of residence in Australia, but they still exhibited a lower level of proficiency in English. Among the other visa categories, relative changes in English skills with duration of residence were not significant.

Fourth, the interaction terms for Cohort 2 show that most visa groups in this cohort have English skills that are relatively inferior to those of the Independent-visaed groups. Or put another way, relative to the other categories, Independent-category immigrants in Cohort 2 are more proficient in English than the same visa group in Cohort 1. The interaction terms for Skilled – Australian Sponsored immigrants in Cohort 2 are, however, insignificant. This implies that their position relative to that of Independent-visaed immigrants remained the same as it was among immigrants in Cohort 1. It improved, however, relative to the other three classes of immigrants in Cohort 2 compared to Cohort 1. Thus, the analysis reveals, in Cohort 2 compared to Cohort 1, a widening of the difference between the English skills of immigrants who were points-tested and those who were not points-tested for entry into Australia.

Fifth, among the other characteristics included in the model of English proficiency, only three have effects that differ across waves or cohorts. The age at migration variable is consistently associated with negative interaction effects. That is, the older an immigrant at the time of arrival in Australia, the poorer their English language skills and the less likely they are to improve their English skills with increases in the duration of their residence in Australia. This effect is more pronounced for members of the second cohort than it is for members of the first cohort. The positive impact of having previously visited Australia on English proficiency is more pronounced, and more persistent, for immigrants in the second cohort than it is for immigrants in the first cohort. Finally, the birthplace fixed effects suggest that the European/USSR reference group tends to improve their relative standing with increases in the duration of their residence in Australia. They also have relatively superior English skills in the second cohort than in the first.

A sixth finding is the lower reported English language proficiency for women in Cohort 1, Wave 1, which does not diminish with duration of residence in Australia or change in the Cohort 2.

What do these results mean for the interpretation of the impact of immigration policy on the English-speaking skills of immigrants?

The main implication is that between Cohorts 1 and 2, the English skills of Independent-visaed immigrants have improved markedly. The English skills of the Skilled – Australian Sponsored group have also improved. These are the groups of immigrants directly affected by the changes in the points tests documented in Chapter 1. Moreover, in Cohort 2, the gaps between the English skills of immigrants who were points-tested for entry into Australia and other immigrants widen over the first few years in Australia, rather than narrow as was the case for immigrants in Cohort 1.

Of course, part of these apparent policy effects might be associated with individual fixed effects. Whether these should be netted out of the estimates is a moot point, as these might be exactly the factors on which the immigration process is selecting. The importance of the individual fixed effects was examined using a linear probability model.

The results from this approach[21] show that the apparent improvement in English skills with increases in the length of residence in Australia is reduced, though evidence of marked improvement remains. The estimated differentials in English proficiency associated with visa category are compressed for Cohort 1. However, in Cohort 2, the control for fixed effects is associated with a compression of the differentials in English proficiency across the points-tested visa categories, and a widening of the differentials in English proficiency among the non-points-tested visa categories. The control for fixed effects is also associated with a widening of the differential in English proficiency between the points-tested and non-points-tested categories in Cohort 2, and with a slight diminution in this differential in Cohort 1.

A final examination of the effects of immigration policy involved splitting the Independent-visaed immigrants in the second cohort into two sub-categories. The first of these comprises the post-July 1999 visa category (sub-class 136). These immigrants were processed under the more stringent language requirements outlined in Chapter 1. The second comprises all other Independent immigrants, who would have had their immigration applications assessed under the earlier criteria. Estimation of the probit specification of Table 5.8 reveals, however, no significant differences between the English skills of these two classes of immigrants. In part this might be due to the almost universal English language proficiency of the different groups of Independent immigrants.

Table 5.9 presents a summary of the findings from this analysis.

Table 5.9 indicates that cohort effects have substantial positive effects on English language skills in this analysis. A difference between differences approach can be applied to the findings in Table 5.9 to assess the impact of changes to the ORE list, and of the introduction of points for English skills among the Skilled – Australian Sponsored immigrants.

Table 5.9 Quantification of the role of English language ability in immigrant selection in LSIA Cohort 1 and Cohort 2

Cohort 1 compared to Cohort 2

Visa category	Differences between cohorts measures	Impact on probit index of (2)[a]	Implications of impact in (3)
(1)	(2)	(3)	(4)
Non-points-tested (Family, Humanitarian)	Cohort effects	Positive effect of between 0.609 and 1.203	Cohort effects give improvement in English skills
Independent	Impact of changes in ORE[b] list + cohort effects	Positive effect of 1.625	Both cohort effects and changes in ORE are associated with improvements in English skills
Skilled – Australian Sponsored	Impact of points for English ability + impact of change in ORE list + cohort effects	Positive effect of 1.795 on probit index	Points for English ability as well as cohort effects and changes in ORE associated with improvement in English skills

Pre- and post-July 1999 Cohort 2

Visa category	Difference between pre- and post-July 1999 Cohorts	Impact on probit index of (2)	Implications of impact in (3)
(1)	(2)	(3)	(4)
Independent	Impact of minimum English threshold	Minimal, if any impact	Change not of any consequence

Notes:
a From the column headed $\varphi_1 LSIA2_i X_i$ in Table 5.8;
b ORE = Occupations Requiring English.

Comparison of the second and first rows of Table 5.9 (that is, Independent versus non-points-tested immigrants) reveals the impact of changes to the ORE list. This is positive, and quantitatively as important as the cohort effects given in the first row of the table. Comparison of the third and second rows (that is, Skilled – Australian Sponsored versus Independent immigrants) reveals the impact of the introduction of points for English skills among the Skilled – Australian Sponsored immigrants. This is shown to be positive, but quite minor. Nevertheless, the conclusion that needs to be drawn from this analysis is that immigration policy can affect immigrants' language skills.

The estimates: Migrating Unit Spouses

Finally, the determinants of English-speaking proficiency among Migrating Unit Spouses were examined. These spouses were assigned the same visa category as the Principal Applicant. In addition, several other variables – for example, the main reason for choosing state settled being family or friends, and whether there had been post-arrival contact with ethnic agencies – were not available for the Migrating Unit Spouses. In these cases information provided by the Principal Applicant was used.

The general patterns in the results for Migrating Unit Spouses are similar to those described above for Principal Applicants, and only brief comments on the links between English-speaking skills and visa categories are provided here.[22]

The ranking of English-speaking skills across visa categories for Migrating Unit Spouses is the same as it is for Principal Applicants, although the language skills of the two points-tested categories (Independent and Skilled – Australian Sponsored) do not differ significantly in the case of Migrating Unit Spouses. The similarity in the ranking for Principal Applicants and their Migrating Unit Spouses presumably comes about through assortative mating (on measured and unmeasured factors) and the complementarities in the learning of English among family members that has been emphasised by Chiswick, Lee and Miller (2005a, 2005b).

The differences in English language proficiency across visa categories among the first cohort of Migrating Unit Spouses (MUS) do not vary with duration in Australia. Non-points-tested immigrants (Humanitarian, Family) among the second cohort have relatively poorer English-speaking skills than was the case among the first cohort. The superior English skills of the spouses of points-tested immigrants imply a double advantage to an immigration policy that favours Principal Applicants with superior English language skills.

SUMMARY AND CONCLUSION

Immigrants' language skills are important for understanding the determinants of their economic well-being. The analyses above provide an account of the dynamics of the processes through which immigrants acquire the English language skills that have been shown in previous research to be of fundamental importance to their economic well-being. It does this by exploiting several features of the Longitudinal Survey of Immigrants to

Australia (LSIA). First, in this survey, unlike census data, the visa classes of the immigrants are known. Second, information is available for two cohorts of immigrants: the first representative of arrivals between 1993 and 1995; the second representative of arrivals between 1999 and 2000. The first panel was followed for 3.5 years after arrival and the second for 1.5 years. The changes in the role of English language skills in immigrant selection affected some visa classes, but not others, over this time period. This permits an assessment of the effect of immigrant selection policy on the English language skills of immigrants.

There are clear differences across visa classes in the English language skills of immigrants at the time of arrival. Specifically, immigrants who entered Australia under points-tested visa categories (Independent and Skilled – Australian Sponsored) have English-language skills superior to the skills of immigrants in the non-points-tested categories (Family and Humanitarian based visas). Humanitarian visaed immigrants have quite limited English skills at arrival. The English skills of all immigrants improve with time spent in Australia, with the most rapid improvement being experienced by the visa groups with the poorest skills at arrival.

The English skills of immigrants in the second arrival cohort (1999–2000) are, in general, superior to those in the first arrival cohort, with the differences being greater for immigrants in the points-tested categories. It was in these categories that there was an increase in the English language requirements for a visa.

These broad patterns are evident in both cross-tabulations (Tables 5.3 and 5.5) and in the multivariate statistical analyses that follow a standard cross-sectional approach (Table 5.6). The statistical analyses also identify a set of variables that influence the English language skills of immigrants. The variables that have negative impacts on immigrants' English proficiency are age at migration, being a female, the presence of family and friends as the main factor influencing location decisions, and living with other immigrant family members. The variables that have positive impacts on immigrants' English proficiency are educational attainment, having cross-country/culture contact in the former home country, having previously visited Australia, an expectation of staying in Australia, and duration of residence in Australia.

The detailed statistical analyses that exploited the longitudinal dimension of the data set (Table 5.8) employed a difference between differences approach that enables the impact of immigrant selection policy to be quantified. This showed that the various expansions to the Occupation Requiring English (ORE) list have had a marked impact on the English language skills of points-tested immigrants. It also revealed that the introduction of points for English skills among the Skilled – Australian Sponsored immigrants in 1997 had a relatively minor effect.

Thus, it is readily apparent that immigration policy can affect immigrants' language skills, and hence both their initial economic success in Australia and the speed of their subsequent adjustment. This effect occurs both directly, in terms of the higher levels of proficiency among Principal Applicants, and indirectly, via the superior language skills of the spouses of points-tested immigrants. Given the positive links between the English skills of parents and children documented in Chiswick, Lee and Miller (2005b), the overall effect of these government policy changes will be more favourable than documented here. Having a minimum threshold such as in the ORE list, or the core criteria of the July 1999 reforms, appears to be a more effective policy instrument than simply using English as one of a number of attributes attracting points. This is a major lesson that other governments could learn from Australia's 'natural experiments' reported on here.

NOTES

1 The names of the visa categories have changed over time. For example, the Skilled – Australian Sponsored category was formerly termed the Skilled – Australian Linked category, and before that the Concessional Family category. The names in place in the late 1990s are used in this study. A brief history of the evolution of the visa categories during this period is provided in Chapter 1.

2 The spouses of Principal Applicants in the points tested categories may have been indirectly affected by this policy change, as points were now awarded when the spouse met certain core requirements.

3 Potential immigrants can be viewed as seeking the 'cheapest/easiest' visa they can obtain. In the Skilled – Australian Sponsored group, this is formally recognized in the processing of applications, with the points for spouses being compared and the higher score used.

4 See Department of Immigration and Multicultural Affairs (1999), Attachment A, reproduced in part in Table 5.1.

5 It is noted that the changes in language requirements could have had an impact on the mix of immigrant source countries, as immigrants from the United States, United Kingdom and Canada presumably would have found it easier to meet the entrance requirements. However, changes in source countries due to this reason cannot be disentangled from changes due to other reasons.

6 Persons born in the English-speaking developed countries (New Zealand, United Kingdom, United States and Canada) are excluded from the data.

7 A similar pattern of an inverse relationship between the initial level and the subsequent increase is found for immigrant earnings – see, for example, Chiswick (1979).

8 Complete results are available from the authors upon request.

9 This is the measure of proficiency introduced above when discussing Tables 5.3 to 5.5. It is noted that this involves aggregating some of the underlying language categories, and may be seen as involving a loss of information. However, Kominski (1989, p.336) has observed in relation to United States Census language data on how well individuals speak English that 'The data do not detail a firm discrimination between the four different categories of the 'how well' question, but there are clear differences between the very best speakers of English and the very worst'. This suggests that the use of the binary indicator will not be a major limitation.

10 This should not be seen as a limitation, as the analyses reported by Chiswick, Lee and Miller (2003a, 2005a, 2006), and by Chiswick and Miller (1996, 1999), show that the birthplace-

related variables have limited explanatory power in analyses for Australia, once country of birth fixed effects are included in the analysis.

11 Another efficiency variable is the extent of the difference between the origin language and English. This behavioural variable is not used in the current study as many of its effects are captured by the birthplace variables. For a development of this work, see Chiswick and Miller (2005).

12 Variable definitions are available from the authors on request.

13 Chiswick and Miller (1998b), for example, report that up to 15 per cent of a group of legalized aliens in the United States who reported that they could read or speak English in specific situations indicated that they could not do so three years later. It could not be determined whether this was an actual deterioration in skills, a change in the reference point as to what is speaking very well or well, or merely measurement error in either situation.

14 Person-specific fixed effects can also be incorporated into this model through the addition of the term $\lambda\mu_i$. The probit fixed effects model can, however, only be estimated on a sub-sample comprising individuals who change language state across waves of data collection. Given this limitation, only brief comments from the application of fixed effects estimators will be provided.

15 The estimated coefficients from the three models listed in Table 5.6 are not numerically comparable. However, given that the partial effect for the kth variable in the probit model is given as $\phi(X\beta)\beta_k$, broad comparisons can be drawn between the estimates for the OLS model (which record marginal effects) and the probit model with the approximation: $\widehat{\beta}_{LP} = a\widehat{\beta}_{\phi}$, where $\widehat{\beta}_{LP}$ denotes the estimates of the parameters for the linear probability (OLS) model, $\widehat{\beta}_{\phi}$ is the estimates of the parameters for the probit model and a is the probability distribution function for the standard normal evaluated at an index that equates to the mean level of English proficiency in the sample. For this sample, an appropriate value of a is 0.375.

16 The variable that records whether a spouse who was not part of the migrating unit is present in the household is statistically insignificant across all estimating models. The benchmark marital status category is not being currently married.

17 Except for the estimated coefficient of variable on 'Middle East and North Africa' in the OLS model.

18 See SAS Institute Inc (1994) for details on the test implemented.

19 These predictions are calculated at the mean values for all variables in the ordered probit model other than educational attainment.

20 Estimates from OLS and ordered probit models corresponding to Equation (3) are available from the authors.

21 Available from the authors on request.

22 Further analysis available from the authors on request.

6. Immigrant Health in the Period After Arrival in Australia

Steven Kennedy and James Ted McDonald

INTRODUCTION

It is well accepted that most immigrants are healthier than their native-born compatriots with similar characteristics, despite that many immigrants come from poorer countries than the country to which they are migrating (see for example, McDonald and Kennedy 2004, Perez 2002, Jasso et al. 2004). This is true of immigrants in Australia as well, where the 'healthy immigrant' effect is well known and has been documented in a number of studies including those by Biddle et al. (2004), Mathers (2003), Australian Institute of Health and Welfare (2002), Strong et al. (1998) and Donovan et al. (1992). However, it is also becoming increasingly well known that after arrival in their new country of residence, immigrants experience a quicker deterioration in their health than native-born residents. Biddle et al. (2004) show that for most immigrants to Australia after about 20 years the health gap – the degree to which they are healthier than the native born – has mostly dissipated, although there is considerable variation by country of birth. For example, immigrants from Asia and other non-English speaking countries tend to exhibit a larger health gap and slower decline in health with years in Australia than other immigrants.

The processes that might be driving the immigrant native-born health gap and subsequent deterioration in immigrant health can be considered in four groups. First, there are those explanations that relate to immigrant selection effects. Selection effects can be associated with observable factors that make immigrants more likely than the average person in the source country to migrate, such as higher education or language skills. Jasso et al. (2004) present a simple theoretical model where the decision to migrate reflects the extent to which (income) gains from migration exceed the costs. In such a model, the decision to migrate will depend on the 'skill' level of migrants and the returns to skill across countries. For example, the model suggests that more highly skilled migrants will come from countries where the costs of migration are high. Furthermore, because health is likely to be associated with skill, selection on skill is likely to be associated with selection on health. However, for some groups of migrants, older persons for example, these effects might be small. Selection effects could also relate to unobservable factors – such as more motivated people tending to migrate – and so relate to the prospective returns from migrating. Selection effect models suggest variations in health levels for different migrant groups, although they do not directly inform the subsequent trajectory in health.

Related to this, health policies associated with the application to migrate might also be an important factor. In this case, simply having a health test that potential immigrants must pass before migration could explain why immigrants are healthier than the native-born, since those individuals who expect to pass the test would be most likely to apply, ceteris paribus. Australian immigration health policies are described in more detail in the next section.

A second set of explanations for the immigrant health gap and health trajectories relate to behaviours adopted in the new country. McDonald and Kennedy (2005) find that most immigrants to Canada have a lower prevalence of obesity on arrival in Canada but that gradually over time this prevalence approximates the native-born level. They also find that there is substantial variation in obesity rates by country of birth, and ethnic networks play an important role. In this chapter variation in immigrant health trajectories is examined by visa category and region of origin in order to gain insights into the trajectories of health following migration. If it is the case that the adoption of behaviours in the new country drives the subsequent trajectories of health, then immigrants who come to Australia from vastly different environments might exhibit different trajectories from those who come from similar countries, particularly if the time to convergence to native-born levels is the same across immigrant groups. However, it is difficult to predict the effects of the adoption of new behaviours on very different immigrant groups and a full understanding requires a direct examination of immigrant health behaviours. Understanding how immigrant health changes with time in a new country also offers unique insights into how the Australian physical and social environment might affect health and therefore has health policy implications not only for immigrants but also for the general population.

The third set of explanations for the healthy immigrant effect reflects what could broadly be called measurement issues. In most health datasets, health conditions are self-reported, and this is the case for the data used in this chapter. It could be the case that as immigrants adjust to their new environment and interact with the health system, they become aware of illnesses that they were not aware of previously. As for health behaviours, if this were an important factor behind the relatively fast decline in immigrant health, variation across different immigrant groups would be expected, reflecting variations in the health systems from which they migrated and how these systems compare with Australia. In this chapter two measures of health, self-assessed health status and prevalence of chronic disease, are analysed. Both measures can be thought of primarily as measures of physical health although the prevalence of chronic disease, in particular, should reflect diagnosing-of-disease related factors.

The fourth category of explanations relates to the provision of health services and health policies. For example, if it were the case that immigrants have more difficulty accessing health services than native-born persons, their health would be expected to deteriorate relatively more quickly. Once again, variations among immigrant groups would also be expected if this factor is indeed influential, with those immigrant groups that do not speak English likely to have more difficulties accessing services than those who do. LeClere et al. (1994) find evidence of a health-service-access effect in a study of immigrants to the United States.

In this chapter, variations in immigrant health in the period immediately after arrival in Australia are explored using the two Longitudinal Survey of Immigrants to Australia (LSIA) cohorts. In particular, the focus of our study is on how health varies for different groups of immigrants during their first 18 months in Australia. There are two particular advantages to using the LSIA data. First, since the LSIA is longitudinal, health changes over time are able to be tracked for specific persons, rather than having to rely on synthetic cohort analysis; and secondly, unlike other datasets the LSIA has information on the visa category in which individuals migrated, as well as data on their education and language skills at migration. The study also explores how immigrant health varies across different arrival cohorts. The particular arrival period for the immigrant cohort will reflect different macroeconomic conditions that might exert a direct effect on immigrant health through, for example, stress about employment opportunities that might be limited owing to recent arrival in Australia. As well, the arrival period will reflect immigration policy in terms of number and composition of immigrant inflows. Thus, any observed differences in health outcomes across immigrant cohorts might also reflect factors related to immigrant selection by the Australian Government.

The study does not directly address the question of why immigrants are healthier on arrival in Australia than are their native-born compatriots. However, in providing information on how immigrant health changes with time in Australia and documenting the factors associated with poor health, insights are provided into what might be driving the health gap between immigrants and the native born. Furthermore, variations in health across immigrant groups will suggest what factors are affecting immigrant health and its subsequent decline, and guide public health policies that might ameliorate the relatively rapid decline in immigrant health.

This study finds evidence of substantial differences in the initial level of immigrant health, with immigrants from skill-related visa categories being substantially healthier than are those from non-skill related categories, even after controlling for the main immigrant selection criteria of age, education, and language ability. It also finds that for most immigrants health does deteriorate in the 18 months after arrival in Australia, even after allowing for other factors that are associated with changes in health such as ageing and economic circumstances. Notably, the decline in health is found to be similar for immigrants from different visa categories, with different English language speaking abilities, and for different regions of origin. The only significant exception is for self-assessed health status by visa category in the first cohort. This result provides some evidence against a number of theories put forward to explain why health deteriorates after arrival in Australia, including persistent barriers to access of health services and improved diagnosis of disease. The results presented are ambiguous in relation to the convergence in lifestyle choices related to health, such as diet, exercise and smoking. It is also found that while there are changes in health measures between the two cohorts, the changes are not consistent across different measures of health.

AUSTRALIAN IMMIGRATION HEALTH POLICY

All immigrants to Australia, including the spouses of Principal Applicants, must pass a set of health tests. The objective of the health tests as described by the Department of Immigration and Multicultural and Indigenous Affairs (DIMIA 2005) is to 'minimise the risks to public health in the Australian community; contain public expenditures on health and community services; protect access by Australians to health and community services'. The extent to which the outcome of the health test bears on the outcome of the application to migrate varies by visa status. For example, the health requirements for 'some close family members or humanitarian applicants' can be waived as long as the persons do not represent a public health risk (DIMIA 2005). The decision to waive aspects of the health tests is that of the Minister for Immigration. It is not the decision of the examining Medical Officer.

While some immigrants may be able to migrate despite being somewhat less healthy than others, exactly the same sets of health tests are applied to all immigrants. The only disease that precludes migration is tuberculosis and even in this case, as long as immigrants are treated on their arrival in Australia they can still migrate.

According to DIMIA, the decision regarding the health requirement, aside from the public health risk, goes primarily to the potential cost to Australia of possible health related services. The decision is made by the Medical Officer conducting the test and other immigration officials cannot overrule the recommendation of the Medical Officer. Although, as noted earlier, the Minister can choose to waive a negative health test result, a positive assessment cannot be overruled, nor can the application be questioned on health grounds if the Medical Officer's assessment is positive.

There were no changes to the health tests for immigrants over the periods in which Cohorts 1 and 2 were surveyed. In fact, there have been no changes to the health tests since the mid 1970s, when health tests were tightened with the introduction of Medicare.

In the context of health service use, Kliewer and Butler (1995) find that immigrants to Australia use fewer health services than do other Australians. Unfortunately, there are no publicly available statistics on applications to migrate to Australia that have been rejected because of failed health tests, so it is difficult to evaluate the extent to which the health requirements are binding. Laroche (2000) finds that the prevalence of rejected applications because of health tests is quite small for Canada, and with the health tests for Australia and Canada being similar the effect may also be small for Australia.

MODELLING IMMIGRANT HEALTH

There are a number of approaches to translating individual characteristics and economic factors into health outcomes but by far the most common in the health economics literature is Grossman's (1972) health capital model. In this model, individuals maximise their lifetime utility with respect to wealth, time, and technical constraints. The arguments of the utility function are healthy time and other goods. As this is a household production model, individuals produce these goods under the technical constraints of production functions, where market goods and time are used to produce health investment, and market goods and time are also used to produce other goods. Optimisation takes place in the face of wealth and time constraints. In this model, health is a capital stock that depreciates over time, but can be increased through investment. Thus, health is both an investment good and a consumption good, as individuals consume health (healthy time) directly as well as invest in health to increase future returns from the health capital stock.

The difficulties in translating this model into data are many, but the most profound lies in finding data on health inputs and prices that vary across individuals. Thus, much research augments the Grossman style health production function and takes on a more descriptive approach. In many analyses health is simply a function of individual characteristics and economic factors such as income. The major difficulty in this approach is the obvious endogeneity that is present between variables such as income and health (Ettner 1996, Smith 1999).

An alternative to the production function approach to modelling health is the 'population health perspective', for example, as discussed by Dunn and Dyck (2000). This approach focuses on the social and economic characteristics of individuals and populations when examining health. It has much in common with augmented Grossman health production functions and is the approach used in this chapter. While it is difficult to identify causal effects using these descriptive approaches, one can still carefully piece together associations between health and individual and economic characteristics, and parcel out the associations of various variables.

In line with the population health approach taken in this chapter, immigrant health is examined using three sets of characteristics. The first (and the main focus of this study) is a set of immigrant characteristics that includes visa category, region of origin, English-speaking ability, and whether the immigrant is the Principal Applicant or accompanying spouse. In many studies of immigrant health information on visa category is not available and can only be captured indirectly through country of birth and arrival cohort variables. Being able to follow the health experiences of immigrants disaggregated by visa category is a significant feature of this research and enhances the relevance of the results to policy makers who typically think of immigration policy in terms of visa groupings. Furthermore, distinct variations in the health of immigrants migrating to Australia under different types of visas are expected, particularly given the manner in which the importance of the health test varies for different visa categories. For example, the Minister has the power to waive negative health tests outcomes for Humanitarian immigrants but this does not apply to immigrants entering under skilled migration visa categories. Variations in the health of immigrants by region might also be expected. One source of this variation is likely to be the general economic conditions and effectiveness of the health system in immigrants' home countries. An immigrant's ability to speak the language of the new country of residence might also affect his health and subsequent health trajectories, particularly the ways in which this may affect his interaction with the Australian health system.

Individual characteristics such as age, gender, marital status and education form the second set of characteristics used to model health. Not surprisingly, (physical) health declines with age and while the mortality rate is usually higher for males than for females, females generally report poorer health than males. Marital status in part reflects the support immigrants will receive should they fall ill, and it is often found that married persons report better health than single persons but particularly separated or divorced persons. Also, education is known to be strongly related to health, with those with higher education reporting significantly better health (Grossman and Kaestner 1997).

The third set of characteristics used to model health is economic in nature. Variables included here are household income and labour force status. The difficulty in using these variables to explore health variation is that not only are they likely to affect health but also health may affect them, particularly in the longer run (for example, if persistent health problems result in early retirement from the workforce). A typical strategy to alleviate this problem would be to use instrumental variables; however, finding suitable instruments is extremely difficult. In this study, these variables are included so at least their association with health can be examined and their influence on health is partly controlled for when examining the relationship between health and other variables.

THE DATA AND MEASURES OF HEALTH

The focus of this chapter is on all (adult) immigrants, including Principal Applicants and Migrating Unit Spouses (MUS) of Principal Applicants, in both LSIA cohorts. Health is measured in two ways. The first measure is based on self-reports of chronic disease. In the LSIA, respondents were asked if they had any long term health conditions that restricted physical activity or work. A long term health condition is defined to be any condition that has lasted or is likely to last six months. A dichotomous variable is constructed, which equals 1 when one or more chronic diseases are reported or 0 otherwise. Chronic diseases include arthritis or rheumatism, hearing problems or deafness, blindness or impaired vision, nerves or stress problems, heart disorder, loss of limb or any other part of the body, diabetes, hepatitis or other liver disorders, asthma, tuberculosis, any permanent loss of memory or loss of mental ability, kidney disorder and any other long term condition that restricts physical activities or doing work.

The second measure of health is self-assessed health status where the respondent is asked: 'Over the last four weeks, in general has your health been very good, good, fair, poor or very poor?' In this study, a dichotomous variable is derived from self-assessed health status where the responses fair, poor or very poor are coded as 1 and the responses very good and good as 0. Hereafter a score of 1 on the dichotomous variable version of self-assessed health status is referred to as poor health. Self-assessed health status is a well accepted measure of health and has been found to be a good predictor of morbidity and mortality (see Idler and Kasl 1995 and McCallum et al. 1994). For a discussion of the measurement issues that may arise with modelling health using self-assessed health status, (see Crossley and Kennedy 2002).

The non-health variables used in this study and the descriptive features of the LSIA cohorts are discussed in the Technical Appendix.

Descriptive statistics

In Tables 6.1 and 6.2 the prevalence rate of chronic disease and the percentage of immigrants reporting poor health status for the Principal Applicants and Migrating Unit Spouses for each wave and cohort are presented by gender, visa category, region of origin and English-speaking ability.[1] The prevalence of chronic disease clearly increases between six and 18 months in Australia

Table 6.1 Percentages of Principal Applicants with chronic disease or reporting poor health

	Chronic disease				Poor health			
	Cohort 1		Cohort 2		Cohort 1		Cohort 2	
	Wave 1	Wave 2	Wave 1	Wave 2	Wave 1	Wave 2	Wave 1	Wave 2
All	6.6	10.2	8.4	9.9	9.8	13.3	8.2	8.0
Males	5.0	8.3	8.8	10.5	6.2	9.7	7.0	6.0
Females	8.3	12.4	8.1	9.2	13.8	17.3	9.5	10.0
Visa category								
Family	6.9	11.7	8.0	8.7	10.4	13.2	8.3	6.9
Skilled – Australian Sponsored	3.4	6.3	2.9	4.1	4.3	9.7	4.3	4.0
BS/ENS	2.0	5.5	3.4	5.0	5.1	9.0	3.3	5.1
Independent	1.4	2.8	5.3	6.0	4.6	9.1	5.2	5.3
Humanitarian	14.3	16.7	33.1	43.1	18.1	22.0	26.5	31.5
Region of origin								
Oceania/Antarctica	4.7	6.1	2.4	3.6	5.9	5.1	4.6	4.9
Europe & USSR	7.4	11.0	6.2	9.3	7.9	13.0	5.2	4.5
Middle East & North Africa	4.8	11.0	17.5	21.9	7.8	10.2	13.8	16.1
Southeast Asia	10.2	12.7	13.4	12.8	17.9	20.6	15.8	8.4
Northeast Asia	2.3	9.4	5.3	7.1	8.6	10.1	7.6	8.9
Southern Asia	3.2	5.3	7.4	8.1	4.1	10.7	9.0	7.3
North America	8.3	12.9	7.9	9.2	10.6	9.5	5.4	5.5
South/Central America and Caribbean	5.0	5.7	3.6	6.7	7.3	18.3	2.0	13.3
Other Africa	7.5	6.6	9.3	6.1	7.7	8.5	6.7	4.5
English-speaking ability								
English only	6.0	8.6	5.3	6.1	6.0	10.8	5.2	5.8
English well or very well	4.6	6.7	5.7	8.4	6.0	8.9	5.3	5.7
English not well or at all	8.7	16.6	15.3	18.8	16.2	21.6	15.2	15.4

Note:
The sample of Principal Applicants in Cohort 1 was 5,192 and for Cohort 2 was 3,124. Means are calculated from weighted data.

Source: Longitudinal Survey of Immigrants to Australia.

for most groups and for both cohorts. For example, the prevalence of chronic disease in all Principal Applicants in Cohort 1 increases from 6.6 per cent in Wave 1 to 10.2 per cent in Wave 2. The differences by visa categories, in the prevalence of chronic disease between cohorts appear minor, except for Humanitarian immigrants in the second cohort who report a substantially higher prevalence of chronic disease. Richardson et al. (2002a) found that

Table 6.2 Percentages of Migrating Unit Spouses with chronic disease or reporting poor health

	Chronic disease				Reporting poor health			
	Cohort 1		Cohort 2		Cohort 1		Cohort 2	
	Wave 1	Wave 2	Wave 1	Wave 2	Wave 1	Wave 2	Wave 1	Wave 2
All	7.8	9.8	8.4	10.3	9.4	14.6	8.1	10.9
Males	6.6	15.2	6.7	10.8	4.4	11.1	6.3	6.5
Females	8.0	8.6	9.1	10.1	10.5	15.3	8.9	12.7
Visa category								
Family	16.8	20.5	31.2	38.1	11.3	23.0	19.5	22.3
Skilled – Australian Sponsored	2.2	4.6	2.0	5.8	4.4	9.0	4.4	6.02
BS/ENS	2.6	5.6	4.3	5.2	8.6	7.2	6.1	3.9
Independent	1.8	4.1	2.8	1.9	6.7	9.2	4.2	7.7
Humanitarian	16.1	16.0	29.8	36.9	15.6	23.0	24.2	31.5
Region of origin								
Oceania/Antarctica	na	na	na	na	0.0	0.0	4.2	4.9
Europe & USSR	8.7	12.5	6.6	4.3	9.8	14.9	9.3	8.8
Middle East & North Africa	14.9	12.0	26.5	31.7	10.8	15.9	17.9	25.3
Southeast Asia	15.8	13.6	18.0	23.3	19.0	31.5	16.1	29.7
Northeast Asia	2.2	3.6	5.2	4.6	7.1	11.3	6.0	2.6
Southern Asia	3.3	5.6	6.6	13.8	5.2	8.5	6.8	9.2
North America	3.0	2.2	1.5	4.8	7.0	2.6	3.3	6.7
South/Central America & Caribbean	6.0	5.8	0.0	0.0	12.2	3.5	1.2	34.6
Other Africa	3.0	11.1	5.8	5.6	3.3	11.1	4.5	3.5
English-speaking ability								
English only	4.3	8.1	4.5	4.5	5.4	9.5	4.6	8.2
English well or very well	3.6	6.4	3.1	5.6	4.7	8.8	5.1	7.0
English not well or at all	12.9	14.5	17.7	29.2	15.1	24.9	16.0	25.4

Note:
The sample of Migrating Unit Spouses in Cohort 1 was 1,769 and for Cohort 2 was 1,057. Means are calculated from weighted data.

Source: Longitudinal Survey of Immigrants to Australia.

Humanitarian immigrants reported substantially higher levels of psychological distress (as measured by the General Health Questionnaire 12) in Cohort 2 than Cohort 1, which may well go some way to explaining the differences in the prevalence of chronic disease between the two cohorts. Richardson also found that the higher levels of psychological distress in Cohort 2 for Humanitarian immigrants were experienced by immigrants from a range of countries rather than reflecting a higher proportion of immigrants from a particular country.

The pattern of chronic disease prevalence increasing across waves for both cohorts is seen in immigrants from all regions of origin and English-speaking categories. The differences in the prevalence of chronic disease by region and English-speaking ability categories most likely underpin differences in health across visa category. For example, Humanitarian immigrants are likely to have come from regions such as the Middle East and North Africa and immigrants from these regions tend to have relatively poor health.

The fact that the prevalence of chronic disease increases so consistently across waves for nearly all groups of immigrants is a striking result. The interval between Wave 1 and Wave 2 is only one year and, while ageing is likely to explain a part of the increasing prevalence of chronic disease, the regression analysis that follows shows that the greater part of the increase is net of ageing effects.

In addition to the differences in the prevalence of chronic disease between cohorts and across waves, there is substantial variation in the initial level of chronic disease prevalence. As expected, Humanitarian immigrants and, more generally, immigrants in non-skill visa categories tend to report a higher prevalence of chronic disease. This may reflect the degree to which the health tests bear on the applications of different groups of immigrants, with those immigrants from visa categories where the tests are less binding reporting poorer health.

The descriptive statistics for self-assessed health status are broadly similar to those for chronic disease, with health deteriorating with time in Australia for most groups and for both cohorts. For Principal Applicants in Cohort 1, the proportion of immigrants reporting their health as fair, poor or very poor increased from 9.8 per cent in Wave 1 to 13.3 per cent in Wave 2. Self-assessed health status did not deteriorate for Principal Applicants in the second cohort, mostly reflecting an improvement in reported health for males.[2] This is not the case for spouses in Cohort 2 where the pattern of deteriorating health was still evident (Table 6.2). Furthermore, somewhat surprisingly, immigrants in Cohort 2 in general report better self-assessed health status than those in Cohort 1 – although the differences are minor and are in contrast to the results for chronic disease. This issue is explored in more detail in the section examining factors behind declining health.

EMPIRICAL MODELS OF IMMIGRANT HEALTH

To examine in more detail the patterns in health present in the descriptive statistics, regressions are conducted jointly for Principal Applicants and Migrating Unit Spouses.[3] In these regressions, the two measures of health and self-assessed health status are regressed against the three sets of variables described earlier – immigrant characteristics, individual characteristics and economic factors – and Wave 1 and Wave 2 (six and 18 months in Australia).

For chronic disease, probit regressions are estimated in order to determine the effect on the probability of reporting one or more chronic diseases of factors in the three main sets of characteristics outlined above. Results are shown in Table 6.3. In order to observe the change in probability from the probit regressions, marginal effects are calculated for each regression at the mean of continuous variables and for the change in dummy variables. For each regression, tests are conducted on each set of dummy variables to determine whether as a group they are significant. For example, a test is conducted on the inclusion of the set of region dummy variables. In all cases, the sets of dummy variables presented in the regression results are significant.

For both cohorts there is a significant increase in the probability of reporting a chronic disease between Waves 1 and 2 (six and 18 months after arrival) (see Table 6.3). In Cohort 1 the probability of reporting a chronic disease increases by 2.4 percentage points while for Cohort 2 it increases by 3.7 percentage points.

Variations in the probability of reporting a chronic disease by visa category are as for the descriptive results, with Humanitarian immigrants in both cohorts more likely to report a chronic disease. The visa category next most likely to report a chronic disease is the Family stream category. It should be noted that these differences by visa category are present after holding constant English proficiency, education and age, the three of the main determinants for admission to Australia on the points system. Thus, the visa category results are likely to be reflecting unobserved skill or income-based factors relevant to the migration decision and important to health and also the likelihood of waivers of the health requirement in the non-skill visa categories. There are some differences between cohorts, with immigrants in the Humanitarian category in Cohort 2 being around three times more likely to report a chronic disease compared with those in Cohort 1 (when compared with the reference category of Family stream). Furthermore, the immigrants in the categories Skilled – Australian Sponsored, Business Skills/Employer Nomination Scheme and Independent are much less likely to report chronic disease in Cohort 2 compared with the Family stream category than they are in Cohort 1.

Table 6.3 Probit regressions on chronic disease

	Cohort 1		Cohort 2			Cohort 1		Cohort 2	
	Marginal effects	*t* - statistic	Marginal effects	*t* - statistic		Marginal effects	*t* - statistic	Marginal effects	t - statistic
Wave 2	0.024	6.26	0.037	5.49	Higher degree	-0.026	-3.14	-0.024	-1.44
Spouse	-0.007	-1.42	-0.018	-2.2	Postgraduate diploma	-0.025	-2.82	-0.028	-1.46
					Bachelor degree	-0.020	-2.75	-0.026	-1.85
Skilled – Australian Sponsored	-0.014	-2.28	-0.046	-3.36	Technical or professional qualifications	-0.023	-3.33	-0.048	-3.85
BS/ENS	-0.018	-2.57	-0.055	-4.77	Trade	-0.008	-0.86	-0.031	-1.98
Independent	-0.019	-2.85	-0.026	-1.9	More than 12 years of schooling	-0.018	-2.68	-0.038	-2.98
Humanitarian	0.037	5.34	0.099	6.62	10 – 11 years of schooling	-0.021	-2.79	-0.012	-0.74
					7 – 9 years of schooling	-0.002	-0.2	-0.007	-0.45
Oceania/Antarctica	-0.002	-0.15	0.044	1.67					
Middle East & North Africa	-0.002	-0.29	0.002	0.14	Employed	0.000	0.03	-0.056	-3.78
Southeast Asia	0.007	1.26	0.024	1.49	Not in labour force	0.010	1.71	0.007	0.53
Northeast Asia	-0.008	-1.16	-0.011	-0.75					
Southern Asia	-0.017	-2.45	-0.014	-0.96	\$97–\$154 a week	0.024	3.78	0.019	1.46
North America	0.022	1.57	-0.012	-0.74	\$155–\$230 a week	0.011	1.6	0.033	2.65
South/Central America & Caribbean	-0.003	-0.37	0.008	0.49	\$231–\$308 a week	0.004	0.47	-0.009	-0.61
Other Africa	-0.007	-0.96	-0.008	-0.42	\$309–\$385 a week	-0.015	-1.74	-0.007	-0.41
					\$386–\$481 a week	-0.010	-1.14	-0.013	-0.72
English well or very well	-0.013	-2.2	0.005	0.45	\$482–\$577 a week	0.008	0.7	0.019	0.96
English not well or at all	-0.003	-0.55	0.032	2.42	\$578–\$673 a week	0.004	0.3	0.043	1.89
					\$674–\$769 a week	0.006	0.42	0.005	0.21
Age	0.000	0.32	0.006	3.53	\$770–\$962 a week	0.004	0.28	0.018	0.78
Age squared	0.000	2.62	0.000	-0.27	More than \$962 a week	0.009	0.72	0.030	1.39
Female	0.011	2.38	-0.003	-0.34					
Married	-0.002	-0.34	-0.006	-0.55	Number of observations	12,956		7,719	
Widowed/separated/divorced	0.026	2.68	0.014	0.89	Pseudo R squared	0.1577		0.2682	

Note:
Omitted Categories: Wave 1, Family Stream, Europe & USSR, English only, male, never married, six years or less of schooling, unemployed, less than \$96 a week.

Table 6.4 Probit regressions on poor health

	Cohort 1		Cohort 2			Cohort 1		Cohort 2	
	Marginal effects	*t*-statistic	Marginal effects	*t*-statistic		Marginal effects	*t*-statistic	Marginal effects	*t*-statistic
Wave 2	0.035	6.86	0.029	4.56	Higher degree	0.013	0.90	0.001	0.07
Spouse	-0.023	-3.37	-0.014	-1.8	Postgraduate diploma	-0.004	-0.25	-0.027	-1.44
					Bachelor degree	-0.013	-1.21	0.006	0.41
Skilled – Australian Sponsored	-0.011	-1.22	-0.001	-0.06	Technical or professional qualifications	-0.007	-0.67	-0.027	-2.14
BS/ENS	-0.004	-0.43	-0.016	-1.28	Trade	-0.015	-1.06	-0.007	-0.45
Independent	0.004	0.38	0.009	0.66	More than 12 years of schooling	-0.027	-2.61	-0.035	-2.92
Humanitarian	0.062	6.47	0.105	7.08	10–11 years of schooling	-0.010	-0.84	-0.005	-0.36
					7–9 years of schooling	0.002	0.14	0.003	0.20
Oceania/Antarctica	-0.035	-1.85	0.052	1.96					
Middle East & North Africa	-0.009	-1.03	0.024	1.49	Employed	-0.006	-0.56	-0.051	-3.71
Southeast Asia	0.033	4.07	0.022	1.4	Not in labour force	0.007	0.92	-0.018	-1.60
Northeast Asia	0.004	0.48	0.020	1.22					
Southern Asia	-0.015	-1.59	0.015	0.96	$97–$154 a week	0.028	3.36	0.028	2.23
North America	-0.010	-0.56	0.031	1.83	$155–$230 a week	0.018	1.85	0.037	3.05
South/Central America & Caribbean	0.003	0.23	0.004	0.24	$231–$308 a week	0.008	0.79	-0.008	-0.56
Other Africa	-0.023	-2.29	0.008	0.41	$309–$385 a week	0.007	0.56	0.009	0.58
					$386–$481 a week	-0.013	-1.06	0.021	1.22
English well or very well	-0.023	-2.97	-0.018	-1.69	$482–$577 a week	0.018	1.25	0.013	0.74
English not well or at all	0.015	1.73	0.045	3.44	$578–$673 a week	-0.002	-0.09	-0.001	-0.03
					$674–$769 a week	-0.004	-0.20	0.016	0.75
Age	-0.001	-0.50	0.003	1.76	$770–$962 a week	-0.008	-0.50	-0.017	-0.85
Age squared	0.000	2.02	0.000	-0.65	More than $962 a week	0.018	1.12	0.011	0.59
Female	0.057	9.44	0.030	4.10					
Married	-0.001	-0.16	0.010	0.98	Number of observations	12,951		7,719	
Widowed/separated/divorced	0.017	1.38	0.034	2.05	Pseudo R squared	0.0807		0.1566	

Note:
Omitted Categories: Wave 1, Family Stream, Europe & USSR, English only, male, never married, six years or less of schooling, unemployed, less than $96 a week.

The relationship between region or country of birth and chronic disease varies between cohorts. In Cohort 1, immigrants from Northeast and Southern Asia tend to have a lower probability of reporting a chronic disease, although this is not the case for Cohort 2. In general, the effects of region of origin are small compared with other factors, suggesting that the significant differences in immigrant health by region of origin that have been found in other research may in fact be reflecting differences in the distribution of visa classes across regions of origin. For other immigrant characteristics there is also variation between Cohorts 1 and 2. Immigrants in Cohort 2 who speak English poorly, or not at all, are found to have a higher probability (3.2 percentage points) of reporting chronic disease relative to immigrants who speak only English, but this is not the case in Cohort 1. Interestingly, in Cohort 1, immigrants who speak English well or very well actually have a lower probability (1.3 percentage points) of reporting a chronic disease compared with those who only speak English. For both cohorts, spouses have a lower probability of reporting a chronic disease compared with Principal Applicants, although the difference is small and is not significant in Cohort 1.

For the set of individual characteristics the association with chronic disease is largely as expected. The probability of reporting a chronic disease increases with age, is higher for females (although this is only true in Cohort 1) and is higher for immigrants who are widowed, separated or divorced compared with never married (although again true only for Cohort 1). For both cohorts the probability of reporting a chronic disease tends to fall with higher educational qualifications. In fact, the effects of education are very similar for both cohorts and tend to be large in magnitude compared with differences across other characteristics.

The relationship between economic factors and chronic disease is also largely as expected. For Cohort 2, employed immigrants report a lower probability of chronic disease compared with other immigrants. However, this difference is not significant for Cohort 1. The relationship between household income and chronic disease is far less clear for both cohorts although the set of dummy variables is significant in each case.

The probit regression results for self-assessed health status are similar to those for chronic disease (see Table 6.4). As for chronic disease prevalence, self-assessed health status deteriorates for both immigrant cohorts between Waves 1 and 2 (an increase in the probability of reporting poor health of 3.5 and 2.9 percentage points for Cohorts 1 and 2). The decline in self-assessed health status across waves for Cohort 2 is in contrast to the descriptive statistics for Principal Applicants and shows that after controlling for other characteristics the pattern of deterioration in health with time in Australia is consistent across the measures of health.

Immigrant characteristics are similarly associated with self-assessed health status as for chronic disease, with Humanitarian immigrants in both cohorts reporting significantly poorer health. However, the pattern among other immigrant categories is somewhat different with immigrants in the Family stream visa category being no more likely to report poorer health compared with the other non-Humanitarian categories. Immigrants who speak English poorly or not at all tend to report significantly poorer self-assessed health status in both cohorts, although this may be more indicative of factors related to language than health issues. For example, there may be issues in the translation of the health category responses and cultural issues in assessing what is meant by good or fair health.

The relationship between self-assessed health status and region of origin is difficult to discern, although interestingly immigrants from Southeast Asia report poorer self-assessed health status in Cohort 1, as they do for chronic disease. Individual and economic characteristics are, in general, related similarly to self-assessed health status as they are to the prevalence of chronic disease. However, the relationships are not as clear as for chronic health, with education, for example, not showing a clear positive with health. The self-assessed health status measure may contain more measurement error than the chronic disease measure and this may be a factor in the regression analysis (see Crossley and Kennedy 2002). In general, however, both measures show a consistent pattern of deteriorating health with time in Australia.

WHAT ARE THE FACTORS BEHIND DECLINING HEALTH?

The regressions presented thus far find that health deteriorates for both cohorts between Waves 1 and 2 or six and 18 months after arrival in Australia.[4] In this section, an examination is undertaken as to whether these patterns vary by visa category – the group of immigrant categories across which there is the most variation in both chronic health and self-assessed health status. In order to observe possible variation in the deterioration in health, the Wave 2 variable (the 18-month period) is interacted with each visa category. For chronic health, the set of interacted variables is significantly different from zero at just above the 5 per cent level of significance (see Table 6.5), indicating that health does not deteriorate at the same pace for all visa categories for Cohort 1.

Examining the results in more detail for Cohort 1 indicates that for chronic conditions it is the health trajectory of Humanitarian immigrants that is significantly different from the other visa categories: a joint test of the significance of the interactions between Wave 2 and the non-Humanitarian visa categories is not rejected (as shown in Table 6.7).[5] For self-assessed

Table 6.5 Probit regressions on chronic health and interactions with Wave 2

	Cohort 1		Cohort 2	
	Marginal effects	*t* - statistic	Marginal effects	*t* - statistic
Visa				
Skilled – Australian Sponsored	-0.018	-2.14	-0.044	-2.3
BS/ENS	-0.024	-2.58	-0.053	-3.4
Independent	-0.016	-1.71	-0.013	-0.7
Humanitarian	0.050	5.41	0.093	5.37
Interactions with Wave 2				
Skilled – Australian Sponsored	0.010	0.79	-0.006	-0.19
BS/ENS	0.016	1.09	-0.008	-0.32
Independent	-0.006	-0.51	-0.026	-1.13
Humanitarian	-0.016	-2.03	0.009	0.56
Region of origin				
Oceania/Antarctica	-0.004	-0.20	0.014	0.44
Middle East & North Africa	-0.002	-0.24	-0.012	-0.60
Southeast Asia	0.014	1.71	0.002	0.09
Northeast Asia	-0.019	-1.90	-0.029	-1.55
Southern Asia	-0.017	-1.63	-0.019	-0.97
North America	0.042	2.07	-0.036	-1.92
South/Central America & Caribbean	0.007	0.62	-0.019	-0.92
Other Africa	-0.002	-0.23	-0.036	-1.48
Interactions with Wave 2				
Oceania/Antarctica	0.004	0.13	0.062	1.22
Middle East & North Africa	0.001	0.07	0.035	1.05
Southeast Asia	-0.011	-1.15	0.051	1.66
Northeast Asia	0.025	1.54	0.051	1.51
Southern Asia	0.000	-0.01	0.012	0.38
North America	-0.022	-1.28	0.072	2.07
South/Central America & Caribbean	-0.017	-1.25	0.070	1.86
Other Africa	-0.008	-0.61	0.087	1.73
English-speaking ability				
English well or very well	-0.018	-2.19	0.001	0.08
English not well or at all	-0.007	-0.93	0.017	1.06
Interactions with Wave 2				
English well or very well	0.010	0.9	0.007	0.36
English not well or at all	0.008	0.8	0.031	1.67

Notes:
Only visa, region of origin and English language speaking ability and related interactions with wave 2 are reported in this table. Full regression results are available from the authors on request. Omitted Categories: Wave 1, Family stream, Europe & USSR, English only, male, never married, six years or less of schooling, unemployed, less than $96 a week.

BS/ENS – denotes Business Skills/Employer Nomination Scheme.

Table 6.6 Probit regressions on poor health and interactions with Wave 2

	Cohort 1		Cohort 2	
	Marginal effects	*t* - statistic	Marginal effects	*t* - statistic
Visa				
Skilled – Australian Sponsored	-0.033	-2.9	0.017	0.92
BS/ENS	-0.004	-0.31	-0.015	-0.92
Independent	-0.012	-1.04	0.018	1.02
Humanitarian	0.051	4.23	0.096	5.64
Interactions with Wave 2				
Skilled – Australian Sponsored	0.054	3.01	-0.032	-1.48
BS/ENS	0.000	-0.01	-0.003	-0.12
Independent	0.035	2.07	-0.017	-0.81
Humanitarian	0.017	1.23	0.012	0.76
Region of Origin				
Oceania/Antarctica	-0.019	-0.66	0.024	0.74
Middle East & North Africa	-0.006	-0.50	0.030	1.38
Southeast Asia	0.042	3.66	0.004	0.23
Northeast Asia	0.013	1.02	0.016	0.75
Southern Asia	-0.020	-1.41	0.020	0.93
North America	0.026	1.02	0.012	0.59
South/Central America & Caribbean	0.028	1.66	-0.012	-0.58
Other Africa	-0.006	-0.39	-0.032	-1.29
Interactions with Wave 2				
Oceania/Antarctica	-0.037	-0.99	0.050	1.04
Middle East & North Africa	-0.005	-0.29	-0.012	-0.44
Southeast Asia	-0.013	-0.99	0.039	1.32
Northeast Asia	-0.015	-0.96	0.008	0.28
Southern Asia	0.007	0.36	-0.009	-0.32
North America	-0.055	-2.20	0.037	1.23
South/Central America & Caribbean	-0.038	-2.14	0.037	1.08
Other Africa	-0.034	-1.88	0.112	2.12
English-speaking Ability				
English well or very well	-0.019	-1.73	-0.002	-0.14
English not well or at all	0.021	1.91	0.034	2.19
Interactions with Wave 2				
English well or very well	-0.008	-0.60	-0.030	-1.86
English not well or at all	-0.011	-0.89	0.016	0.97

Notes:
Only visa, region of origin and English language speaking ability and related interactions with wave 2 are reported in this table. Full regression results are available from the authors on request. Omitted Categories: Wave 1, Family stream, Europe & USSR, English only, male, never married, six years or less of schooling, unemployed, less than $96 a week.

BS/ENS – denotes Business Skills/Employer Nomination Scheme.

Table 6.7 Probit regressions for Cohorts 1 and 2, testing joint significance of interactions with Wave 2

	Chronic health		Poor health	
	Chi-square statistic	Probability	Chi-square statistic	Probability
Cohort 1				
Interactions with Wave 2				
Visa	9.21	0.056	11.14	0.018
Region of origin	8.36	0.399	12.73	0.122
English-speaking ability	0.92	0.629	0.79	0.673
Non-Humanitarian Visa	2.26	0.519		
Cohort 2				
Interactions with Wave 2				
Visa	2.25	0.690	4.59	0.334
Region of origin	8.28	0.406	13.52	0.095
English-speaking ability	3.55	0.169	10.91	0.004

Notes:
Omitted categories in pooled regression: Wave 1, Family stream, Europe & USSR, English only, male, never married, six years less of schooling, unemployed, less than $96 a week.

These results are based on the regressions presented in Tables 6.5 and 6.6.

Table 6.8 Pooled probit regressions for Cohorts 1 and 2, testing equality of coefficients across cohorts

	Chronic health		Poor health	
	Chi-square statistic	Probability	Chi-square statistic	Probability
Visa	12.98	0.011	7.73	0.102
Region of origin	13.21	0.067	23.28	0.003
English-speaking ability	4.37	0.112	5.82	0.054
Education	11.06	0.198	14.29	0.074
Income	6.85	0.739	8.26	0.604
Employment	12.74	0.002	9.97	0.007
Marital status	1.50	0.471	0.86	0.651
	t-statistic	Probability	*t*-statistic	Probability
Wave	-0.15	0.885	-0.52	0.605
Female	-2.04	0.041	-2.77	0.006
Age	2.34	0.019	1.42	0.156
Age squared	-1.54	0.123	-1.49	0.137

Notes:
Omitted categories in pooled regression: Wave 1, Family stream, Europe & USSR, English only, male, never married, six years or less of schooling, unemployed, less than $96 a week.

These results are based on the regressions presented in Tables 6.5 and 6.6.

health, the interaction terms by visa category are again jointly significant in Cohort 1, but there is no clear pattern in the differences in health trajectories by visa category (Table 6.6). For Cohort 2 the set of interaction terms is not significantly different from zero at conventional levels for either measure of physical health. Thus, for this cohort of immigrants health declines at a comparable pace across visa categories despite the fact that immigrants from different visa groups have a significantly different prevalence of chronic disease and self-assessed health status on arrival in Australia.

Interestingly, interactions of the Wave 2 variable with English-speaking ability and region are found to be insignificantly different from zero for both cohorts and for both health measures. Thus, there appears to be little significant variation in the pace of the deterioration in health across different groups of immigrants as indicated by either region of origin or degree of language fluency.

These results in general run counter to explanations of the deterioration in immigrant health that predict variation in the deterioration of health for different immigrant groups. For example, they are inconsistent with the hypothesis that immigrants with little English ability or immigrants markedly unfamiliar with a Western-style health system experience increasing diagnosis of existing health conditions with time in Australia. Similarly, the results are inconsistent with the explanation that a persistent difficulty in accessing health services for particular immigrant groups underpins the decline in their health. Furthermore, the lack of variation across region of origin categories is also inconsistent with explanations related to changes in health behaviour, since immigrants from regions with significantly different health behaviours exhibit similar declines in physical health over time. Admittedly, however, the relatively short window of time considered in the LSIA might not be sufficient to allow changed behaviours to lead to observed changes in physical health. (McDonald and Kennedy (2005) find significant but fairly slow convergence in the prevalence of immigrant overweight and obesity rates to native-born levels for immigrants to Canada.)

As noted earlier in this chapter, most studies find that immigrant health deteriorates net of ageing effects and our results support this conclusion. For example, Jasso et al. (2004) find that the health gap narrows for most immigrants to the United States but that it persists for some groups of immigrants. Biddle et al. (2004) find that for Australia the health gap varies across immigrant groups and that the decline in health (chronic disease in their study) also varies. McDonald and Kennedy (2004) find much the same patterns for immigrants to Canada. Thus, the unique finding in this chapter is the lack of variation in the decline in health for very different groups of immigrants. It may be the case that the 18-month period over which immigrant health is followed is not long enough for substantial variation across immigrant groups to emerge. However, a decline in health that is similar across all groups of immigrants (for example, immigrants from different visa categories and regions of origin) is also consistent with explanations of health patterns that have similar effects across groups of immigrants.

Differences between cohorts

In this section, differences in health patterns between cohorts are examined to try to gain insights into any effects related to the prevailing macroeconomic conditions or other entry year effects present for each cohort. In order to provide an indication of the difference in macro conditions, it should be noted that in 1994, when most of Cohort 1 was first surveyed, the Australian unemployment rate was 8 to 10 per cent while in 2000 it was around 6 per cent (see Chapter 1). If macroeconomic conditions affect immigrant health net of the direct effect on their personal circumstances, differences between the cohorts might arise, even after controlling for differences in average characteristics. As well, the annual immigrant intake was lower in 1999–2000 than in 1993–95, and was increasingly focused on skills-based immigrants.[6] Although the regressions include controls for visa group and other immigrant characteristics, changes in immigration policy might still exert an effect on immigrant health through selection effects based on unobservable characteristics important to physical health.

In the examination of the descriptive statistics earlier in this chapter it was noted that, on average, chronic disease was worse in Cohort 2 but that self-assessed health status was overall quite similar. To control for the differences in the characteristics of each cohort, the data are pooled and the core regression model re-estimated after including a control for Cohort 2. This allows the identification of differences in the level of health between the two cohorts while holding the average characteristics of both cohorts constant. For both chronic health and self-assessed health status, the regression results confirmed the earlier descriptive results. Chronic health is significantly worse in Cohort 2 (3.7 percentage points higher) while for self-assessed health status there is no significant difference. For the second cohort, they arrived at a time when fewer total immigrants were accepted, and when general economic conditions were better, than was the case for the first cohort. Both of these factors might suggest that the second cohort should be in better health on arrival, ceteris paribus. However, as there is no clear pattern for the two health measures, it is difficult to derive conclusions about arrival cohort or macroeconomics effects on initial health status on arrival in Australia.

The pooled regression model is extended by interacting the indicator variable for Cohort 2 with all other explanatory variables. This fully interacted model is then used to test for differences between cohorts. For example, a test of the inclusion of a set of dummy variables interacted with the

Cohort 2 variable indicates whether there is significant variation in the effect of these variables between cohorts.

For health trajectories following migration, the equality of the Wave 2 coefficients is tested for both chronic health and self-assessed health status, and the results indicate that the coefficients are not significantly different from each other (or the variable interacted with the Cohort 2 variable is insignificant) for both measures of health (see Table 6.8). That is, the deterioration in health is – after controlling for other characteristics – the same for both cohorts. Again, it appears that regardless of the measure of physical health or the year of arrival, the rate of decline of immigrant health is statistically and quantitatively the same.

Each of the other variables or sets of descriptive variables are also tested for equality between cohorts. Characteristics that have the same effect on the prevalence of diseases for both cohorts include region of origin, English-speaking ability, income, education and marital status, while visa category and employment status had significantly different effects. For self-assessed health status the effects of visa category, English-speaking ability, income, education and marital status were the same, while the effects of employment status and region of origin were different.

To provide an overall assessment of between-cohort differences while holding the association between explanatory variables and health constant, the equality of all coefficients between regressions is also tested. In this case instead of using the fully interacted model, the separate regressions are compared and Hausman specification and likelihood ratio tests used. The results of these tests suggest that overall the set of coefficients are significantly different. This may mean that different macroeconomic circumstances do affect immigrant health, but only indirectly through the relationship of health with other variables. However, this is at best a tentative conclusion.

Differences between Principal Applicants and Migrating Unit Spouses

The final extension considered is to estimate models of physical health separately for Principal Applicants and for spouses (see Tables 6.9 and 6.10). It might be expected that the positive health gaps for skilled immigrants would be larger (relative to Family stream immigrants) for Principal Applicants than their spouses, since it is the characteristics of the former on which the application to migrate is based. This turns out to be true only for chronic conditions and only for Cohort 1: while skilled Independent Principal Applicants are significantly less likely to have a chronic condition on arrival than Family stream Principal Applicants in Cohort 1, there are no significant differences between the Migrating Unit Spouses of applicants in those classes. However, for Cohort 2, skilled Independent Principal Applicants and

Table 6.9 Probit regressions on chronic health: Selected results for Principal Applicants and Migrating Unit Spouses

	Principal Applicants				Migrating Unit Spouses			
	Cohort 1		Cohort 2		Cohort 1		Cohort 2	
	Marginal effects	*t* - statistic	Marginal effects	*t* - statistic	Marginal effects	*t* - statistic	Marginal effects	*t* - statistic
Wave 2	0.025	5.09	0.038	4.19	0.020	2.68	0.039	2.64
Skilled – Australian Sponsored	-0.006	-0.78	-0.059	-3.31	-0.011	-0.70	-0.036	-1.00
BS/ENS	-0.031	-3.72	-0.058	-3.80	-0.007	-0.40	-0.063	-2.18
Independent	-0.026	-2.82	-0.012	-0.63	-0.004	-0.23	-0.052	-1.48
Humanitarian	0.038	4.20	0.135	6.38	0.035	1.83	0.057	1.45
Oceania/Antarctica	0.006	0.35					0.041	0.71
Middle East & North Africa	-0.002	-0.31	0.010	0.48	0.000	0.02	-0.037	-1.20
Southeast Asia	0.015	2.00	0.030	1.37	0.001	0.09	0.060	1.39
Northeast Asia	0.000	-0.01	0.011	0.47	-0.003	-0.19	0.011	0.26
Southern Asia	-0.014	-1.49	0.007	0.30	-0.023	-1.91	-0.021	-0.56
North America	0.029	1.54	0.000	-0.02	0.002	0.08	-0.012	-0.30
South/Central America & Caribbean	-0.025	-2.49	0.050	1.98	-0.027	-1.83	-0.028	-0.82
Other Africa	0.017	1.50	0.031	1.19	-0.008	-0.57	0.041	0.71
English well or very well	0.008	0.99	0.008	0.53	0.016	1.24	-0.055	-1.87
English not well or at all	0.006	0.94	0.014	0.79	0.006	0.55	-0.015	-0.44

Note:
Omitted categories: Wave 1, Family stream, Europe & USSR, English only, male, six years or less of schooling, unemployed, or less than $96 a week.

Table 6.10 Probit regressions on poor health: Selected results for Principal Applicants and Migrating Unit Spouses

	Principal Applicants				Migrating Unit Spouses			
	Cohort 1		Cohort 2		Cohort 1		Cohort 2	
	Marginal effects	*t* - statistic	Marginal effects	*t* - statistic	Marginal effects	*t* - statistic	Marginal effects	*t* - statistic
Wave 2	0.028	4.14	0.025	2.97	0.037	3.58	0.039	2.75
Skilled – Australian Sponsored	-0.009	-0.74	-0.015	-0.81	0.022	0.79	-0.002	-0.05
BS/ENS	-0.018	-1.27	-0.003	-0.18	0.026	0.87	-0.025	-0.79
Independent	-0.004	-0.28	-0.002	-0.09	0.047	1.50	0.013	0.35
Humanitarian	0.085	6.30	0.129	6.23	0.076	2.49	0.075	1.88
Oceania/Antarctica	-0.012	-0.53	0.035	0.99	-	-	0.037	0.70
Middle East & North Africa	0.004	0.33	0.013	0.59	-0.012	-0.66	0.008	0.24
Southeast Asia	0.045	4.07	0.019	0.88	0.033	1.92	-0.001	-0.04
Northeast Asia	0.028	2.19	0.017	0.75	-0.018	-1.06	0.002	0.06
Southern Asia	0.013	0.91	0.019	0.90	-0.039	-2.35	-0.033	-1.03
North America	-0.002	-0.08	0.025	1.10	-0.011	-0.30	-0.011	-0.32
South/Central America & Caribbean	0.014	0.87	0.000	-0.02	-0.049	-2.33	-0.042	-1.36
Other Africa	-0.011	-0.74	0.012	0.50	-0.021	-1.02	0.011	0.18
English well or very well	0.024	2.13	-0.013	-0.93	0.019	1.13	-0.006	-0.20
English not well or at all	0.031	3.38	0.039	2.24	0.055	3.72	0.062	1.96

Note:
Omitted categories: Wave 1, Family stream, Europe & USSR, English only, male, six years or less of schooling, unemployed, less than $96 a week.

their spouses are both less likely to have a chronic condition than Family stream immigrants. For self-assessed health status, there are no discernible differences between Skilled and Family stream Principal Applicants and their spouses in either cohort. The results for both cohorts also indicate that the relatively poor health experienced by Humanitarian immigrants on arrival in Australia is common to both Principal Applicants and their spouses.

For health trajectories, the consistency of the rate of decline in health for both Principal Applicants and Migrating Unit Spouses is again present across both cohorts and both measures of health. Regardless of cohort, Principal Applicant status, measure of health, region of origin and language fluency, the decline in health is significant and of comparable magnitude. This result is even more surprising for the spouses of Principal Applicants where the mechanisms that underlie differences in the level of health among immigrants from different visa groups would be expected to be more subdued. The consistency of decline in health seems robust to almost all variation in immigrant characteristics.

CONCLUDING COMMENTS

This chapter has examined immigrant health in the period soon after arrival in Australia using two measures of physical health that are commonly used in the immigrant health literature: the prevalence of chronic disease, and self-assessed health status. The study finds that a number of factors are important determinants of an immigrant's health on arrival in Australia. When measured by the prevalence of chronic conditions, immigrants' health status at the time of migration varies substantially by visa category, with Skilled immigrants generally healthier and Humanitarian immigrants less healthy than comparable Family stream immigrants. The significance of visa category is interesting since three of the main characteristics on which skilled immigrants are approved for migration – education, language and age – are already controlled for in the regression analyses. This may point to the importance of unobserved human capital characteristics of those accepted into Australia as skilled immigrants that are also key determinants of health.

It is also found that immigrant health declines between six and 18 months for both immigrant cohorts examined in this study. The deterioration in health is comparable for immigrants from different visa categories, from different regions of origin, and with different degrees of English language fluency. Our results derived using panel data do confirm the results of other papers that have used pooled cross-section data and suggest immigrant health declining relatively quickly is a real phenomenon and not an artefact of cross-section data and related methods.

The fact that health declines so consistently across immigrants groups runs against a number of explanations of why health declines relatively quickly for immigrants compared with the native-born. In particular, it does not support arguments that focus on difficulties in accessing health systems and differences in the diagnosis of disease. The consistent decline could be in accord with a health behaviours explanation if it is the case that the adoption of behaviours affects all immigrants similarly. However, as noted in the introduction the effects of the common adoption of health behaviours are hard to predict and require a closer examination of particular health behaviours. Finally, the results found in this chapter are also in accord with the notion that something about the process of immigration to a new country itself – such as stress – has potentially long term negative health consequences. The mental health and welfare of recent immigrants is also a promising avenue for future research.

An examination of the differences in health status between the two immigrant cohorts finds that after controlling for the characteristics of each cohort, the prevalence of chronic conditions is worse for Cohort 2 but self-assessed health status is largely the same for both cohorts. Since period of arrival will reflect macroeconomic conditions, immigration policy with respect to the size and composition of the immigrant intakes, and other immigration and economic policy changes, decomposing these effects might reveal what is driving the significant health differences between cohorts. This remains a task for future research.

The consistent decline in health for many groups of immigrants does not, however, lead easily to straightforward policy conclusions. If we were able to determine that the process of migration affects health, it is difficult to conceive of a public health policy that might ameliorate the decline in health given such large variation in immigrant groups ranging from Humanitarian immigrants to highly skilled English-speaking immigrants. Perhaps the most telling policy conclusion arising from this analysis is the potential for the 'healthy immigrant' phenomenon – including the initial health gap between immigrants and the native-born and subsequent decline in immigrant health – to illuminate the effect of the Australian environment on the health of all Australians. Furthermore, increasing our understanding of what is driving immigrant health has the potential to provide unique insights into the health dimension of our way of life.

NOTES

1. Means are derived using population weights.
2. However, when a mean of the self-assessed health status is derived using an ascending 5 score scale (0 for very poor health, 1 for poor health and so on), this effect is not present. Furthermore, in the regression analysis that follows it is found that health actually deteriorates after controlling for other factors.

3 In the following the section the assumption of Principal Applicants and Migrating Unit Spouses having similar health relationships is relaxed when each is modelled separately.

4 In fact, in models estimated for Cohort 1 where there is data for 42 months after arrival in Australia it is found that both chronic health and self-assessed health status continue to deteriorate. The full results are available from the authors on request.

5 The result indicates that while Humanitarian immigrants in Cohort 1 are initially significantly more likely to have a chronic condition than other immigrants, the probability of experiencing a chronic condition increases relatively more slowly than for the other visa categories.

6 According to the Report 'Australian Immigration Consolidated Statistics Number 21', immigration from offshore (the group from which the LSIA is sampled) was only 60,070 in 1999–2000, compared with 64 179 in 1993–1994 and 70 964 in 1994–1995. As well, 51 per cent of immigrants from offshore were in the Skilled categories in 1999–2000 compared with 39 per cent in 1993–1994 and 1994–1995.

7. Immigrants' Housing Outcomes in the Early Years of Settlement

Siew-Ean Khoo

INTRODUCTION

All immigrants require accommodation on arrival in their new country of residence and immigrants' housing arrangements form an important aspect of their settlement experience. Recently arrived migrants, who tend to have higher unemployment rates, may have difficulty in finding affordable housing, particularly if they do not have relatives or friends (Hassell and Hugo 1996, Junankar et al. 1993). The housing arrangements and choices of immigrants can have implications for the demand and supply of housing, particularly in the major cities where most immigrants tend to settle (Junankar et al. 1993). Therefore, the issue of immigrants and housing has been the subject of a number of studies (for example, Hassel and Hugo 1996, Junankar et al. 1993, National Population Committee 1990, Ray et al. 2004, Tonkins et al. 1993).

Past research has shown that recent immigrants tend to have higher housing costs than other members of the community (Econsult 1992, Ferris and Silberburg 1982). Studies have also indicated that immigrants to Australia usually progress from shared or rental housing on arrival to buying and eventually owning their own homes, in a similar way to other Australian residents (Junankar et al. 1993). Data for the cohort of immigrants interviewed in the first Longitudinal Survey of Immigrants to Australia (Cohort 1) confirm this pattern of progression from renting to buying to owning their own homes during the first few years of settlement (VandenHeuvel and Wooden 1999). This study also found differences in the home ownership rate by type of immigrant, with immigrants in the Business Skills visa category having the highest rate and those in the Humanitarian visa category having the lowest. Immigrants in the Skilled Independent and Humanitarian visa categories were also more likely to be living in apartments while those in the Family stream and the Business Skills and Employer Nomination Scheme were more likely to be living in separate houses. Housing costs also vary with visa category. Based on their findings, VandenHeuvel and Wooden (1999) suggested that changes in the composition of the immigrant intake could affect the demand for various types of housing.

A comparison of the two LSIA cohorts of immigrants on their housing choices within the first six months of arrival showed that there was no difference between the two cohorts in the type of housing (houses or apartments) in which they lived (Richardson et al. 2002a). The proportion renting privately (over half) or living rent-free with family or friends (one-fifth) was also the same for the two cohorts at six months after arrival even though the second cohort had a greater proportion employed and a lower proportion unemployed compared with the first cohort. The study also found that migrants in the Humanitarian visa category were more likely than other migrants to have a significant level of financial stress, as indicated by their having to pay a high proportion of their income in rent.

Previous studies have identified many areas for additional research on the issue of recently arrived migrants and their housing situation. These include the issues of housing costs and affordability and the factors affecting immigrants' housing arrangements, which are examined in this chapter. The availability of longitudinal data for two different cohorts of immigrants from the LSIA also presents an opportunity to compare their housing situation to determine if the timing of their arrival affects the housing situation of recently arrived migrants. The two cohorts faced quite different economic conditions in Australia at the time of their arrival, as discussed in earlier chapters, which could have had implications for their housing situation. The first cohort arrived in 1993–1995 just as the Australian economy was recovering from the recession of the early 1990s. The second arrived during 1999–2000 when the economy was performing well. The housing market of the later period was more robust than that of the earlier period. Studies comparing the labour market experiences of the two cohorts soon after their arrival have indicated that the second cohort had much better labour market outcomes than the first cohort as measured by their employment to population ratio and unemployment rate (Cobb-Clark 2003, Richardson et al. 2002a).

This chapter addresses three main issues relating to immigrants' housing outcomes during the first few years of settlement:

1. The rate of home ownership and the factors that influence the transition to home ownership;
2. Housing costs by tenure status and how they may change during the early years of settlement as migrants change their status from renters to home buyers and owners;
3. Housing affordability as measured by the percentage of income spent on housing costs and the factors associated with recent immigrants' experience of financial stress in relation to housing costs.

The chapter compares the two cohorts of immigrants on these housing outcomes. If differences are observed in home ownership rates, housing costs and housing affordability between the two cohorts, an attempt is made to determine whether they relate to differences in the characteristics and composition of the two cohorts or to the different circumstances they faced at the time of their arrival. As described in the earlier chapters, the first and second cohorts were selected according to slightly different selection criteria in relation to skills and English language proficiency. The second cohort also had a higher proportion of skilled migrants than the first cohort, and a smaller proportion of family reunion migrants. There were also changes to government policy concerning access to income support programs during the interval between the arrival of the two cohorts. While the first cohort faced a six-month waiting period before they could access income support programs, the second cohort had to wait for two years before they could access welfare payments.[1] This change might have resulted in members of the second cohort who were self-selected as being less likely to be dependent on government-provided income support payments. The analyses in this chapter therefore provide an indication of the relative importance of (1) migrant characteristics and the composition of the immigrant intake as determined by immigration policy and selection criteria and (2) the socioeconomic conditions associated with the time of arrival in influencing immigrants' housing outcomes in the early years of settlement.

The importance of location in influencing housing outcomes is also examined since most immigrants to Australia tend to settle in the gateway cities of Sydney and Melbourne where housing is more expensive; very few go to the smaller cities where housing costs are generally lower. More than 90 per cent of immigrants to Australia settle in the major cities and other urban areas. The state of New South Wales has 34 per cent of Australia's population but attracts more than 40 per cent of recent immigrants, with most settling in the Sydney metropolitan area. In contrast, the smaller states of South Australia and Tasmania have consistently received much less than their share of immigrants compared to their share of Australia's total population. How migrants' housing outcomes compare across different locations may have implications for policy initiatives that attempt to divert new immigrants away from large cities such as Sydney and Melbourne to smaller cities and regional areas.

DATA AND METHOD

In the LSIA, data on housing was obtained from interviews with the Principal Applicant only. The Principal Applicant is the person who applied for the visa to migrate. Any spouse or dependent children or close relatives who migrate on the same visa application with the Principal Applicant are members of the migrating unit. It is likely that all persons in the migrating unit will live in the same household on arrival in Australia.

While three waves of interviews were conducted with the first cohort, only two waves of interviews were conducted with the second cohort. Therefore, for a comparable longitudinal analysis of both cohorts, only data from the first two waves of interviews (conducted at 3–6 months and 15–18 months after arrival) were used. The data used in the analyses in this chapter were for 4,469 Principal Applicants in Cohort 1 and 2,649 Principal Applicants in Cohort 2 who participated in both waves of interviews. They were drawn from and represented 64,448 and 27,832 people who arrived in Australia as Principal Applicants on immigrant visas during the years 1993–1995 and 1999–2000 respectively.

The two LSIA samples were stratified according to visa category and region or country of birth and covered all immigrants who settled in capital cities and other major urban centres. More than 95 per cent of adult migrants in the two cohorts settled in the areas covered by the surveys. Because of the stratified nature of the data, weights have been estimated to be applied in data analyses so that the findings are representative of the immigrant cohorts. The results presented in this chapter are based on weighted data.

The indicators of immigrants' housing outcomes examined are home ownership and the transition to home ownership, housing costs and housing affordability (the percentage of income spent on housing costs). The availability of longitudinal data provides for an examination of the transition to home ownership and changes in housing costs and housing affordability during the one-year period between the first and second wave interviews. Information collected in the LSIA on housing costs relates to weekly mortgage, rent or board paid by the Principal Applicant (and spouse if present).

The concept of housing affordability, as used by the Australia Bureau of Statistics in its 1988 and 1999 Housing Surveys, measures housing costs as a percentage of the average weekly income. In this study affordability has to be estimated, since the data collected in the LSIA on both housing costs and income are available only in ranges of values rather than a specific numeric amount. Migrants in the survey were asked to indicate which income and housing costs categories their weekly income and housing costs fall within. To calculate the percentage of weekly income spent on mortgage or rent, an individual's housing cost is assumed to be the mid-range value of each mortgage or rent category while the individual's income is assumed to be the end value of each income range.[2] This reduces the likelihood of overestimating the percentage of income spent on housing when housing cost is divided by income. The housing costs and incomes of the Principal Applicant and spouse (if present) are used to calculate the index. It has been suggested that housing stress can be viewed as having to pay more than 40 per cent of gross income in rent or mortgage payments (Richardson et al. 2002a). On this measure, about

18 per cent of the second LSIA cohort experienced housing stress, with the proportion much higher for Humanitarian migrants (Richardson et al. 2002a).[3]

Three types of factors that are likely to influence immigrants' housing outcomes are examined. These are demographic and socioeconomic characteristics of the migrant or migrant's household, visa category and other circumstances associated with the migration process, and location.

Demographic and socioeconomic characteristics examined in this study are the migrant's age, marital status, education and household income. Surveys have shown that housing occupancy status, and particularly home ownership, is related to age (ABS 2000). Younger adults are more likely to rent and the home ownership rate tends to increase with age. Marital status may also be related to housing arrangements, as married people are more likely to be home owners than unmarried people. People with higher educational qualifications may have better employment outcomes than those with lower qualifications and therefore are more likely to be able to afford to buy a house. Higher income is also likely to be correlated with higher rates of home ownership.

The LSIA has information about the migrant's visa category, the number of people who migrated with the Principal Applicant and the amount of money that they brought along at the time of migration or transferred soon after, all of which can affect their housing situation soon after arrival. As mentioned earlier, migrants entering under different types of visas – Family stream, Skilled[4] or Humanitarian – have different housing arrangements and different housing costs. The housing demands and choices of migrants may also depend on the number of people migrating as a unit. The housing situation of a single person migrating alone is likely to be different from that of a family unit of four people. The amount of money that immigrants bring with them is also likely to affect their housing situation. Those who bring more money may be more likely to buy a house or apartment soon after arrival, or conversely, those planning to buy a house soon after arrival or anticipating having high housing costs will bring more money with them.

As mentioned earlier, the location of residence as a factor influencing immigrants' housing outcomes is also examined. Houses are more expensive and rents are higher in Sydney and Melbourne than in other cities in Australia (ABS 2000). Migrants choosing to settle in places where housing is more expensive may be less able to buy a house or apartment than those settling in places where house prices are lower.

Table 7.1 compares the two cohorts of immigrants according to these factors. Besides their different periods of arrival in Australia, the two cohorts also differ from each other in other ways. A larger percentage of immigrants in the second cohort was aged between 25–44 years and a larger percentage was married at the time of arrival compared with those in the first cohort. Immigrants in the second cohort were better educated on average than those in the first cohort, with a higher percentage having university degrees and

Table 7.1 Characteristics of immigrants in Cohorts 1 and 2

Characteristics	Cohort 1	Cohort 2
	%	%
Age at arrival		
15–24	17.4	13.3
25–34	46.2	50.0
35–44	20.5	23.4
45–54	6.3	8.3
55+	9.6	5.1
Marital status at first interview		
Currently married	71.7	76.1
Not currently married	28.3	23.9
Highest education		
Higher degree	11.8	19.8
Degree	20.5	22.9
Trade certificate/diploma	29.4	26.9
No post-school qualification	38.4	30.3
Household income at first interview		
Up to $25,000	29.1	18.4
$25,001–$50,000	24.3	25.4
$50,001 or more	19.1	33.6
Not stated	27.5	22.6
Visa category		
Family	57.1	53.3
Skilled – Australian Sponsored	8.0	10.1
BS/ENS	3.4	5.3
Independent	17.3	24.0
Humanitarian	14.2	7.4
Number of people in migrating unit		
One	59.2	57.2
Two	14.5	14.4
Three	10.6	12.1
Four or more	15.7	16.3
Average $'000 brought on migration	19.8	39.0
State of residence		
New South Wales	42.8	43.3
Victoria	25.9	25.1
Queensland	11.6	10.8
South Australia	5.1	4.9
Western Australia	11.4	13.2
Tasmania	0.7	0.9
Northern Territory	0.6	0.6
Australian Capital Territory	2.0	1.3
Number of respondents	4,469	2,649
Weighted population	64,448	27,832

Source: Longitudinal Survey of Immigrants to Australia.

higher degrees and a lower percentage with no post-school qualifications. This is most likely due to the higher proportion of skilled migrants in the second cohort, a specific outcome of policy changes after 1996 that place more emphasis on skilled migration and reduce the proportion of family reunion migration. As shown in earlier chapters, as a consequence a greater percentage of the second cohort was employed at six months after arrival and their labour market outcomes were generally much better than those of the first cohort. There was also a greater percentage of higher income households among the second cohort than the first cohort, no doubt related to their better labour market outcomes. These differences in migrant characteristics would suggest that the two cohorts were likely to have different housing outcomes.

The composition of the two cohorts in terms of their visa categories is also different. As noted earlier, policy changes have resulted in a larger proportion of Independent, and the Business Skills and Employer Nomination migrants and lower percentages of Family stream and Humanitarian migrants in the second cohort compared with the first cohort. There was also a slightly higher percentage of immigrants in the second cohort who were accompanied by two or more family members (therefore having a total of three or more people in the migrating unit). A rather surprising difference relates to the amount of money brought in at the time of migration. The average amount of funds brought in by the second cohort was twice that brought in by the first cohort.[5]

Differences in location by state of residence were small. In both cohorts, 43 per cent resided in New South Wales and 25 per cent in Victoria. Since the LSIA was conducted only in major cities, the migrants in New South Wales and Victoria were mainly those settling in Sydney and Melbourne, the capital cities of the two states respectively.

Following descriptive analyses of the relation between these factors and immigrants' housing arrangements, the transition to home ownership and housing costs and housing affordability, multivariate regression analyses were conducted to investigate whether the housing outcomes of the two cohorts were still different after controlling for their different profiles, migration circumstances and location of residence. Any observed cohort effect would reflect the influence of other factors not accounted for in the analysis. These would include external factors such as the state of the housing market and other aspects of the prevailing economic conditions associated with the different time periods of arrival of the two cohorts in Australia.

HOUSING ARRANGEMENTS

The housing arrangements of the two cohorts of migrants at about six and 18 months after arrival in Australia are shown in Figure 7.1. There was no difference between the two cohorts in the percentage living in homes that they owned or were renting at six months after arrival. However, the percentage that had bought a home within six months of arrival and was paying it off was nearly twice as high in the second cohort as in the first. This percentage increased for both cohorts a year later. While the increase was larger for the first cohort than the second cohort, the second cohort was still ahead by 8 percentage points at the second interview. Migrants living rent-free (the second most common living arrangement for new migrants at 3–6 months after arrival) were mainly those living with relatives and were mostly (75–80 per cent) migrants in the Family stream category.

Figure 7.1 Housing arrangements of migrants in Cohorts 1 and 2 at six and 18 months after arrival

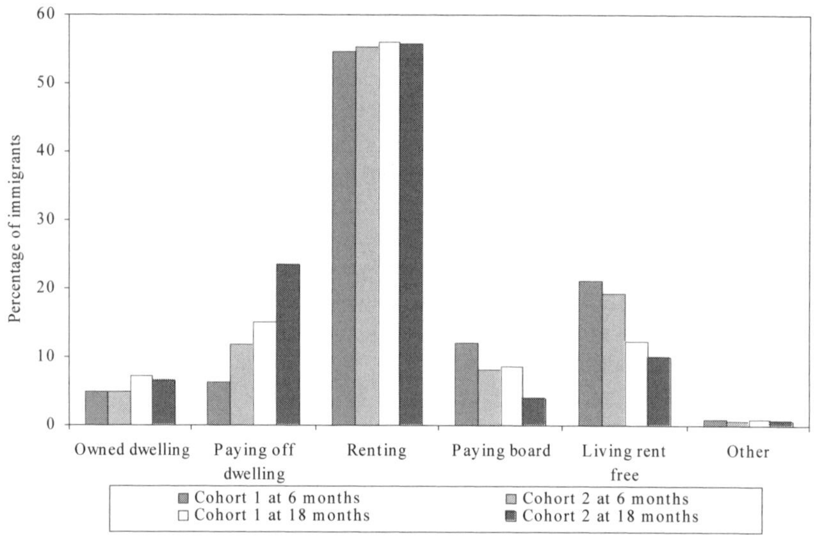

Source: Longitudinal Survey of Immigrants to Australia.

As expected, immigrants' housing arrangements vary by their age, marital status, education, income, visa category and location of residence (Table 7.2). Migrants aged 35–54 years were more likely to be living in their own homes than those younger or older. This was true for both cohorts.

Also as expected, married migrants were more likely to be living in homes they owned or were paying off compared with migrants who were not married. There was not much difference by marital status in the percentage renting, but migrants who were not married were more likely to live rent-free with friends or relatives. A higher percentage of both married and single migrants in the second cohort were home owners when interviewed within six and 18 months after arrival compared with those in the first cohort.

Table 7.2 Percentage of migrants who owned or were paying off their homes at six and 18 months after arrival

Migrants' characteristics	At 6 months after arrival		At 18 months after arrival	
	Cohort 1	Cohort 2	Cohort 1	Cohort 2
Age at arrival	%	%	%	%
15–24	9	8	16	17
25–34	9	16	20	31
35–44	17	20	34	34
45–54	16	28	30	40
55+	15	16	20	22
Marital status				
Married	14	20	27	34
Not married	5	8	11	15
Highest education				
Higher degree	11	17	22	27
Degree	10	14	23	29
Trade certificate/diploma	13	20	27	34
No post-school qualification	10	17	19	29
Household income at interview				
Up to $25,000	10	15	17	25
$25,001–$50,000	10	17	21	29
$50,001 or more	18	24	36	38
Not stated	8	8	13	17
Visa category				
Family	15	20	26	31
Skilled – Australian Sponsored	10	11	24	29
BS/ENS	30	43	49	64
Independent	5	13	21	28
Humanitarian	1	0	3	6
Number of people in migrating unit				
One	11	16	21	27
Two	13	20	27	32
Three	10	14	22	29
Four or more	10	19	25	39
State of residence				
New South Wales	9	9	18	14
Victoria	9	18	18	27
Queensland	15	25	31	43
South Australia	15	22	23	31
Western Australia	18	30	39	53
Tasmania	19	36	43	52
Northern Territory	13	16	34	42
Australian Capital Territory	16	19	22	33
Total	11	16	22	30

Source: Longitudinal Survey of Immigrants to Australia.

Migrants in higher income households were more likely to live in their own home than those with lower household incomes. The percentage owning or paying off their homes increased for low income as well as for higher income households between the first and second interviews. However, the more educated migrants did not have higher home ownership rates

Differences in housing arrangements by migrants' visa category emerged as expected. Migrants in the Business and Employer Nomination category were the most likely to own or be paying off their homes during the early years of settlement. They also showed the largest percentage point increase in home ownership between the first and second interviews. In contrast, very few migrants in the Humanitarian category owned or bought a home during the early years of settlement. The number of people in the migrating unit did not have a significant effect on housing arrangements.

In both cohorts, a lower percentage of migrants who settled in New South Wales (mainly in Sydney) owned or bought a home compared with migrants who settled elsewhere. The home ownership rate was highest for both cohorts settling in Tasmania. As shown in Table 7.1, less than 1 per cent of immigrants in both cohorts settled in Tasmania. Migrants settling in Western Australia (mainly in Perth, the state capital) had the next highest rate of home ownership, followed by those settling in Queensland. House prices are lower in these states than in New South Wales. The LSIA data showed that the value of dwellings occupied by migrants in Tasmania was much lower than those occupied by migrants in New South Wales.

Table 7.3 presents the results of logistic regression analyses showing the log odds of a migrant being a home owner associated with migrant characteristics, migration circumstances and location of residence.[6] The analyses also show whether the two cohorts still differ significantly from each other after these factors have been taken into account.

At six months after arrival, the rate of home ownership varies by marital status, household income, visa category, amount of funds brought on arrival, location of residence and cohort. Married migrants, those living in households with income of more than $50,000 and migrants who brought more money with them were more likely to own or buy a home soon after arrival. Conversely, Humanitarian migrants and Independent migrants were less likely, when compared with Business Skills and Employer Nomination migrants, to own or buy their homes. Also, those settling in New South Wales and Victoria were much less likely to be home owners than those settling elsewhere in Australia.[7] The regression results also show the first cohort had a significantly lower rate of home ownership than the second cohort, even after controlling for their different profiles. This suggests that the conditions faced by the second cohort had been more conducive to becoming home owners soon after arrival than those faced by the first cohort.

Table 7.3 *Log odds of owning or paying off a home at six and 18 months after migration*

	Home ownership at			
	6 months		18 months	
	Estimate	Std. error	Estimate	Std. error
Constant	-2.709*	0.286	-2.36*	0.261
Migrant's age at arrival				
15–24	-0.484	0.185	0.089	0.162
24–34	0.068	0.159	0.472	0.153
35–44	0.495	0.166	0.935*	0.153
45–54	0.211	0.197	0.634*	0.180
55+	-		-	
Marital status at first interview				
Currently married	0.772*	0.122	0.760*	0.092
Not currently married	-		-	
Highest education				
Higher degree	-0.011	0.134	-0.445*	0.113
Degree	-0.175	0.117	-0.158	0.094
Trade certificate/diploma	0.058	0.100	-0.050	0.083
No post-school qualification	-		-	
Household income at first interview				
Up to $25,000	0.189	0.120	0.178	0.109
$25,001–$50,000	0.206	0.118	0.391*	0.101
$50,001 or more	0.861*	0.112	1.005*	0.098
Not stated	-		-	
Visa category				
Family	0.315	0.205	0.261	0.187
Skilled – Australian Sponsored	-0.448	0.220	-0.124	0.194
BS/ENS	-		-	
Independent skilled	-0.614*	0.202	-0.165	0.182
Humanitarian	-2.910*	0.490	-1.605*	0.243
Number in migrating unit				
One	0.334	0.162	0.079	0.123
Two	0.411	0.163	0.247	0.124
Three	0.107	0.169	-0.008	0.128
Four or more	-		-	
$'00,000 brought at migration	0.479*	0.042	0.977*	0.073
State of residence at interview				
New South Wales	-0.843*	0.091	-0.855*	0.072
Victoria	-0.422*	0.097	-0.599*	0.081
Other	-		-	
Cohort				
Cohort 1	-0.270*	0.082	-0.124	0.067
Cohort 2	-		-	
Likelihood ratio chi-square	911		1448	
df	22		22	
N	7116		7116	

Notes:
- = reference category
* p<0.001

At about 18 months after arrival the cohort effect had disappeared. There was no significant difference in the home ownership rate between the two cohorts after controlling for their different characteristics and migration circumstances. The factors affecting the home ownership rate at this time include age, marital status, education, household income, migration category, funds brought at migration and location of settlement. The number of people in the migrating unit had no significant effect on home ownership status.

The analyses confirm that home ownership is much less likely for Humanitarian migrants than other migrants and that married migrants, and migrants who brought more money with them, are much more likely to be home owners during the early years of settlement. Home ownership is also positively correlated with household income, but not with education once other factors are taken into account. This contrasts with a recent study in the United States that shows the importance of migrants' educational attainment on their home ownership (Ray et al. 2004).

TRANSITION TO HOME OWNERSHIP

The longitudinal data allows the examination of which migrants are more likely to change their housing tenure from renting, or living rent-free with relatives and friends, to buying their own home during the one-year interval between the first and second wave interviews. It is also possible to investigate whether there is any difference between the two cohorts in their transition to home ownership during this period of settlement. Figure 7.2 summarises the changes in housing arrangements observed for the two cohorts. There was little difference between the cohorts in the proportion transiting to home ownership. There was also not much difference between the two cohorts in terms of other changes in housing arrangements. About two-thirds of both cohorts did not change their housing status, with 44 per cent of both cohorts renting at both six and 18 months after arrival.

The transition to home ownership is also modelled using logistic regression to examine the factors that are associated with migrants becoming homebuyers during the first 1–2 years of settlement (Table 7.4). Migrants who were aged 35–44 years, who were married or had brought more money with them were more likely to become home buyers than others. The transition to home ownership was positively correlated with household income. There was no relation to education once income was controlled. Humanitarian migrants were less likely to become home owners than other migrants and the negative effect on home ownership of living in New South Wales and Victoria (mainly in Sydney and Melbourne) was again demonstrated. The results also showed no difference between the two cohorts

Table 7.4 Log odds of becoming home owners in the one-year interval between the two interviews

	Estimate	Std. error
Constant	-2.387*	0.292
Migrant's age at arrival		
15–24	0.097	-0.198
24–34	0.356	0.177
35–44	0.736*	0.183
45–54	0.584	0.210
55+	-	-
Marital status at first interview		
Currently married	0.668*	0.114
Not currently married	-	-
Highest education		
Higher degree	-0.506	0.138
Degree	-0.021	0.111
Trade certificate/diploma	-0.043	0.100
No post-school qualification	-	
Household income at first interview		
Up to $25,000	-0.771*	0.121
$25,001–$50,000	-0.062	0.104
$50,001 or more	0.389*	0.101
Not stated	-	
Visa category		
Family	0.089	0.207
Skilled – Australian Sponsored	0.251	0.211
BS/ENS	-	-
Independent	0.320	0.198
Humanitarian	-0.999*	0.258
Number in migrating unit		
One	-0.164	0.140
Two	-0.001	0.139
Three	-0.129	0.141
Four or more	-	-
$'00,000 brought at migration	0.103*	0.031
State of residence		
New South Wales	-0.646*	0.085
Victoria	-0.535*	0.098
Other	-	-
Cohort		
Cohort 1	0.106	0.080
Cohort 2	-	-
Likelihood ratio chi-square	421	
df	22	
N	7,114	

Notes:
- = reference category
* $p<0.001$.

Figure 7.2 Comparison of migrants' housing arrangements at Wave 1 and Wave 2

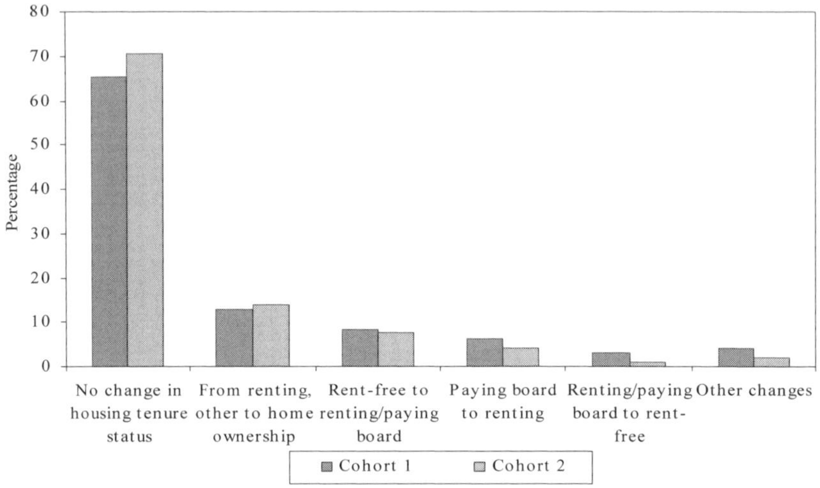

Source: Longitudinal Survey of Immigrants to Australia.

in their transition to home ownership once differences in their profile and composition had been taken into account. Observed differences between the two cohorts in the rate of home ownership and the transition to home ownership were due to differences in their characteristics and visa composition, brought about by policy changes. The different times of arrival and the differences in the state of the economy and the housing market did not appear to affect migrants' transition to home ownership.

HOUSING COSTS

Housing costs are a significant budget item for both renters and mortgage holders. In the survey migrants were asked to indicate the amount of mortgage payment or rent they (and their spouse) paid each week. A comparison of the weekly mortgage payments shows that the second cohort had a higher median mortgage payment at six months after arrival than the first cohort, but there was no difference between the two cohorts one year later after adjustment was made for inflation (Table 7.5).[8] Renters in the second cohort had a higher median rent payment than renters in the first cohort at both six and 18 months after arrival, even after adjusting for inflation.[9] The median rent payment was lower generally than the median mortgage payment.

Table 7.5 Housing costs at Wave 1 and Wave 2 (% of migrants in Cohort 1 and Cohort 2)

Weekly payment	Wave 1		Wave 2	
	Cohort1	Cohort 2	Cohort 1	Cohort 2
	%	%	%	%
Mortgage				
<$50	1.3	0.1	0.5	0.5
$50–$99	10.9	5.3	4.7	4.9
$100–$149	21.9	13.8	18.2	13.1
$150–$199	15.1	16.1	18.2	14.3
$200–$299	27.4	28.5	32.4	31.3
$300–$499	13.5	13.5	16.7	18.5
$500+	5.0	11.7	6.8	11.9
Not stated	5.8	8.4	2.5	5.5
Median	$203	$223*	$226	$226*
N	288	223	677	502
Rent				
<$50	2.9	1.8	2.2	1.3
$50–$99	17.4	10.0	17.4	9.0
$100–$149	39.2	25.3	38.0	23.2
$150–$199	27.7	31.6	28.9	31.7
$200–$299	8.8	21.3	11.4	25.2
$300–$499	1.8	7.4	1.4	7.6
$500+	0.7	2.3	0.7	1.9
Not stated	1.5	0.3	0.1	0.1
Median	$138	$146*	$140	$151*
N	2553	1400	2642	1385

* Cohort 2 median mortgage payment in 1993 dollars, after adjusting for inflation between 1993 and 1999 as measured by the Consumer Price Index. The increase in CPI based on rents only was used to adjust the median rent payment to 1993 dollars.

Source: Longitudinal Survey of Immigrants to Australia.

Table 7.6 shows the results of logistic regression analyses modelling the probability of having high housing costs, which are defined as mortgage payment of $300 or more per week or rent payment of $200 or more per week. These thresholds are higher than the median mortgage or rent payments and represent the top 20–30 per cent of housing costs. The analyses show that Business Skills and Employer Nomination migrants, migrants with higher educational qualifications, those who have higher household income, or those who brought more money with them were more likely to have higher housing costs than other migrants. It was also clear that migrants living in New South Wales were the most likely to pay mortgages of at least $300 per week or rents of at least $200 per week. Migrants living in South Australia and Tasmania were the least likely to pay these amounts. Given this situation it is rather ironic that, in spite of the high housing costs, New South Wales is

Table 7.6 Log odds of experiencing high housing costs: Mortgagees and renters at six and 18 months after migration

	Mortgages of $300+ pw		Rent of $200+pw	
	Wave 1	Wave 2	Wave 1	Wave 2
Constant	-2.973	-3.498	-2.734*	-2.772*
Principal Applicant's age at arrival				
15–24	0.604	2.149	0.040	0.157
24–34	1.864	1.810	0.725	0.211
35–44	1.659	1.873	0.718	-0.063
45–54	0.437	1.750	0.938	0.445
55+	-	-	-	-
Marital status at first interview				
Currently married	-0.405	0.144	0.029	-0.068
Not currently married	-	-	-	-
Highest education				
Higher degree	0.694	0.825*	0.963*	0.432*
Degree	0.586	0.524	0.580*	0.251
Trade certificate/diploma	-0.558	0.000	0.547*	0.293
No post-school qualification	-	-	-	-
Household income at first interview				
Up to $25,000	-1.287	-1.458*	-0.26	-0.657
$25,001–$50,000	-0.972	-0.991*	0.157	0.038
$50,001 or more	0.570	0.515	1.454*	1.333*
Not stated	-	-	-	-
Visa category				
Family	-0.386	-1.242*	-0.905*	-0.915*
Skilled – Australian Sponsored	-1.400	-0.855	-1.387*	-1.469*
BS/ENS	-	-	-	-
Independent skilled	-0.266	-0.669	-1.567*	-1.358*
Humanitarian	-	-1.603	-2.302*	-1.987*
Number in migrating unit				
One	-1.107	0.165	-0.858*	-0.475
Two	-0.346	0.432	-0.588*	-0.004
Three	-1.211	-0.446	-0.698*	-0.493
Four or more	-	-	-	-
$'00,000 brought at migration	0.591*	0.129	0.781*	1.688*
State of residence				
New South Wales	2.114*	1.813*	2.546*	3.285*
Victoria	0.866	1.139	1.058	1.734*
Queensland	1.247	1.497*	1.395*	2.014*
South Australia & Tasmania	-	-	-	-
Western Australia	1.090	0.691	0.804	1.690*
NT and ACT	2.305	0.946	0.756	2.817*
Cohort				
Cohort 1	-0.509	-0.374	-1.159*	-1.085*
Cohort 2	-	-	-	-
Likelihood ratio chi-square	156	247	1043	1112
df	24	25	25	25
N	468	1125	3875	3981

Notes:
- = reference category
* p<0.01

Table 7.7 Change in housing costs for migrants between six and 18 months after arrival

	Change in housing costs			No. of respondents	Total population
	No change	Decrease	Increase		
	% of migrants				
Migrants with mortgages at both times					
Cohort 1	51.2	20.4	28.5	241	3219
Cohort 2	44.7	27.3	28.1	188	2838
Migrants renting at both times					
Cohort 1	68.2	9.4	22.4	2102	28431
Cohort 2	67.1	9.8	23.1	1116	12449
Migrants who were not home owners at 6 months but become so at 18 months after arrival					
Cohort 1	11.7	9.5	78.7	409	6112
Cohort 2	17.6	14.1	68.3	290	3433

* Chi-square tests show differences between the two cohorts are not significant ($p>0.05$).

the most favoured place to live for recently arrived immigrants while South Australia and Tasmania have difficulty attracting their share of immigrants. The 1999 Australian Housing Survey showed that housing costs were also lowest in the capital cities of these two states (ABS 2000).

After controlling for differences between the two cohorts in personal and migration characteristics, no significant difference was observed between the two cohorts in relation to their having a high mortgage payment. However, renters in the second cohort were much more likely to have rents of at least $200 per week than were renters in the first cohort. This confirms the findings shown in Table 7.5 that Cohort 2 migrants had higher median rent payments than Cohort 1 migrants, even after adjusting for inflation. There could be a number of reasons for this cohort difference. A possible reason might be that the second cohort had different housing preferences from the first cohort and were more likely to live in higher rent suburbs or rent larger houses or apartments than the first cohort.

Do housing costs change for migrants during the early years of settlement? Table 7.7 examines this question separately for migrants who were paying mortgages or rents at the time of the first and second interviews and for those who changed their housing status in the interim period from renter to home buyer. The majority of migrants who did not change their housing status – they had mortgages at Waves 1 and 2 or they were renting at both points in time – reported little or no change in their housing costs.[10] For migrants who did not change their housing status as mortgagees or renters, there was no difference between the two cohorts in the proportion who experienced a decrease or an increase in their housing costs.

However, among migrants who changed their housing status from renting, boarding or living rent-free at six months of arrival to having a mortgage one year later, at least two-thirds reported an increase in housing costs. The percentage reporting an increase in housing costs was also larger for migrants in Cohort 1 than in Cohort 2. Logistic regression analysis for this group that controls for migrant characteristics, visa category and state of residence also confirms this finding. The analysis also showed that migrants in South Australia and Tasmania were the least likely to face an increase in housing costs when they changed their housing status from renting or other tenure arrangements to becoming a home owner with a mortgage. This is another indication of the favourable housing situation in the capital cities of these two states for new immigrants choosing to settle there. Migrants in the Independent and Skilled – Australian Sponsored categories were more likely to increase their housing costs when they changed housing status compared with other migrants. This suggests that these migrants might have improved their economic outcomes to a greater extent during this period of settlement than other migrants, enabling them to afford an increase in housing costs by purchasing their own home.

HOUSING AFFORDABILITY

Housing costs need to be examined in relation to income to ascertain whether migrants are having difficulty with high housing costs in the early years of their settlement. The standard measure of housing affordability is the percentage of household income devoted to housing costs. In this chapter, the measure of housing affordability is based on only the Principal Applicant's (and spouse's if present) gross weekly income rather than the household income since data collected on housing costs refer to the costs paid by the Principal Applicant (and spouse) only.[11] It has been suggested that households spending more than 30 per cent of their income are believed to face affordability problems and those spending more than 50 per cent of their income on housing would have severe affordability problems (Ray et al. 2004). The threshold used in this chapter to indicate financial stress in meeting housing costs is 40 per cent or more of income spent on housing, in accordance with earlier analysis of LSIA data by Richardson et al. (2002).

Table 7.8 examines housing costs paid by the Principal Applicant (and spouse) as a percentage of their income for those who were paying mortgages or rents at six and 18 months after arrival.[12] On average new migrants spent about 30–40 per cent of their gross income on mortgage or rent payments, which would indicate some affordability problems. There was little difference between the two cohorts and between renters and mortgagees in terms of the proportion of their income spent on housing on average. The 1999 Australian Housing Survey showed that households in the second lowest income quintile with mortgages or renting privately spent about 30 per cent of their income on housing (ABS 2000). The comparative percentages for households in the lowest and highest income quintiles were 64 and 12 respectively.

A higher proportion of migrants in the first cohort were paying at least 40 per cent of their income on housing compared with migrants in the second cohort. This was observed at both six and 18 months after arrival for both mortgagees and renters. The difference between the two cohorts in terms of the percentage of their income spent on housing also appeared to widen slightly over time. At 18 months after arrival, migrants in Cohort 1 were paying on average 5 percentage points more of their income in mortgages or rents than migrants in Cohort 2, compared with a difference of 2 percentage points at six months after arrival.

Table 7.8 Percentage of migrants according to percentage of income spent on mortgages or rents

	Percentage of income spent on mortgage or rent				Mean % income spent on housing	Number of respondents
	0%	1–19%	20–39%	40%+		
	% of migrants					
Migrants with mortgages at 6 months after arrival						
Cohort 1	34.0	19.7	17.3	29.0	27	227
Cohort 2	29.0	18.1	27.7	25.2	29	213
Migrants with mortgages at 18 months after arrival						
Cohort 1	11.7	14.2	34.3	39.8	41	672
Cohort 2	12.8	22.9	32.9	31.4	36	481
Migrants with rent payments at 6 months after arrival						
Cohort 1	20.2	18.6	28.3	33.0	33	2,437
Cohort 2	18.9	27.5	26.4	27.2	31	1,400
Migrants with rent payments at 18 months after arrival						
Cohort 1	8.9	23.0	34.8	33.3	36	2,638
Cohort 2	12.4	30.5	32.0	25.1	31	1,383

Note:
Percentage distribution is based on weighted sample.

Source: Longitudinal Survey of Immigrants to Australia.

There was also an increase in the percentage with housing affordability problems during the one-year period between the first and second interviews for mortgagees in both cohorts – but not for renters. Many migrants had taken out mortgages between the first and second interviews. It would appear that for many Cohort 1 migrants who did this the mortgage payments were at least 30 per cent of their income, putting them in a problematic situation in terms of housing affordability.

Differences in housing affordability were observed by visa category (Figure 7.3). Among migrants with mortgages, those in the Family stream category were the most likely to have housing affordability problems, while few migrants in the skilled visa categories, particularly in the second cohort, were in this situation.[13] Nearly 40 per cent of migrants in the Family stream and Humanitarian categories who were renters were paying at least 40 per cent of their income on housing.

When the two cohorts were compared in regression analyses controlling for differences in migrant characteristics and composition, there were no significant differences between them in terms of housing affordability problems (Table 7.9). There were also no significant differences by age or education. Married migrants were less likely to have housing affordability problems than unmarried migrants at six months after arrival but there was not much difference a year later. As expected, migrants living in lower income households were more likely to have housing affordability problems and this was particularly so among renters.

The regression analyses confirm earlier observations that Family stream migrants were the most likely to experience housing affordability problems. Family stream and Humanitarian migrants who were renters had a much greater likelihood of paying at least 40 per cent of their income on housing than skilled migrants, although the situation of Humanitarian migrants in relation to other migrants appeared to improve between the two interviews.

Location was again an important factor in migrants having problems with housing affordability. Migrants who were renters in New South Wales were the most likely to have a problem with housing affordability. Migrants in South Australia and Tasmania were the least likely to have mortgage payments exceeding 40 per cent of their income.

The positive relation between funds transferred on arrival and housing affordability among renters might be explained by the possibility that migrants who brought more money might have lower recurrent income. These migrants might not really be in a financially stressed situation, having brought in sufficient funds to pay for their housing costs.

Do migrants' housing costs as a percentage of their income increase or decrease during the early years of settlement? The availability of longitudinal data makes it possible to examine whether this percentage changes and in

Figure 7.3 Percentage of migrants paying 40 per cent or more of income in housing costs, at six and 18 months after arrival, by visa category

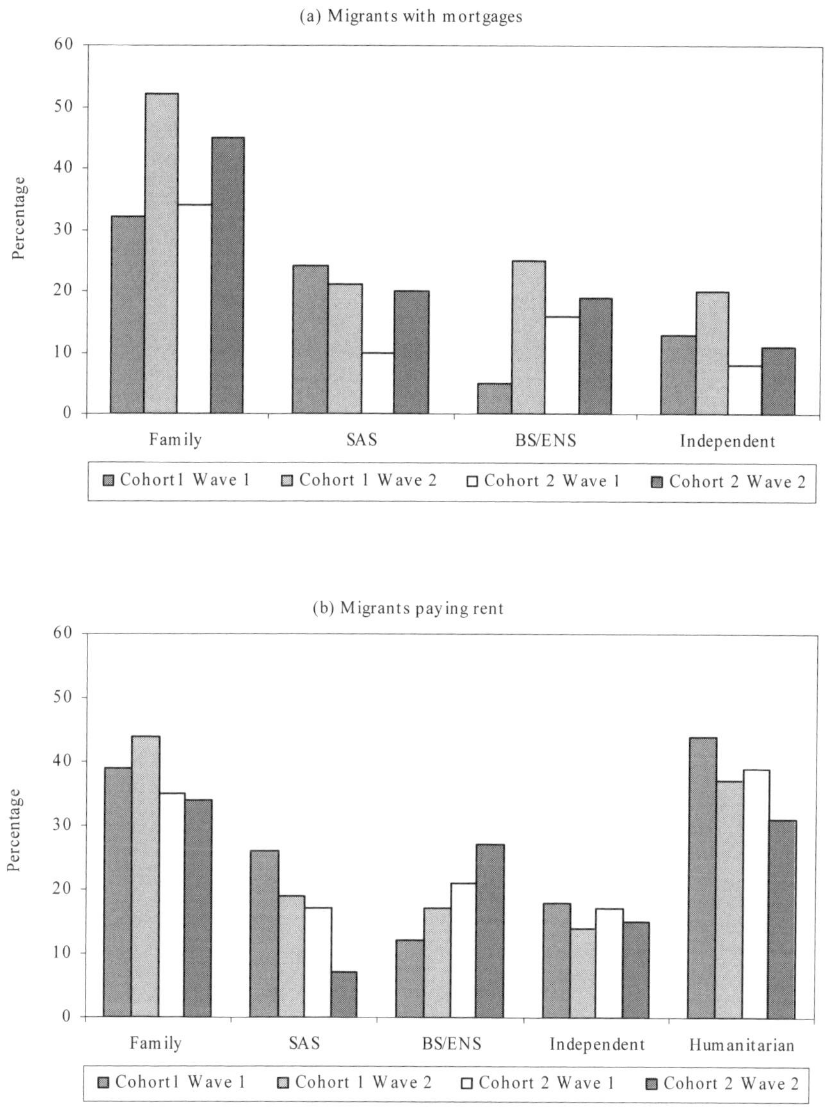

Source: Longitudinal Survey of Immigrants to Australia.

Table 7.9 Log odds of paying 40 per cent or more of income on housing, by migrants' tenure status

	Migrants with mortgages		Migrants in rental housing	
	Wave 1	Wave 2	Wave 1	Wave 2
Constant	-2.760	-2.847*	-1.563*	-1.560*
Migrant age at arrival				
15–24	1.325	0.892	-0.350	0.092
24–34	1.006	0.187	-0.416	-0.159
35–44	1.275	0.442	-0.363	0.009
45–54	-	0.488	-0.241	0.047
55+		-	-	-
Marital status at first interview				
Currently married	-1.613*	0.163	-0.527*	-0.078
Not currently married	-	-	-	
Highest education				
Higher degree	0.239	0.277	0.047	0.071
Degree	-0.802	0.015	0.036	-0.071
Trade certificate/diploma	0.276	0.244	-0.056	-0.148
No post-school qualification	-	-		
Household income at first interview				
Up to $25,000	0.428	-0.040	0.660*	0.771*
$25,001–$50,000	-0.197	0.042	-0.186	-0.442*
$50,001 or more	-0.085	-0.236	-0.908*	-1.222*
Not stated	-	-	-	-
Visa category				
Family	1.598	1.075*	1.558*	1.128*
Skilled – Australian Sponsored	0.543	0.027	0.454	-0.321
BS/ENS	-	-	-	-
Independent skilled	-0.595	-0.065	0.181	-0.327
Humanitarian		0.556	1.058*	0.479
Number in migrating unit				
One	-0.142	0.521	-0.418*	0.251
Two	-0.146	-0.308	0.152	0.451*
Three	0.073	0.186	0.272	0.343
Four or more	-	-	-	-
$'00,000 brought at migration	-0.171	0.111	0.158*	0.306*
State of residence				
New South Wales	1.322	0.731	0.816*	0.559*
Victoria	0.730	0.854*	0.434	0.196
Queensland	2.341*	0.543	0.554*	-0.066
South Australia & Tasmania	-	-	-	-
Western Australia	1.352	0.192	0.299	-0.137
Northern Territory & Australian Capital Territory	-0.326	1.113	0.339	0.249
Cohort				
Cohort 1	-0.269	0.269	0	0.156
Cohort 2	-	-	-	-
Likelihood ratio chi-square	77	174	499	750
df	23	25	25	25
N	421	1137	3806	3982

Notes:
\- = reference category
* p<0.01

which direction for those migrants who remained as mortgagees or renters during the first 1–2 years of settlement and those who changed their housing tenure from renters to mortgagees (Table 7.10). For migrants who had mortgages or were renting and did not change their housing status, about 20 per cent experienced no change in their housing costs in relation to income. A greater number had a decrease in their housing costs in relation to income than had an increase. The percentages experiencing an increase or a decrease were similar for both cohorts. For migrants whose status changed from renters to mortgagees, only 10 per cent experienced no change in the housing affordability index while 50–60 per cent faced an increase in housing costs in relation to their income. Again the same pattern of change was observed for both cohorts. The figures in Table 7.10 show that migrants are more likely to see their housing affordability index increase if they transition from renting to having a mortgage. But the different economic conditions and state of the housing market faced by the two cohorts during their early settlement period did not appear to have any effect on whether their housing costs as a percentage of their income increase or decrease during this period.

Table 7.10 Change in the housing affordability index by housing status

	Change in housing affordability index			Average change in index
	Decrease	No change*	Increase	
	% of migrants			
Migrants with mortgages at 6 and 18 months after arrival				
Cohort 1	44.7	20.7	34.5	9.9
Cohort 2	42.2	20.5	37.3	5.7
Migrants renting at 6 and 18 months after arrival				
Cohort 1	45.0	16.7	38.3	2.1
Cohort 2	44.4	20.5	34.8	-1.6
Migrants renting at 6 months and owning at 18 months after arrival				
Cohort 1	32.6	10.0	57.4	8.0
Cohort 2	38.0	9.6	52.4	7.5

Notes:
* No change can include those who did not report an income at both interviews.
Chi-square tests show differences between the two cohorts are not significant ($p>0.05$).

Source: Longitudinal Survey of Immigrants to Australia.

CONCLUSION

This chapter has set out to determine if immigrants' housing outcomes in the early years of settlement are more likely to be affected by factors such as their demographic and socioeconomic characteristics, visa category of migration and location of residence or by cohort effects associated with the period of their arrival that may be related to the prevailing economic conditions. A comparison of two cohorts of immigrants who arrived in Australia about six years apart, under different selection criteria for skilled migration and facing different economic conditions, allows us to assess the relative importance of composition and cohort effects in influencing housing outcomes.

The main findings (summarised in Table 7.11) are that composition effects – and therefore public policy that influences migrant cohort composition – are important in affecting migrants' transition into home ownership and the home ownership rate during the first few years of settlement. Cohort effects that might be related to timing of arrival seem to have no significant influence on migrants' transition to home ownership.

The observed differences between the two migrant cohorts in their rates of home ownership and transition to home ownership during the early years of settlement can be explained by differences in their demographic and socioeconomic characteristics, visa composition and the amount of funds brought with them. Once these factors were taken into account in regression analyses, there was no significant difference between the two cohorts in their home ownership rate or propensity to become home owners during the one-year period of observation between the first and second interviews. This indicates that migrants' characteristics were more important in influencing migrants' housing tenure status than the macroeconomic conditions they faced at the time of arrival and that different cohorts of immigrants adjust to different conditions on arrival as part of their settlement process.

The cohort that arrived in 1999–2000 faced higher housing costs than the cohort that arrived in 1993–1995. This was particularly so among renters, even after adjusting for inflation in rents between 1993 and 1999 and controlling for differences in cohort characteristics. It is possible that part of the cohort effect might be due to cohort differences in housing preferences. For example, migrants in Cohort 2 might have preferred more spacious housing or living in higher-rent suburbs compared with migrants in Cohort 1. The analyses in this chapter have not taken into account any differences in housing characteristics and locality in examining housing outcomes.

There was, however, no difference between the two cohorts on the measure of housing affordability once differences in cohort composition had been taken into account. The more favourable economic conditions and the housing market boom of the late 1990s did not appear to affect housing affordability among the second cohort of migrants compared with the first cohort, possibly because the better labour market outcomes of the second cohort, as shown in previous chapters, might have offset any increase in housing costs. Family stream and Humanitarian migrants in both cohorts were more likely to spend more on housing in relation to their income than other migrants. As for Australian residents generally, migrants in low-income households in both cohorts were also more likely to have problems with housing affordability.

Table 7.11 Summary of findings

Indicator	Findings	Conclusion
Home ownership at six and 18 months after arrival	Cohort effect significant at six months but not at 18 months after arrival after controlling for differences in composition.	Cohort effect important soon after arrival, but not in longer term. Evidence of policy effect.
Transition to home ownership between six and 18 months after arrival	No difference between cohorts after controlling for differences in composition	Cohort effect not important. Evidence of policy effect.
Housing costs	Cohort 2 renters had higher housing costs after controlling for differences in composition	Evidence of both policy and cohort effects
Change in housing costs during the first 18 months of settlement	No observed difference between the two cohorts	No evidence of policy or cohort effects.
Housing costs>40% of income	No difference between cohorts after controlling for differences in composition	Cohort effect not important. Evidence of policy effect.
Change in housing affordability index during the first 18 months of settlement	No observed difference between the two cohorts.	No evidence of policy or cohort effects.

There was no evidence of composition or cohort effects on *changes* in housing costs or housing affordability during the early period of migrant settlement. The percentages of migrants experiencing an increase or a decrease in housing costs or housing affordability were the same for both cohorts after controlling for housing tenure status. Migrants were more likely to increase their housing costs and pay more for housing in relation to their income if they changed status from renting to having a mortgage than if they maintained the same housing status.

All the data modelling shows the importance of location in influencing housing outcomes. Migrants settling in the Sydney metropolitan area in New

South Wales had a lower rate of home ownership, were less likely to buy a house during the early years of settlement, had higher housing costs and were more likely to have housing affordability problems than migrants settling elsewhere. The housing outcomes were the most favourable for migrants settling in South Australia and Tasmania. Yet a large proportion of new immigrants each year are attracted to Sydney and very few choose to settle in South Australia or Tasmania. Obviously housing costs are not very important in influencing migrants' residential location decisions. LSIA data have shown that this decision is more commonly based on the presence of family and friends and perceptions of employment opportunities (Richardson et al. 2002). Evidently migrants are prepared to pay more for housing to live in larger cities with more employment opportunities and family and social networks than in smaller cities where they do not have such networks. The lower housing costs and higher rate of home ownership in smaller cities are not enough to compensate for living away from family and friends and where the jobs are.

The findings described in this chapter – that immigrants' housing outcomes are related to their personal characteristics, visa category and location of residence but not to when they arrive in Australia – are not surprising. They suggest that immigration policies that determine the selection criteria of migrants and the composition of migration cohorts can have an impact on migrants' housing outcomes, particularly in relation to home ownership, just as earlier chapters have shown that they also affect language skills and labour market outcomes. Immigration policy affecting the selection criteria of migrants and the composition of migration cohorts, therefore, can have implications for housing demand and the housing market, particularly in the gateway cities favoured by new migrants. While migrants arriving at different times may face different economic conditions and while this may affect their housing costs, it does not seem to affect their transition to home ownership and the proportion of their income spent on housing. It would appear that migration cohorts reconcile their housing costs and tenure status to the economic and housing conditions they face on arrival. Whether their housing costs increase or decrease with settlement appears to be dependent primarily on whether they change housing tenure status. There was no difference between the two cohorts on this measure for those who did not change their housing status in spite of differences in their composition and period of arrival.

NOTES

1 Immigrants in the Humanitarian visa categories were not subjected to the two-year waiting period for access to welfare payments.

2 There were 13 income categories in the LSIA survey questionnaire, so the range of each income group was not very broad. The last open-ended category posed a problem. A value twice that of the beginning of the open-ended category has been assumed in these cases.

3 Richardson et al. took into consideration the income of all family members and imputed an income for family members where no information was available. In calculating the index of housing stress in this paper only the stated income of the Principal Applicant migrant and spouse has been used, as the question on housing costs asked how much was paid by the Principal Applicant and spouse. A higher proportion of migrants will experience housing stress according to this calculation compared with Richardson et al.'s calculation.

4 The Skilled stream includes the Skilled Independent, Business Skills and Employer Nominated visa categories.

5 In calculating the average amount of funds transferred by migrants, it was assumed that those who did not answer the question brought in zero funds. Without this assumption, the average amount would have been much higher for both cohorts, but the second cohort still brought in twice as much on average as the first cohort. Further examination of the data showed that it was mainly the Business migrants who were responsible for the large increase in the average amount transferred by the two cohorts: their average doubled from $164,000 to $337,000. Skilled migrants in the second cohort also brought in more money on average than those in the first cohort ($37,000 compared to $23,000). The average amount of funds brought in by Family stream migrants increased only slightly between the two cohorts ($14,000 to $16,000) and there was a small decrease in the already small amount of funds brought in by Humanitarian migrants (from $600 to $300)

6 Regression coefficients were estimated using SAS version 8. In these analyses, the data were weighted and then normalised.

7 Differences among the other states were not significant compared with New South Wales and Victoria; therefore the other states were combined into a single reference category for analysis.

8 The increase in the Consumer Price Index (CPI) between 1993 and 1999 was 12.8 per cent based on the weighted average of eight capital cities (http://www.ato.gov.au/print.asp?doc=/content/cpi.htm).

9 The increase in the CPI based on rents only was 16.4 percentage points between 1993 and 1999. This was used to adjust the median rent payment for Cohort 2 to 1993 dollars.

10 Change was defined as a movement from one housing cost grouping to another. If migrants' housing costs increased from $200 to $250 no change in housing costs would have been recorded in the survey since the migrants would be recorded as having housing costs within the $200–$299 range at both points in time.

11 Only information on gross income was collected; information was not collected on net income and it was not possible to estimate their income net of taxes.

12 Migrants who paid 0 per cent of their income on housing were those who did not state their income or reported no income.

13 There were very few Humanitarian migrants with mortgages within the first two years of arrival.

PART FOUR

CONCLUSION

8. Public Policy and Immigrant Settlement: How Much Does Immigrant Selection Matter?

Deborah A. Cobb-Clark and Siew-Ean Khoo

INTRODUCTION

Immigration is the component of demographic change that is most directly under the control of policy makers. Other elements of demographic change – fertility, mortality, emigration – are certainly influenced by a broad range of education, health or labour market policies, but usually only indirectly. Immigration officials, on the other hand, directly choose the number of immigrants and the circumstances under which they are to be accepted. Not surprisingly then, there is a great deal of interest in the ways in which immigration policy might matter not only for immigrants themselves, but also for the economic and social well-being of society more broadly.

This book centres on understanding the way that Australian immigrant selection and settlement policies affect a broad range of immigrant outcomes including labour market status, English language acquisition, health and housing. Though the focus is on a set of specific policy changes taking place in Australia in the mid- to late 1990s, the conclusions have much wider implications. Many countries are placing a greater weight in the selection process on productive skills as a way of achieving national objectives regarding immigration. These changes stem from the belief that immigrants selected for their skills find settlement easier and provide greater economic benefits than immigrants admitted on the basis of their family relationships or out of humanitarian concerns.

Against this backdrop, there is much to be learned from Australia. Australia is after all a nation of immigrants. Nearly one in four individuals (23 per cent) enumerated in the 2001 Australian Census were foreign born, while an additional 18 per cent were second generation, having been born in Australia to at least one foreign-born parent.[1] Moreover, Australia's unique position as an island-continent implies that immigrant selection lies firmly in the hands of policy makers. Although there is some illegal migration, mainly through abuse of legal non-immigrant visas, Australia's national immigration policy is not undermined by large-scale, undocumented migration (as is the case in the United States) or greatly limited by the policies of other countries (as is the case in the European Union).[2]

Most importantly, the type of the policy changes taking place in Australia, combined with the strengths of the Longitudinal Survey of Immigrants to Australia (LSIA) data, provide us with a truly unique opportunity to study directly the impact of selection policy on the settlement of immigrants. As Chiswick and Miller discuss in Chapter 1, the Australian Government began in the mid-1990s to place greater weight on productivity-related characteristics in the selection decision. The LSIA data provide information about immigrant outcomes immediately before and immediately after this change in government policy. Moreover, information about the administrative details of the migration application (that is, visa class, Principal Applicant status etc.) allows us to identify the individuals who were and were not required to meet the selection criteria. Unlike other data sources such as the census or labour force surveys, the LSIA is specifically designed to capture in some detail the early settlement experiences of immigrants. These features of the LSIA data are instrumental in allowing us to assess the impact of this policy change across a wide range of outcomes.[3]

THE POLICY CONTEXT IN THE 1990s

A number of factors contributed to the more successful settlement of those arriving in Australia in the later part of the 1990s in comparison to those who arrived approximately five years earlier. In particular, the early 1990s were a time of relatively high unemployment and generally falling labour market participation rates. Wage rigidities stemming from a history of centralised wage bargaining imply that adjustment in the Australian labour market occurs primarily along the employment rather than the wage dimension (Miller and Neo 2003). Consequently, immigrants arriving at the beginning of the decade faced a much larger hurdle in accessing the Australian labour market. It is perhaps not surprising that immigrants entering between 1993 and 1995 (LSIA Cohort 1) had an unemployment rate of 22.3 per cent 18 months after arrival, as shown in Chapter 2.

Migrants arriving between 1999 and 2000 (LSIA Cohort 2) were much better prepared for the challenges of entering the Australian labour market. A higher proportion of immigrants entered on a skills-based visa, reflecting the overall expansion of the skilled immigration program and the relative scaling back of the admittance of family-based and humanitarian migrants. Further, changes in selection policy in the mid-1990s were targeted towards strengthening the characteristics – English language ability, education, labour market experience – that previous research had shown to be important for labour market success. Individuals in Cohort 2 were more educated, spoke better English, and had more recent labour market experience. As demonstrated in Chapter 3, Principal Applicants in Cohort 2 took only half as much time as Cohort 1 to find their first job and, 18 months after migration, the unemployment rate amongst Cohort 2 immigrants was 9.9 per cent, as shown in Chapter 2.

Given these results, it seems almost self-evident that immigration policy led to an improvement in immigrants' labour market outcomes. At the same time, changes in immigration policy were coupled with changes in welfare policy that tightened access to taxpayer-funded income-support programs. The inability to access public assistance almost certainly influenced migration decisions, reduced any benefit-induced unemployment and increased Cohort 2's incentives to enter the labour market quickly and find a job. Moreover, improvements in labour market conditions over the decade would have made finding this job easier.

It is an open question then whether it is immigration policy itself or labour market conditions and income-support policy that is most directly responsible for the improvement in immigrants' labour market position. We would also like to know the extent to which these changes in selection policy led to improvements in related outcomes. While the chapters in Part 2 of the book focus on the former issue, the chapters in Part 3 focus on the latter.

IS SELECTION POLICY SIMPLY ABOUT ALLOCATION ACROSS VISA TYPES?

There is one consistent conclusion from the various analyses that make up this book: visa category matters. The type of visa an immigrant holds tells us a great deal about his or her chances of labour market success (as we might expect), and is also important for understanding dimensions of immigrant settlement. Immigrants holding skills-based visas are better able to communicate in English (Chapter 5), are less likely to have a chronic disease or be in poor health (Chapter 6), and are less likely to be burdened with high housing costs immediately after migration (Chapter 7). Humanitarian immigrants, in contrast, have relatively poor English skills, poor health, and poor housing outcomes.

Given this strong link between visa status and outcomes, there is an enormous potential for selection policy to affect immigrant settlement simply by altering the visa composition of the immigrant flow. The particular difficulties faced by refugees could be avoided, for example, if no humanitarian immigrants were admitted. In most cases, however, it is not this simple.

Immigrant selection policy is about more than achieving economic outcomes for migrants. In particular, selection policy must also meet a variety of other, often conflicting, goals regarding the provision of social justice through the reunification of families and the acceptance of global responsibility through the admittance of refugees. Moreover, potential immigrants will seek the easiest or cheapest visa to enter Australia. If the bar is raised for one type of visa, the potential applicant will try another. Is there scope then for selection policy to affect immigrant outcomes beyond the impact on overall composition across visa categories?

Based on our analysis of changes in Australian selection policy in the 1990s, the answer appears to be a resounding yes. While visa composition effects are important, they are by no means the only mechanism through which immigration policy affects immigrant settlement. There is also evidence that immigration policy does influence the human capital characteristics of new arrivals.[4] For example, changes to the Occupations Requiring English (ORE) list had a positive and substantial impact on the English language ability of new arrivals, while the introduction of points for English skills among Skilled – Australia Sponsored immigrants also had a positive (though more minor) effect. It seems clear that Australian policy has had an effect on the language skills of immigrants, as demonstrated in Chapter 5.

Moreover, English language skills along with other human capital characteristics (education, labour market experience, region of origin) play an important role in immigrant settlement – even after we account for visa category. The employment-to-population ratio is higher and the time taken to find the first job is lower amongst native English speakers for example (as observed in Chapters 2 and 3), while more highly educated immigrants have better housing outcomes (Chapter 7). These human capital characteristics have a direct effect on improving settlement outcomes over and above the indirect effect they have through determining an individual's visa class.

HOW MUCH DOES SELECTION POLICY MATTER FOR IMMIGRANT SETTLEMENT?

In addition to identifying the relationship between immigrant skills and settlement outcomes, the various chapters in this book also attempt to quantify how much changes in the skill distribution might matter for immigrant settlement. How much of the improved labour market outcomes of new arrivals can we attribute to the changes in their characteristics?

Our answer is that changes in the human capital characteristics of immigrants over the 1990s contributed substantially to the improvement in their labour market and housing outcomes. All of the change in men's labour market participation rate, and more than three-quarters of the change in the participation rate of women, can be attributed to changes in productivity-related characteristics, as demonstrated in Chapter 2. It is interesting, however, that changes in immigrant skills are equally important in understanding the increased participation of both women who are tied movers and women who are primary movers, as observed in Chapter 4.

Changes in characteristics are less important in understanding employment outcomes, particularly those of women. Changing characteristics explain approximately half of the between-cohort difference in the unemployment rates of men, but none of the difference in the unemployment rates of women (Chapter 2). Moreover, Principal Applicants arriving at the end of the 1990s found their first job twice as quickly (approximately four months on average) as those Principal Applicants entering between 1993 and 1995. Differences in productivity-related characteristics account for between 28 and 40 per cent of this improvement for men, but only 10 to 22 per cent of the improvement for women (Chapter 3).

Thus, while inter-cohort differences in labour market participation rates are largely driven by disparities in the characteristics of immigrants themselves, differences in employment outcomes stem more from differences in the labour market returns to characteristics. In other words, an individual with a given set of human capital and demographic characteristics was less likely to be unemployed at the end of the 1990s than at the beginning. This change in the likelihood of finding work (conditional on one's characteristics) is the result of the general improvement in labour market conditions which made finding employment easier for immigrants and native-born alike. Moreover, the limitations on access to social assistance may have also contributed to increased employment by altering migration incentives, reducing any benefits-induced unemployment, altering the incentives for extended job search and altering the return migration rate of immigrants. Labour market outcomes are clearly related to the overall labour market conditions at the time of labour market entry.

At the same time, immigrants' demographic and socio-economic characteristics, visa composition and access to funds appear to drive housing outcomes, as shown in Chapter 7. Once these differences are taken into account, there is no difference in the home ownership rate or housing affordability of the two cohorts. This implies that the housing boom of the late 1990s did not make housing less affordable for new arrivals. Housing outcomes are more about the characteristics of immigrants themselves than when they arrived, demonstrating again the importance of immigration policy in relation to the selection of migrants and the composition of migration cohorts.

Australia's policy of requiring health checks for all immigrants prior to migration means that newly arrived immigrants are generally in better health than the resident population. However, as shown in Chapter 6, immigrants suffer declining health over time, even after allowing for the effect of ageing, and this decline seems to occur at about the same pace for all migrants regardless of their visa category, region of origin, economic circumstances and period of arrival. Selection policy appears not to have mattered in this aspect of settlement. After arrival all immigrants have access to Medicare, the universal health care system in Australia, and this might have contributed to the similarity in their health trajectory after migration.

The less favourable settlement outcomes observed for Humanitarian migrants are not unexpected considering that their admittance is based on claims of refugee status and other humanitarian concerns, not on selection criteria focusing on economic skills and productivity. To assist them in their settlement and in becoming active participants in the economy and in Australian society, the government provides a range of settlement services that include an adult English language program, accommodation support, health services such as torture and trauma counselling, and links to community support programs (Department of Immigration and Multicultural Affairs 2000). For refugees and other Humanitarian migrants, settlement policy is likely to be of greater relevance to their settlement outcomes than selection policy.

CONCLUSION

This book set out to examine whether government policies relating to immigrant selection criteria or the general macroeconomic environment immigrants face on arrival have a greater influence on their settlement outcomes. The conclusion from analysing longitudinal data for two cohorts of immigrants is that policy matters more for many outcomes than macroeconomic conditions. While better labour market conditions do contribute to better employment outcomes for new migrants, immigration policy that specifically affects the human capital characteristics of immigrant cohorts has a wide impact.

In particular, the effect of policy on immigrant settlement goes beyond the labour market. Labour market success is an important settlement outcome that has broader ramifications, leading to social mobility and greater engagement with the host society. It is therefore important that new migrants have the necessary skills and qualifications to enter the labour market quickly and receive positive returns on their human capital.

With many countries now trying to recruit skilled immigrants, the conclusions in this book regarding the role of public policy for immigrant settlement are important ones. Governments can have a role in immigrant selection, and through that on immigrant settlement. A structured immigration policy that has carefully considered criteria for the selection of economic migrants can deliver positive outcomes for the migrants themselves and for the broader host community.

NOTES

1 In comparison, 18.1 per cent of the Canadian and 11.2 per cent of the US population was foreign-born in 2001 (OECD, 2005).

2 The exception here is the 1973 Trans-Tasman Travel Agreement that allows New Zealand citizens to migrate to Australia without a visa. This agreement implies that immigration to Australia is potentially affected by immigration and citizenship policies in New Zealand.

3 See the Technical Appendix for more details about the LSIA data.

4 It is interesting that the demographic composition (that is, average age, gender ratio, marital status) of new arrivals did not change much over the 1990s (see the Technical Appendix).

Technical Appendix: Longitudinal Survey of Immigrants to Australia

Deborah A. Cobb-Clark

BACKGROUND

The Longitudinal Survey of Immigrants to Australia (LSIA) documents the settlement experiences of two cohorts of recent immigrants to Australia. More than 300 questions about the settlement process – including labour market adjustment, housing arrangements, health status and so on – are asked in each wave of the survey. LSIA data are particularly useful for understanding the role of selection criteria in facilitating immigrant settlement because of the availability of accurate information about detailed visa categories. [1] LSIA data are also well suited for shedding light on the experiences of different family members because it is a household rather than an individual-based survey. Detailed information is collected from all those spouses of Principal Applicants migrating as part of the same household, while limited information is collected for other household members as well. As Principal Applicants are distinguished from accompanying family members, researchers are able to specifically identify those individuals meeting the selection criteria for immigration. Moreover, by studying the same individuals over time, the LSIA allows for a fuller understanding of the process through which immigrants settle into life in Australia. These advantages of the data are critical to the various analyses in this book.

There are, however, two important limitations of the LSIA data for studying the process of immigrant settlement. First, the LSIA includes only immigrants and does not provide us with a comparison sample of native-born individuals. While comparisons can be made between different types of immigrants – that is, between those with different qualifications and skills, holding different visas, or in different family structures – it is not possible to say anything about immigrant status per se. Second, the Cohort 1 data span the first three and a half years after migration, while Cohort 2 reflect only the first 18 months. As such the data provide information about the early

Table A1: Visa status, demographic characteristics and human capital endowments

LSIA immigrants by gender and cohort
(Means[a] and Standard Deviations)

	Cohort 1						Cohort 2					
	Total		Men		Women		Total		Men		Women	
Visa Status												
Family – Principal Applicant	0.454	(0.498)	0.381	(0.486)	0.514	(0.500)	0.399	(0.490)	0.325	(0.468)	0.463	(0.499)
Family – Spouse	0.032	(0.175)	0.011	(0.105)	0.048	(0.215)	0.015	(0.122)	0.007	(0.085)	0.022	(0.145)
SAS – Principal Applicant	0.062	(0.241)	0.098	(0.298)	0.032	(0.176)	0.078	(0.268)	0.100	(0.300)	0.059	(0.236)
SAS – Spouse	0.039	(0.194)	0.018	(0.135)	0.056	(0.230)	0.046	(0.209)	0.045	(0.206)	0.046	(0.210)
IND – Principal Applicant	0.135	(0.342)	0.223	(0.416)	0.063	(0.243)	0.189	(0.391)	0.280	(0.449)	0.109	(0.312)
IND – Spouse	0.068	(0.252)	0.022	(0.147)	0.106	(0.308)	0.108	(0.311)	0.063	(0.243)	0.147	(0.354)
BS/ENS – Spouse	0.027	(0.162)	0.052	(0.221)	0.007	(0.083)	0.044	(0.206)	0.080	(0.272)	0.013	(0.115)
BS/ENS – Spouse	0.019	(0.137)	0.004	(0.061)	0.032	(0.176)	0.032	(0.177)	0.006	(0.077)	0.055	(0.228)
HUM – Principal Applicant	0.111	(0.315)	0.161	(0.368)	0.071	(0.256)	0.057	(0.232)	0.076	(0.264)	0.041	(0.198)
HUM – Spouse	0.053	(0.223)	0.030	(0.170)	0.071	(0.257)	0.032	(0.177)	0.019	(0.135)	0.044	(0.205)
Weeks since migration	19.1	(6.7)	19.4	(7.0)	18.8	(6.5)	21.9	(5.2)	22.1	(5.3)	21.8	(5.2)
Demographic												
Female	0.548	(0.498)	-	-	-	-	0.537	(0.499)	-	-	-	-
Married	0.769	(0.421)	0.747	(0.435)	0.788	(0.409)	0.792	(0.406)	0.761	(0.426)	0.818	(0.386)
Age	35.2	(12.5)	35.7	(12.0)	34.8	(12.9)	35.0	(10.5)	36.2	(10.3)	34.0	(10.5)
Education												
University	0.322	(0.467)	0.366	(0.482)	0.285	(0.452)	0.427	(0.495)	0.465	(0.499)	0.394	(0.489)
High school	0.269	(0.443)	0.209	(0.406)	0.318	(0.466)	0.216	(0.411)	0.169	(0.375)	0.256	(0.436)
< 10 years	0.128	(0.334)	0.090	(0.287)	0.159	(0.366)	0.079	(0.269)	0.052	(0.223)	0.102	(0.302)
Trade degree	0.274	(0.446)	0.331	(0.471)	0.227	(0.419)	0.275	(0.447)	0.310	(0.463)	0.245	(0.430)
English ability												
Native	0.307	(0.461)	0.345	(0.475)	0.275	(0.447)	0.379	(0.485)	0.430	(0.495)	0.334	(0.472)
English well	0.308	(0.462)	0.326	(0.469)	0.292	(0.455)	0.317	(0.465)	0.331	(0.471)	0.305	(0.461)
English badly	0.386	(0.487)	0.329	(0.470	0.432	(0.495)	0.304	(0.460)	0.239	(0.427)	0.360	(0.480)

	Cohort 1						Cohort 2					
	Total		Men		Women		Total		Men		Women	
Labour market experience in home country												
Professional	0.350	(0.477)	0.416	(0.493)	0.295	(0.456)	0.456	(0.498)	0.544	(0.498)	0.380	(0.486)
Skilled	0.293	(0.455)	0.328	(0.470)	0.264	(0.441)	0.259	(0.438)	0.291	(0.454)	0.230	(0.421)
Unskilled	0.035	(0.185)	0.043	(0.204)	0.029	(0.168)	0.012	(0.109)	0.011	(0.106)	0.013	(0.111)
Not employed	0.316	(0.465)	0.210	(0.407)	0.404	(0.491)	0.268	(0.443)	0.148	(0.355)	0.372	(0.483)
Time Unemployed (months)	0.7	(2.5)	0.8	(2.6)	0.7	(2.5)	0.5	(2.2)	0.6	(2.3)	0.5	(2.1)
English language proficiency group[b]												
Group 1	0.217	(0.412)	0.245	(0.430)	0.194	(0.395)	0.238	(0.426)	0.286	(0.452)	0.197	(0.398)
Group 2	0.268	(0.443)	0.257	(0.437)	0.277	(0.447)	0.314	(0.464)	0.302	(0.459)	0.324	(0.468)
Group 3	0.355	(0.479)	0.369	(0.483)	0.344	(0.475)	0.285	(0.451)	0.287	(0.452)	0.283	(0.451)
Group 4	0.160	(0.367)	0.128	(0.335)	0.186	(0.389)	0.163	(0.370)	0.126	(0.332)	0.196	(0.397)

Notes:

a Means are in percentages except for time since migration (weeks), age (years), and time unemployed (months).

b Group 1 is those countries rating 98 per cent or higher on the English proficiency index. Group 2 is those countries with a rating of 80 per cent or higher, while Group 3 is countries with a rating between 50 per cent and 80 per cent. Countries with a rating of less than 50 per cent make up Group 4 (DIMA, 1999). See text for other variable definitions.

settlement process rather than about long-run equilibrium behaviour. The shortness of the two panels leaves many important questions regarding long-term immigrant settlement unanswered.

TECHNICAL DETAILS

The LSIA data – Cohort 1 and Cohort 2 – comprise two separate immigrant entry cohorts.[2] Cohort 1 generalises to those Principal Applicants aged 15 and older arriving in Australia over a two-year period between September 1993 and August 1995. A total of 5,192 Principal Applicants and 1,837 Migrating Unit Spouses[3] were interviewed in the first wave of Cohort 1. A further 3,124 Principal Applicants and 1094 Migrating Unit Spouses were sampled in Wave 1 of Cohort 2. These individuals represent the cohort of Principal Applicants over the age of 15 years arriving between September 1999 to August 2000. Both Cohort 1 and Cohort 2 are stratified random samples and weights are provided which allow the stratification to be taken into account.[4] Each survey covered the capital cities of all eight Australian states and Territories as well as selected major urban areas.[5] New Zealand citizens, individuals under the age of 15, and people granted visas while in Australia are outside the scope of both Cohort 1 and Cohort 2.

Face-to-face interviews were conducted with both Principal Applicants and Migrating Unit Spouses. The form of the questionnaire is the same for Principal Applicants and spouses, although Principal Applicants report additional information for other members of the household and for the household as a whole. With minor exceptions, the surveys are also the same across cohorts. Wave 1 interviews for both Cohort 1 and Cohort 2 were timed to occur approximately six months after arrival. The first LSIA cohort was re-interviewed approximately 18 months (Wave 2) and 42 months (Wave 3) after arrival. The second LSIA cohort was re-interviewed only once at approximately 18 months (Wave 2) after arrival.

COMPARISON OF THE TWO LSIA COHORTS

Table A1 compares the characteristics at Wave 1 of individuals in the two LSIA cohorts. The distribution of LSIA immigrants across visa categories highlights the expansion of the skilled immigration program and the relative scaling back of the Family and Humanitarian streams. The proportion of individuals entering on a skills-based visa increased from one in three (35 per cent) in Cohort 1 to one in two (50 per cent) in Cohort 2. Family stream immigrants made up 48 per cent of the first LSIA cohort, but only 41 per cent of the second, while the proportion of Humanitarian immigrants fell by almost half over the five years separating the two entry cohorts.

Not surprisingly, there are large gender differences in the proportion of LSIA immigrants subject to Australia's points test. Principal Applicants in the Skilled – Australian Sponsored and Independent visa categories account for approximately one third of all men in the two LSIA cohorts. In contrast, only 9 per cent of Cohort 1 women and 17 per cent of Cohort 2 women entered Australia as the Principal Applicant in one of the two skill-based programs subject to points testing.

Although the demographic characteristics – average age, gender ratio, and marital status – of the two cohorts are much the same there are striking differences in human capital endowments. Consistent with changes in selection criteria, the cohort of individuals entering Australia in 1999–2000 was more educated and had better English language skills[6] than was the earlier cohort. They also were more likely to have been working in a professional occupation and less likely to have been not employed in the former home country in the year prior to immigration.[7] Overall, almost half (46 per cent) of Cohort 2 had recent labour market experience in a professional occupation at the time of migration. This was true of just over one third (35 per cent) of individuals in the first cohort. Finally, there are differences in the source countries of the two cohorts. Cohort 2 immigrants were more likely (55 per cent versus 49 per cent) to come from countries where English is widely spoken and with cultural traditions and institutions that closely resemble those of Australia.[8]

Additional information about the characteristics and labour market outcomes for the two LSIA cohorts can be found in Richardson et al. (2001, 2004).

NOTES

1 Information about visa categories comes from Department of Immigration and Multicultural Affairs administrative records and not self-reports.

2 For more information about the technical details of the LSIA data see the DIMIA web page http://www.immi.gov.au/research/lsia; the technical documentation for the data; Cobb-Clark (2001); and Richardson et al. (2001, 2004).

3 For the purposes of the LSIA, the migrating unit includes all individuals migrating to Australia as part of the same visa application. The term 'spouse' includes legal spouses, fiancé(e)s and de facto partners. In both LSIA cohorts more than 95 per cent of those Migrating Unit Spouses present in the household were successfully interviewed.

4 The Cohort 1 sample is stratified by visa category and approximately 50 regions or countries of birth. The sample size of each stratum was chosen so as to achieve a 2.5 per cent absolute standard error for each visa category and a 7 per cent absolute standard error for each region or country of birth in Wave 3. Because sample attrition was less than anticipated, a higher degree of confidence was achieved for some region/country of birth and visa groups. Cohort 2 is also stratified by visa category and region/country of birth, although the visa categories are somewhat more detailed and the region/country of birth somewhat broader than in Cohort 1.

5 In LSIA1 the geographic areas covered by the survey represented approximately 96 per cent of the population of interest. While Cairns was included in the sampling frame for Cohort 1 it was dropped in Cohort 2.

6 LSIA respondents were asked to report about their ability to speak English. Those who reported speaking English 'only' or 'best' are classified as 'native' English speakers. Non-native speakers who reported speaking English 'very well' or 'well' are combined to form the 'English well' category. Non-native speakers who reported speaking English 'badly' or 'not at all' form the 'English badly' category.

7 Although LSIA data do not contain direct measures of labour market experience, LSIA respondents were asked about their labour market experiences in their former home country in the year prior to migration. Individuals employed at some point in the year prior to migration reported their occupation. These occupations have been coded into three major categories: professional, skilled, unskilled. Individuals not employed in the 12 months before migration are coded as 'not employed'. Finally, 'time unemployed' measures the number of months in the year prior to migration that an individual reported being unemployed and looking for work.

8 In Table A1 source countries are divided into English proficiency groups based on the English-speaking ability of recent immigrants to Australia (see DIMA, 1996).

References

Ackland, R. and L.S. Williams (1992), *Immigrants and the Australian Labour Market: The Experience of Three Recessions*, Canberra, Australia: Australian Government Publishing Service.

Antecol, H., D.A. Cobb-Clark and S.J. Trejo (2003a), 'Immigration policy and the skills of immigrants to Australia, Canada, and the United States', *Journal of Human Resources,* **38** (1), 192–221.

Antecol, H., D.A. Cobb-Clark and S.J. Trejo (2003b), 'The skills of female immigrants to Australia, Canada, and the United States', in J.G. Reitz (ed.), *Host Societies and the Reception of Immigrants*, San Diego, CA, USA: Center for Comparative Immigration Studies, University of California.

Australian Bureau of Statistics (ABS) (2000), *1999 Australian Housing Survey: Housing Characteristics, Costs and Conditions*, Canberra, Australia: ABS Catalogue No. 4182.0.

Australian Bureau of Statistics (ABS) (2005), *Labour Force, Australia, Detailed,* Canberra, Australia: ABS, Catalogue No. 6291.0.55.001.

Australian Institute of Health and Welfare (2002), *Australian Health Inequalities Bulletin, Issue 2*. Canberra, Australian: AIHW, Catalogue No. AUS-27.

Baker, M. and D. Benjamin (1997), 'The role of the family in immigrants' labor-market activity: An evaluation of alternative explanations', *American Economic Review*, **87** (4), 705–727.

Bauer, T., M. Lofstom and K.F. Zimmermann (2000), 'Immigration policy, assimilation of immigrants, and natives' sentiments towards immigrants: Evidence from 12 OECD Countries', *Swedish Economic Policy Review*, **7** (2), 11–53.

Beggs, J. and B. Chapman (1988), 'Immigrant wage adjustment in Australia: Cross section and time series estimates', *Economic Record*, **64** (186), 161–167.

Beggs, J. and B. Chapman (1990), 'Search efficiency, skill transferability and immigrant relative unemployment rates in Australia', *Applied Economics*, **22** (2), 249–260.

Biddle, N., S. Kennedy and J.T. McDonald (2004), *Health Assimilation Patterns Among Australian Immigrants*, manuscript, Australian National University.

Bielby, W.T. and D.D. Bielby (1992), 'I will follow him: Family ties, gender-role beliefs, and reluctance to relocate for a better job', *American Journal of Sociology*, **97** (5), 1241–1267.

Birrell, B. and S. Evans (1996), 'Recently arrived immigrants and social welfare', *People and Place*, **4** (2), 1–11.

Biswal, U.D. (1999), 'Testing the family "common preference" model for immigrant and non-immigrant women's labour supply', *Canadian Public Policy*, **25** (1), S95–S114.

Borjas, G.J. (1993), 'Immigration policy, national origin, and immigrant skills: A comparison of Canada and the United States' in D. Card and R. Freeman (eds), *Small Differences that Matter: Labor Markets and Income Maintenance in Canada and the United States*, Chicago, IL, USA: University of Chicago Press, pp. 21–44.

Borooah, V. and J. Mangan (2002), 'An analysis of occupational outcomes for indigenous and Asian employees in Australia', *Economic Record*, **78**, 31–49.

Boyle, P., T.J. Cooke, K. Halfacree and D. Smith (2001), 'A cross-national comparison of the impact of family migration on women's employment status', *Demography,* **38** (2), 201–213.

Chiswick, B.R. (1979), 'The economic progress of immigrants: Some apparently universal patterns', in W. Fellner (ed.)*, Contemporary Economic Problems* 1979, Washington DC, USA: American Enterprise Institute for Public Policy Research, pp. 357–399.

Chiswick, B.R. (1987), 'Immigration policy, source countries, and immigrant skills: Australia, Canada, and the United States', in *The Economics of Immigration. Proceedings of Conference held at the Australian National University*, Canberra, Australia: Australian Government Publishing Service.

Chiswick, B.R., Y.L. Lee and P.W. Miller (2003a), 'Immigrants' language skills: The Australian experience in a longitudinal survey', *Annales d'Economie et de Statistique*, **71–72**, 97–139.

Chiswick, B.R., Y.L. Lee, and P.W. Miller (2003b), *Immigrant Health: An Economic Analysis*, School of Economics and Commerce, University of Western Australia: unpublished.

Chiswick, B.R., Y.L. Lee and P.W. Miller (2005a), 'Family matters: The role of the family in immigrants' destination language acquisition', *Journal of Population Economics*, **18** (1), 1–17.

Chiswick, B.R., Y.L. Lee and P.W. Miller (2005b), 'Parents and children talk: English language proficiency within immigrant families', *Review of Economics of the Household*, **3** (3), 243–268.

Chiswick, B.R., Y.L. Lee and P.W. Miller (2006), 'Immigrants' language skills and visa category', *International Migration Review*. **40** (2), 419–450.

Chiswick, B.R. and P.W. Miller (1992a), 'Language in the immigrant labour market', in B.R. Chiswick (ed.), *Immigration, Language and Ethnicity: Canada and the United States*, Washington DC, USA: American Enterprise Institute, pp. 229–296 and pp. 471–476.

Chiswick, B.R. and P.W. Miller (1992b), *Post-Immigration Qualifications in Australia: Determinants and Consequences*, Canberra, Australia: Bureau of Immigration Research, Commonwealth of Australia.

Chiswick, B.R. and P.W. Miller (1994), 'The determinants of post-immigration investments in education', *Economics of Education Review*, **13** (2), 163–177.

Chiswick, B.R. and P.W. Miller (1995), 'The endogeneity between language and earnings: International analyses', *Journal of Labor Economics*, **13** (2), 246–288.

Chiswick, B.R. and P.W. Miller (1996), 'Ethnic networks and language proficiency among immigrants', *Journal of Population Economics*, **9** (1), 19–35.

Chiswick, B.R. and P.W. Miller (1998a), 'English language fluency among immigrants in the United States', *Research in Labor Economics*, **17**, 151–200.

Chiswick, B.R. and P.W. Miller (1998b), 'Language skill definition: A study of legalized aliens', *International Migration Review*, **32** (4), 877–900.

Chiswick, B.R. and P.W. Miller (1999), 'Immigration, language and multiculturalism in Australia', *Australian Economic Review*, **32** (4), 369–385.

Chiswick, B.R. and P.W. Miller (2002), 'Immigrant earnings: Language skills, linguistic concentrations and the business cycle', *Journal of Population Economics*, **15** (1), 31–57.

Chiswick, B.R. and P.W. Miller (2005), 'Linguistic distance: A quantitative measure of the distance between English and other languages', *Journal of Multilingual and Multicultural Development*, **26** (1), 1–11.

Cobb-Clark, D.A. (2000), 'Do selection criteria make a difference? Visa category and the labor market status of immigrants to Australia', *The Economic Record*, **76** (232), 15–31.

Cobb-Clark, D.A. (2001), 'The Longitudinal Survey of Immigrants to Australia', *Australian Economic Review*, **34** (4), 467–477.

Cobb-Clark, D.A. (2003), 'Public policy and the labor market adjustment of new immigrants to Australia', *Journal of Population Economics*, **16** (4) 655–681.

Cobb-Clark, D.A. and M.D. Connolly (2001), 'A family affair: The labor market experience of immigrant spouses', *Social Science Quarterly*, **82** (4), 796–811.

Cobb-Clark, D.A., M.D. Connolly and C. Worswick (2005), 'Post-migration investments in job search and education: A family perspective', *Journal of Population Economics*, **18** (4), 663-690.

Cobb-Clark, D.A. and T.F. Crossley (2004), 'Revisiting the family investment hypothesis', *Journal of Labor Economics*, **11** (3), 373-333.

Cooke, T.J. and A.J. Bailey (1996), 'Family migration and the employment of married women and men', *Economic Geography*, **72** (1), 38–48.

Crossley, T. and S.K. Kennedy (2002), 'The reliability of self-assessed health status', *Journal of Health Economics*, **21** (4), 643–658.

Daniels, D. (2004), *Social Security Payments for the Unemployed, the Sick and Those in Special Circumstances, 1942 to 2004*, Social Policy Section, Parliamentary Library, Parliament of Australia: Viewed 2 March, 2005, http://www.aph.gov.au/library/pubs/online/special_partb.htm.

Department of Immigration and Multicultural Affairs (1996), 'Classification of countries into English proficiency groups', *Statistical Focus* C96.1A.

Department of Immigration and Multicultural Affairs (1997), *Australian Immigration: Consolidated Statistics, No. 19, 1995–1996*, Canberra, Australia: Commonwealth of Australia.

Department of Immigration and Multicultural Affairs (1999), *Review of the Independent and Skilled – Australian Linked Categories*, Canberra, Australia: Commonwealth of Australia.

Department of Immigration and Multicultural Affairs (2000), *Settlement Services Guide,* Canberra, Australia: Commonwealth of Australia.

Department of Immigration and Multicultural and Indigenous Affairs (2004), http://www.immi.gov.au/statistics/migrant.htm (accessed December 2005).

Department of Immigration and Multicultural and Indigenous Affairs (2005), http://www.dimia.gov.au/allforms/pdf/1071i.pdf (accessed December 2005).

Doiron, D.J. and W.C. Riddell (1994), 'The impact of unionization on male–female earnings differences in Canada', *Journal of Human Resources*, **29** (2), 504–534.

Dolton, P. and G. Makepeace (2004), 'Computer use and earnings in Britain', *Economic Journal*, **114** (494), C117–C129.

Donovan, J., C.M. d'Espaignet and M. van Ommeren (eds) (1992), *Immigrants in Australia: A Health Profile*, Canberra, Australia: Australian Government Publishing Service.

Duleep, H.O. and M.C. Regets (1992), 'Some evidence on the effects of admissions criteria on immigrant assimilation' in B.R. Chiswick (ed.), *Immigration, Language and Ethnic Issues: Canada and the United States*, Washington DC, USA: American Enterprise Institute, pp. 410–439.

Duleep, H.O. and S. Sanders (1993), 'The decision to work by married immigrant women', *Industrial and Labor Relations Review*, **46** (4), 677–690.

Duleep, H.O. and M.C. Regets (1996), 'Admission criteria and immigrant earnings profiles', *International Migration Review*, **30** (2), 571–590.

Duleep, H.O. and M.C. Regets (1999), 'Immigrants and human-capital investment', *American Economic Review*, **89** (2), 186–190.

Dunn, J.R. and I. Dyck (2000), 'Social determinants of health in Canada's immigrant population: Results from the National Health Survey', *Social Science and Medicine*, **51** (11), 1573–1593.

Dustmann, C. and I. Preston (2000), 'Racial and economic factors in attitudes to immigration', *CEPR Discussion Paper Series 2542*, London, UK: Centre for Economic Policy Research.

Econsult (Australia) Pty. Ltd. (1992), 'Recently arrived immigrants', in *Housing Information Study, Background Papers to the Australian National Housing Strategy*, **14**, 75–83.

Edin, P-A., P. Fredriksson and O. Åslund (2004), 'Settlement policies and the economic success of immigrants', *Journal of Population Economics*, **17** (1), 133–155.

Ettner, S. (1996), 'New evidence on the relationship between income and health', *Journal of Health Economics*, **15** (1), 6–85.

Evans, M.D.R. (1984), 'Immigrant women in Australia: Resources, family, and work', *International Migration Review*, **18** (4), 1063–1090.

Evans, M.D.R. and Kelley, J. (1986), 'Immigrants' work: Equality and discrimination in the Australian labour market', *Australia New Zealand Journal of Sociology*, **22** (2), 187-207.

Ferris, W. and R. Silberburg, (1982), 'Immigration and the demand for housing', in D. Douglas (ed.), *The Economics of Australian Immigration: Conference Proceedings, 8–9 February 1982*, Sydney, Australia: University of Sydney, pp. 117–123.

Friedberg, R.M. (2000), 'You can't take it with you? Immigrant assimilation and the portability of human capital', *Journal of Labor Economics*, **18** (2), 221–251.

Graetz, B. (1993), ‘Health consequences of employment and unemployment: Longitudinal evidence for young men and women’, *Social Science and Medicine*, **36** (6), 715–724.

Green, A.G. and D.A. Green (1995), ‘Canadian immigration policy: The effectiveness of the point system and other instruments’, *Canadian Journal of Economics*, **28** (4b), 1006–1041.

Green, A.G. and D.A. Green (1999), ‘The economic goals of Canada’s immigration policy: Past and present’, *Canadian Public Policy*, **25** (4), 425–451.

Green, D.A. (1995), ‘Intended and actual occupations of immigrants’ in D.J. DeVortez (ed.), *Diminishing Returns: The Economics of Canada's Recent Immigration Policy*, Toronto and Vancouver, Canada: C.D. Howe Institute and The Laurier Institution.

Green, D.A. (1999), ‘Immigrant occupational attainment: Assimilation and mobility over time’, *Journal of Labor Economics*, **17** (1), 49–79.

Grossman, M. (1972), ‘On the concept of health capital and the demand for health’, *Journal of Political Economy*, **80** (2), 223–255.

Grossman, M. and R. Kaestner (1997), ‘Effects of education on health’, in J.R. Behrman and N. Stacey (eds), *The Social Benefits of Education*, Ann Arbor, MI, USA: University of Michigan Press, pp. 69–123.

Hassell, D, and G.J. Hugo (1996), *Immigrants and Public Housing*, Canberra, Australia: Australian Government Publishing Service.

Heckman, J.J. (1979), ‘Sample selection bias as a specification error’, *Econometrica*, **47** (1), 153–161.

Houstoun, M.F., R.G. Kramer and J.M. Barrett (1984), ‘Female predominance in immigration in the United States since 1930: A first look’, *International Migration Review*, **38** (4), 908–963.

Idler, E.L. and S.V. Kasl, (1995), ‘Self-ratings of health: Do they also predict change in functional ability?’, *Journal of Gerontology*, **50B**, S344–S353.

Inglis, P. and T. Stromback, (1986), ‘Migrants’ unemployment: The determinants of employment success’, *Economic Record*, **62** (178), 310–324.

Jasso, G. and M.R. Rosenzweig (1995), ‘Do immigrants screened for skills do better than family reunification immigrants?’, *International Migration Review*, **29** (1), 85–111.

Jasso, G., D.S. Massey, M.R. Rosenzweig and J.P. Smith (2004), ‘Immigrant Health – Selectivity and Acculturation’ in N.B. Anderson, R.A. Bulatao, and B. Cohen (eds), *Critical Perspectives on Racial and Ethnic Differences in Health in Late Life*, Washington, USA: National Academies Press, pp. 227–266.

Junankar, P.N. and S. Mahuteau (2005), Do migrants get good Jobs? 'New migrant settlement in Australia', *Economic Record*, **81** (Special Issue), S34–S46.

Junankar, P.N., S. Paul, S. and W. Yasmeen (2004), 'Are Asian Migrants Discriminated Against in the Labour Market? A Case Study of Australia', *IZA Discussion Paper No. 1167*, Bonn, Germany: IZA.

Junankar P.N., D. Pope, C. Kapuscinski, G. Ma, and W. Mudd (1993), *Recent Immigrants and Housing*, Canberra, Australia: Australian Government Publishing Service.

Kalbfleisch, J. and R. Prentice (2002), *The Statistical Analyses of Failure Time Data*, 2nd edn, New York: John Wiley, New York.

Kan, A. (1991), *The Australian Experience of Skilled Migration: The Employer Nomination Scheme in the Manufacturing and the Finance, Property and Business Services Sectors*, Canberra, Australia: Bureau of Immigration Research, Australian Government Publishing Service.

Kennedy, S.K. (2003), 'Immigrant mental health and unemployment', *Social and Economic Dimensions of an Aging Population*, SEDAP Research Paper No. 92, McMaster University, Canada.

Khan, A.H. (1997), 'Post-migration investment in education by immigrants in the United States', *Quarterly Review of Economics and Finance*, **37** (Supplement 1), 285–313.

Killingsworth, M.R. (1983), *Labor Supply*, Cambridge, UK: Cambridge University Press.

Kliewer, E.V. and J.R.G. Butler (1995), *Hospital Morbidity Patterns and Costs of Immigrants in Australia*, Canberra, Australia: National Centre for Epidemiology and Population Health, Australian National University.

Kominski, R. (1989), 'How good is "How well"? An examination of the census English-speaking ability question', in *American Statistical Association Proceedings of the Social Statistics Section*, Atlanta, GA, USA: American Statistical Association pp. 333–338.

Laroche, M. (2000), 'Health status and health services utilisation of Canada's immigrant and non-immigrant populations', *Canadian Public Policy*, **16** (1), 51–73.

Lazear, E.P. (1998), 'Diversity and immigration', *NBER Working Paper 6535, April 1998*, Cambridge MA, USA: National Bureau of Economic Research.

LeClere, F.B., L. Jensen and A.E. Biddlecom (1994), 'Health care utilization, family context, and adaptation among immigrants to the United States', *Journal of Health and Social Behaviour*, **35** (4), 370–384.

LeClere, F.B. and D.K. McLaughlin (1997), 'Family migration and changes in women's earnings: A decomposition analysis', *Population Research and Policy Review*, **16** (4), 315–335.

Long, M.H. (1990), 'Maturational constraints on language development', *Studies in Second Language Acquisition*, **12** (3), 251–285.

MacPherson, D.A. and J.B. Stewart (1989), 'The labor force participation and earnings profiles of married female immigrants', *Quarterly Review of Economics and Business*, **29** (3), 57–72.

Madden, R. and S. Young (1993), *Women and Men Immigrating to Australia: Their Characteristics and Immigration Decisions*, Bureau of Immigration Research, Canberra, Australia: Australian Government Publishing Service.

Mathers, C. (2003), 'Health patterns of immigrants to Australia', *People and Place*, **4** (1).

McCallum, J., B. Shadbolt and D. Wang (1994), 'Self-rated health and survival: A 7-year follow-up study of Australian elderly', *American Journal of Public Health*, **847**, 1100–1105.

McDonald, J.T., and S.K. Kennedy (2004), 'Insights into the 'healthy immigrant effect': Health status and health service use of immigrants to Canada', *Social Science and Medicine*, **59** (8), 1613–1627.

McDonald, J.T., and S.K. Kennedy (2005), 'Is migration to Canada associated with unhealthy weight gain? Overweight and obesity among Canada's immigrants', *Social Science and Medicine*, **61** (12), 2469–2481.

McDonald, P. and R. Kippen (2001), 'The impact of immigration on the ageing of Australia's population' in M.A.B. Siddique (ed.), *International Migration into the Twenty-First Century: Essays in Honour of Reginald Appleyard*, Cheltenham, UK and Northampton, MA, USA: Edward Elgar, pp. 153–177.

Miller, P.W. (1986), 'Immigrant unemployment in the first year of Australian labour market activity', *Economic Record*, **62**, 82–87.

Miller, P.W. (1999), 'Immigration policy and immigrant quality: The Australian point system', *American Economic Review*, **89** (2), 192–197.

Miller, P.W. and L. Neo (1997), 'Immigrant unemployment: The Australian experience', *International Migration*, **35**, 155–185.

Miller, P.W. and L. Neo (2003), 'Labour market flexibility and immigrant adjustment', *Economic Record*, **79** (246), 336–356.

Mincer, J. (1978), 'Family migration decisions', *Journal of Political Economy*, **86** (5), 749–773.

Morrison, D.R. and D.T. Lichter (1988), 'Family migration and female employment: The problem of underemployment among migrant married women', *Journal of Marriage and the Family*, **50** (1), 161–172.

Murphy, J. and L. Williams (1996), 'Social security recipiency among recently arrived immigrants', *People and Place*, **4** (2), 15–20.

National Population Council (1988), *Immigration Selection Systems: A Report of the National Population Council (G. Withers, Chairperson)*, Canberra, Australia: National Population Council.

National Population Council (1990), *Immigration and Housing in the Major Cities. Final Report*. Canberra, Australia: Australian Government Publishing Service.

Norris, K and M. Wooden (1996), 'The changing Australian labour market: An overview', in K. Norris and M. Wooden (eds), *The Changing Australian Labour Market*, Canberra, Australia: Economic Planning Advisory Committee, Australian Government Publishing Service, pp.1–14.

OECD (2005) *OECD Factbook 2005: Economic, Environmental, and Social Statistics*, http://hermia.sourceoecd.org/vl=1716067/cl=14/nw=1/rpsv/factbook/. Accessed March 2005.

Parliamentary Library (1996), *Bills Digest 1995–96: Social Security Legislation Amendment (Newly Arrived Residents' Waiting Periods and Other Measures) Bill 1996*, Canberra, Australia: Parliament of Australia.

Perez, C.E. (2002), Health status and health behaviours among immigrants, *Health Reports*, Statistics Canada, Catalogue No.82-003.

Ray, B.K., D. Papademetriou and M. Jachimowicz (2004), *Immigrants and Homeownership in Urban America: An Examination of Nativity, Socioeconomic Status and Race*. Washington DC, USA: Migration Policy Institute.

Reid, J. and P. Trompf (1990), *The Health of Immigrant Australia: A Social Perspective*, Marrickville, Australia: Harcourt Brace Jovanovich.

Reimers, C.W. (1985), 'Cultural differences in labor force participation among married women', *American Economic Review*, **75** (2), 251–255.

Reitz, J.G. (1998), *Warmth of the Welcome: The Social Causes of Economic Success for Immigrants in Different Nations and Cities*, Boulder, CO, USA: Westview Press.

Richardson, S., F. Robertson and D. Ilsley (2001), *The Labour Force Experience of New Migrants*, Canberra, Australia: Department of Immigration and Multicultural Affairs.

Richardson, S., L. Miller-Lewis, P. Ngo, and D. Ilsley (2002a), *Life in a New Land: The Experience of Migrants in Wave 1 of LSIA 1 and LSIA 2*,

Canberra, Australia: Department of Immigration and Multicultural and Indigenous Affairs.

Richardson, S., L. Miller-Lewis, P. Ngo and D. Ilsley (2002b), *The Settlement Experiences of New Migrants: Paper prepared for the Department of Immigration and Multicultural and Indigenous Affairs*, Adelaide, Australia: National Institute of Labour Studies, Flinders University.

Richardson, S., S. Stack, L. Lester, J. Healy, D. Illsley and J. Horrocks (2004), *The Changing Labour Force Experience of New Migrants; A Report prepared for DIMIA*, Adelaide, Australia: National Institute for Labour Studies, Flinders University.

SAS Institute Inc. (1994), *SAS/STAT User's Guide,* Version 6, Vol. 2, 4th edn, USA: SAS Institute Inc.

Service, E. and F.I.M. Craik (1993), 'Differences between young and older adults in learning a foreign vocabulary', *Journal of Memory and Language*, **32** (5), 608–623.

Shamsuddin, A. (1998), 'Labour supply of immigrant women', *Australian Journal of Labour Economics*, **2** (2), 105–133.

Smith, J.P. (1999), 'Healthy bodies and thick wallets: The dual relation between health and economic status', *Journal of Economic Perspectives*, **13** (2), 145–166.

Sorensen, E., F.D. Bean, L. Ku and W. Zimmermann (1992), *Immigrant Categories and the U.S. Job Market: Do They Make a Difference?* Washington DC, USA: The Urban Institute Press.

Spitze, G. (1984), 'The effect of family migration on wives' employment: How long does it last?' *Social Science Quarterly*, **65** (1), 21-36.

Stalker, P. (2000), *Workers Without Frontiers: The Impact of Globalization on International Migration*, Boulder, CO, USA: Lynne Rienner Publishers, Inc.

Straubhaar, T. and K.F. Zimmermann (1993), 'Towards a European migration policy', *Population Research and Policy Review*, **12** (3), 225–241.

Strong, K., P. Trickett and K. Bhatia (1998), 'The health of overseas-born Australians, 1994–1996', *Australian Health Review*, **21** (2), 124–133.

Thapa, P. (2004), 'On the risk of unemployment: A comparative assessment of the labour market success of migrants in Australia'; *Australian Journal of Labour Economics*, **7** (2), 199–229.

Tonkins, S., L.S. Williams and R. Ackland (1993), *The Relationship Between Visa Category and Demand for Housing: Results from the Longitudinal Survey of Immigrants to Australia (LSIA) Pilot*, Canberra, Australia: Australian Government Publishing Service.

United Nations, Department for Economic and Social Information and Policy Analysis, Population Division, (1995), *International Migration Policies and the Status of Female Migrants*, New York, USA: United Nations.

VandenHeuvel, A. and M. Wooden (1999), *New Settlers Have Their Say: How Immigrants Fare Over the Early Years of Settlement*, Canberra, Australia: Department of Immigration and Multicultural Affairs.

VandenHeuevel, A. and M. Wooden (2000) 'Immigrants' labour market experiences in the early settlement years', *Australian Bulletin of Labour*, **26** (1), 59–69.

Vialet, J.C. and L.M. Eig (1990), *Immigration Act of 1990 (P.L. 101-649)*, Washington DC, USA: Congressional Research Service, Library of Congress.

Watts, M. (2000), 'The dimensions and costs of unemployment in Australia', in S. Bell (ed.), *The Unemployment Crisis in Australia: Which Way Out?*, Cambridge, UK: Cambridge University Press, pp. 21–48.

Withers, G. (2002), 'Population ageing and the role of immigration', *Australian Economic Review*, **35** (1), 104–112.

Wooden, M., R. Holten, G.J. Hugo and J. Sloan (1994), *Australian Immigration: A Survey of the Issues*, Canberra, Australia: Australian Government Publishing Service.

Wooden, M. and A. VandenHeuvel (1997), 'Family composition and the labour supply choices of married immigrant women', *Australian Journal of Labour Economics*, **1** (2), 121–142.

Wright, R.E. and P.S. Maxim (1993), 'Immigration policy and immigrant quality: Empirical evidence from Canada', *Journal of Population Economics*, **6**, 337–352.

Young, C. (1986), *Selection and Survival: Immigrant Mortality in Australia*, Canberra, Australia: Department of Immigration and Ethnic Affairs, Australian Government Publishing Service.

Young, C. (1992), 'Mortality: The ultimate indicator of survival: the differential experience between birthplace groups', in Donovan, J., C.M. d'Espaignet and M. van Ommeren (eds) (1992), *Immigrants in Australia: A Health Profile*, Canberra, Australia: Australian Institute of Health and Welfare, Ethnic Series No.1, Australian Government Publishing Service, pp. 34–70.

Index